Project Risk Management Guidelines

Project Risk Management Guidelines

Managing Risk in Large Projects and Complex Procurements

Dale F. Cooper, Stephen Grey, Geoffrey Raymond and Phil Walker

Broadleaf Capital International

John Wiley & Sons, Ltd

Copyright © 2005   John Wiley & Sons Ltd, The Atrium, Southern Gate, Chichester,
West Sussex PO19 8SQ, England

Telephone   (+44) 1243 779777

Email (for orders and customer service enquiries): cs-books@wiley.co.uk
Visit our Home Page on www.wileyeurope.com or www.wiley.com

Reprinted August 2005, February and June 2006, March and October 2008

Other Wiley Editorial Offices

John Wiley & Sons Inc., 111 River Street, Hoboken, NJ 07030, USA

Jossey-Bass, 989 Market Street, San Francisco, CA 94103-1741, USA

Wiley-VCH Verlag GmbH, Boschstr. 12, D-69469 Weinheim, Germany

John Wiley & Sons Australia Ltd, 33 Park Road, Milton, Queensland 4064, Australia

John Wiley & Sons (Asia) Pte Ltd, 2 Clementi Loop #02-01, Jin Xing Distripark, Singapore 129809

John Wiley & Sons Canada Ltd, 22 Worcester Road, Etobicoke, Ontario, Canada M9W 1L1

Wiley also publishes its books in a variety of electronic formats. Some content that appears
in print may not be available in electronic books.

Library of Congress Cataloging in Publication Data

Project risk management guidelines: managing risk in large projects and complex procurements/
Dale Cooper . . . [et al.].
    p.   cm.
  Includes bibliographical references and index.
  ISBN 0-470-02281-7 (cloth: alk. paper)
  1. Risk management.   2. Project management.   3. Industrial procurement—Management.
  I. Cooper, Dale F.

  HD61.P765 2004
  658.15′5—dc22

                                                                                    2004011338

British Library Cataloguing in Publication Data

A catalogue record for this book is available from the British Library

ISBN 13: 978-0-470-02281-8 (H/B)

Typeset in 10/12pt Garamond by Integra Software Services Pvt. Ltd, Pondicherry, India
Printed and bound in Great Britain by CPI Antony Rowe, Chippenham, Wiltshire

CONTENTS

FOREWORD

Project risk management has come a long way since the 1980s, when Dale Cooper and I worked together on a range of risk management consultancy projects in the UK, Canada and the USA, published together, and became friends as well as colleagues. In particular, the leading edge has moved from bespoke methods and models developed for particular organizations and situations towards generic processes. It has also come a long way since the mid-1990s, when Stephen Grey and I worked together on the Association for Project Management PRAM (Project Risk Analysis and Management) Guide. In particular, the debate about what shape generic processes should take has clarified a number of issues, without leading to a consensus. Project risk management continues to evolve in interesting and useful ways, with no end to this development in sight.

One of the key current dilemmas is the gap between common practice and best practice. Central to this is a widespread failure to understand the relationship between simple approaches that work well in appropriate circumstances, and more complex approaches that pay big dividends when the aspects they focus on deserve attention. Opinions are divided on the scale and nature of this dilemma, and I have some views on how best to approach it which differ from those put forward in this book. However, I think this book is very useful reading for both experts and novices. It addresses the need for simplicity without being simplistic in a direct manner. It has lots of useful practical advice for getting started and dealing with simple situations. It also addresses some of the areas where more sophisticated approaches are well worthwhile, and some of the relevant concepts and tools. In addition, it packages the whole in a structure that works well.

A key feature of this book is the way it postpones addressing quantitative analysis and associated process iterations (multiple pass looping) until after the basic process has been described. Initially I found this a source of concern. However, this book is unusually clear about the limitations of semi-quantitative approaches, the consequence rating tables (Tables 4.3 and 4.4) make this approach unusually rich in insight, and the attractions of the starting position adopted include a close proximity to common practice. There are many routes to best practice, and both the best routes and the nature of the destination are debatable. This book provides a particularly simple basic process as a starting position without overlooking the drawbacks, and it addresses many of the implications of more sophisticated processes later.

Another key feature of this book is the notion that best practice risk management is shaped to particular contexts for efficiency, but the principles are universal and transportable. The chapters on environmental issues and outsourcing, for example, address very different contexts, but they share some basic perspectives.

This is a pragmatic and directly useful book for project risk management novices. It is also a stimulating and challenging book for those with considerable experience of the field.

Chris Chapman
Professor of Management Science
University of Southampton, UK

PREFACE

The risk management processes described in this book had their genesis well over 20 years ago when I accepted a position at the University of Southampton. There I met and worked with Dr Chris Chapman, already an acknowledged expert in project risk, with an established relationship with BP and an extensive client base in Canada. Chris involved me in his consulting activities in North America, primarily associated with quantitative risk analyses of large projects in the hydroelectric and the oil and gas industries. This was a time of innovation, as there were few protocols or models for the kinds of risk analyses that were required for these projects, and the quantitative calculations used a form of numerical integration called the Controlled Interval and Memory approach, developed by Chris, that was implemented in bespoke software. We had to develop different model structures and forms of analysis, and new software had to be written on some occasions to accommodate the new structures. It was highly stimulating, at times exhausting, and great fun, and I learned a huge amount from Chris and the clients with whom we worked.

Many of the projects on which we worked are described in published papers, and some of them are referred to in the case material in this volume. They are all described in our book (Cooper and Chapman, 1987).

After I left Southampton, I worked as a consultant in the finance sector, primarily with international companies in the UK, USA, Hong Kong and Australia. Many of my assignments involved risk in one form or another: risks associated with trading equities, bonds, commodities, currencies and other financial instruments; compliance risks; new business risks as the finance sector in the UK restructured and transformed itself at the time of the so-called Big Bang; and balance sheet and liquidity risks associated with the management of financial assets and liabilities having different bases and maturity structures. I then worked as a senior line manager in the sector, where I had to develop organizational strategy and manage its implementation, as well as run operational business areas.

One of the main lessons I learned from the finance sector, an industry that is often perceived as notoriously risky, is this: if something is too complex to understand and explain then it is probably too risky to undertake, as you won't be able to design and implement the right kinds of operational processes, controls and monitoring to manage the risks effectively. That insight, and the reinforcement I have received from many clients subsequently, has led me to simplify many of the processes and tools I use for risk management. When complexity is needed, then it is really needed and it must be done properly, but simple approaches are often sufficient for making sound decisions.

A large part of this book is based on simple qualitative approaches to project risk. The processes described here had a long gestation; they were first formalized by me in the New South Wales Government *Risk Management Guidelines* in 1993. The first version of the *Australian and New Zealand Standard on Risk Management* (AS/NZS 4360) (1995), extended the same simple framework and became a best-seller, and subsequent revisions have refined it further.

While the emphasis is on simple qualitative methods, more complex quantitative approaches to project risk are not ignored. Quantitative analysis is discussed, largely using case material, to provide a flavour of the way it may be structured and implemented, and the level of sophistication that may be obtained. More detailed treatment would require its own volume – instead, interested readers are referred to the excellent book by my co-author Dr Stephen Grey (1995) and my former colleagues at Southampton, Professor Chris Chapman and Dr Stephen Ward (Chapman and Ward, 1997, 2002).

The material in this book is based on our activities with major projects in a wide variety of organizations, countries and industry sectors and different cultural environments. It reflects our varied consulting and line management experience, working with project sponsors, owners, users and project delivery organizations, and occasionally regulators, in both industry and Government and in a range of jurisdictions. While many of the examples have been generalized and sometimes adjusted, either to clarify their exposition or to remove confidential material, they are all based on real projects with which we have been involved.

We would like to thank all our clients for the insights we have gained while working with them. Many of our assignments have been truly collaborative, and the outcomes reflect the efforts of our clients' teams as much as our own.

The structure of the initial chapters of this book was developed some time ago when I was commissioned by Purchasing Australia, at that time the procurement arm of the Australian Government, to develop a handbook on managing risk in procurement. This was subsequently published as Cooper, 1997. This publication is now out of print. While much has been retained from the earlier work, there have been many additions. These are based on our current consulting practice, as well as recent developments in the way projects are conducted. In particular, outsourcing arrangements and new risk-sharing structures like public–private partnerships have transformed some aspects of project procurement for Governments and large organizations.

Dennis Goodwin, our colleague and a principal consultant at Broadleaf, made major contributions to Chapter 15 on market testing and outsourcing and Chapter 16 on public–private partnerships. Our colleague John Pacholski of Spectrum Corporation, with whom Broadleaf is partnered as Broadleaf Spectrum International for public–private partnership advice, also contributed to Chapter 16. Pauline Bosnich, our colleague and a principal consultant at Broadleaf, made valuable contributions to Chapter 17 on technical tools.

Chapter 18 deals with environmental risk management in a project context. It contains case study material relating to an analysis of mine waste management at the Ok Tedi mine in Papua New Guinea. It has benefited from discussions at the time and subsequently with Ken Voigt of Ok Tedi Mining Limited, who was the manager of the Mine Waste Management Project, and Malcolm Lane of Lane Associates and Dr Adrian Bowden of URS Greiner, who conducted the detailed risk assessment for the project. (I was the owner's auditor for the detailed project risk management process, and I worked closely with Ken, Malcolm and Adrian during the conduct of the risk assessment.) It also contains material we developed for the Australian Department of Defence on the integration of risk management processes into Environmental Management Systems that comply with the ISO 14000 series of environmental standards. Janet Gough of Environmental Risk Management New Zealand, Malcolm Lane and Ken Voigt all made valuable comments on an early draft of this chapter.

The first case study in Chapter 20 is based on work undertaken for a client of Acres International in Canada. Dave MacDonald, then the Head of Planning and Estimating in Acres, and Professor Chris Chapman, Professor of Management Science in the School of Management, University of Southampton, made significant contributions. Extended versions of the material that appears here have been published by Cooper, Macdonald and Chapman (1985), and as Chapter 9 of Cooper and Chapman (1987).

Chapter 21 concerns the pre-design evaluation of a timber development project. It was written jointly with Dr Alessandro Bignozzi, who was the Project Director for the development at the time. Sandro Bignozzi's contribution is gratefully acknowledged.

Chapter 23 draws briefly on case study material that has been described in more detail by Chapman, Cooper, Debelius and Pecora (1985), and in Chapter 5 of Cooper and Chapman (1987).

A version of Chapter 24 was presented by me as an invited paper, Implementing Risk Management in Large Projects, to the 2003 Conference of the Project Management Institute of New Zealand (PMINZ), held in Christchurch, New Zealand, over the period 5–7 November 2003. I was invited and sponsored by the Centre for Advanced Engineering, a not-for-profit organization established in 1987 to commemorate the centenary of the School of Engineering at the University of Canterbury and based at the university. Their support is gratefully acknowledged.

I continue to enjoy stimulating and often vigorous discussions with my colleagues on the Standards Australia and Standards New Zealand Joint Technical Committee OB-007, the committee that continues to develop the Standard AS/NZS 4360 and associated handbooks that enlarge on its application. While it is always risky to name names, as I have enjoyed my interactions with all the members of the committee and its secretariat, I would like to thank particularly our Chair, Professor Jean Cross from the University of New South Wales, Janet Gough from ERMA New Zealand, Kevin Knight from the Queensland Department of Education and Grant Purdy from BHP Billiton.

We would all like to thank our colleagues in Broadleaf Capital International, Dr Sam Beckett, Pauline Bosnich and Dennis Goodwin, for their constructive reviews of early drafts of this book. Their enthusiasm and support is gratefully acknowledged. However, any errors or omissions are entirely our own.

Dr Dale F. Cooper
Pymble

ABOUT THE AUTHORS

Dr Dale F. Cooper

Dale Cooper received his PhD in operational research from the University of Adelaide. He has been a research fellow at the University of London, and a member of the academic staff at the University of Southampton, where he began consulting on risk analyses for major hydroelectric and offshore oil and gas projects in Canada and the USA. He then joined Spicer and Oppenheim Consultants in London, working with finance sector clients in London, New York, Hong Kong and Australia. He returned to Sydney as Joint Managing Director of the stockbroker Pring Dean McNall, and later joined Standard Chartered Bank Australia as National Manager International Services, with responsibilities for the bank's trade finance and priority banking businesses. He was also a member of the bank's Executive Committee.

Dale Cooper established Broadleaf Capital International in 1991. Broadleaf offers high-level assistance and advice on all aspects of strategic and project risk management, including qualitative and quantitative risk assessments and the development and implementation of corporate risk management processes, for large public and private sector clients.

Dale Cooper is a member of the Standards Australia Technical Committee OB-007 that developed the Australian and New Zealand Standard for Risk Management AS/NZS 4360, and he has also contributed to international standards committees. He has numerous professional publications, including *Risk Analysis for Large Projects* (Cooper and Chapman, 1987) and *Applying Risk Management Techniques to Complex Procurement* (Cooper, 1997). Contact him at Cooper@Broadleaf.com.au

Dr Stephen Grey

Stephen Grey received his BSc (Hons) degree from the University of New South Wales and his PhD in applied physics from the University of Leeds. He has worked for the UK Ministry of Defence on rocket propellants, and at STC Defence Systems on major projects, tenders and strategic planning. He moved from STC to its then subsidiary ICL with the specific task of improving the assessment and management of project risk in a commercial environment. He was instrumental in enabling ICL to develop quantitative risk analysis methods that brought the company competitive advantages in bidding and reduced the number of unprofitable projects it accepted.

Stephen Grey joined Broadleaf Capital International as an associate director in 1996. He is a regional director of the Risk Management Special Interest Group of the US Project Management Institute. He is the author of *Practical Risk Assessment for Project Management* (1995). Contact him at Grey@Broadleaf.com.au

Geoffrey Raymond

Geoffrey Raymond received Bachelor of Science and Bachelor of Engineering (Chemical Engineering) degrees from the University of Sydney. He spent ten years with ICI Australia Operations, where he held a range of management positions, including responsibilities for all aspects of batch and continuous plants producing a variety of high-value products. He then moved to Honeywell, where he was responsible for the application of new technology and control systems to automate and enhance the performance of industrial processes.

In 1990 Geoff Raymond joined BHP Engineering, where he developed the Risk Engineering Services and the Waste Management business units, with a focus on the heavy industry and mining sectors. As Manager, Risk Engineering Services, he undertook strategic and technical work, including project risk, safety and environmental assignments around the world. He was invited to make a keynote address to the UN Workshop on Waste Recycling and Waste Management in Developing Countries, Bombay, 1992.

Geoff Raymond joined Broadleaf Capital International as an associate director in 1996. Contact him at Raymond@Broadleaf.com.au

Phil Walker

Phil Walker has a Masters in Business Administration from the University of Southern Queensland, majoring in project management. He had a long career in the Australian Department of Defence, most of which was involved with or in support of major high-technology defence projects, including postings to the USA. His responsibilities have covered all operational and policy aspects of large-scale government procurement and large project acquisitions. His most recent appointments prior to leaving Defence were as C-130J Project Manager, in charge of the billion-dollar acquisition of the new generation Hercules aircraft for the Royal Australian Air Force, from the approval stage through Request for Tender, negotiation and contract signature to delivery of the aircraft, and later as Director of the C-130 Systems Project Office. His position required that he liaise effectively with senior officials and managers at high levels in the Commonwealth and the international defence industry. In February 1999, he chaired the inaugural C-130J Joint Users Conference, hosted by Australia, with international representation from the air forces of the USA, UK, Italy and New Zealand.

Phil Walker joined Broadleaf Capital International as an associate director in 1999. Contact him at Walker@Broadleaf.com.au

Contact details

Information about Broadleaf Capital International is provided on our website – http://www.Broadleaf.com.au – including further general information about project risk management, many of our publications and conference presentations and a short benchmarking survey. If you have specific questions, please contact Dale Cooper at Cooper@Broadleaf.com.au

INTRODUCTION TO PROJECT RISK MANAGEMENT

Scope of this book

This book describes the philosophy, principles, practices and techniques for managing risk in projects and procurements, with a particular focus on complex or large-scale project activities. The approaches contained here may also be applied to simple purchases of goods and services, although with considerable simplification.

Managing risk in projects is important to:

- managers, because it improves the basis for making decisions to meet operational requirements and achieve project and programme objectives;
- project staff, because it helps to identify things that can go wrong in the project process and offers ways to address them effectively;
- end users, because it contributes to satisfying needs and achieving value for money in acquiring major assets and capabilities;
- suppliers and contractors, because a sensible approach to risk in projects leads to better planning and better outcomes for sellers as well as buyers;
- financiers, who must ensure they obtain a financial reward commensurate with the risks involved; and
- insurers, who require comfort that risks are being managed prudently within the project prior to determining whether and how much to charge for financing residual risks.

Benefits of project risk management

Projects, by their nature, are unique and many of the more interesting ones are complex. They frequently take place over an extended period of time and demand the engagement of a wide range of resources, including people, finance, facilities, materials and intellectual property. In most circumstances, projects have defined objectives or an end-state that provides those involved in the project with a clear vision and specification of their goal.

The purpose of project risk management is to minimize the risks of not achieving the objectives of the project and the stakeholders with an interest in it, and to identify and take advantage of opportunities. In particular, risk management assists project managers in setting priorities, allocating resources and implementing actions and processes that reduce the risk of the project not achieving its objectives.

Risk management facilitates better business and project outcomes. It does this by providing insight, knowledge and confidence for better decision-making. In particular, it supports better decisions about planning and design processes to prevent or avoid risks and to capture and exploit opportunities, better contingency planning for dealing with risks and their impacts, better allocation of resources to risks and alignment of project budgets to risks, and better decisions about the best allocation of risk amongst the parties involved in a project activity. Together, these lead to increased certainty and a reduction in overall risk exposure.

Of these benefits, improved outcomes from the capture of opportunities and the reduction in risk exposure provide the main justifications for undertaking risk management. At the management level, better insight is a critical aspect, leading to better decisions. Risk management also provides a framework that avoids sudden surprises and justifies prudent risk reduction and mitigation measures.

The benefits of risk management are not confined to large or risky projects. The process may be formalized in these circumstances, but it is applicable for all scales of project and procurement activity. It can be applied at all stages in the project cycle, from the earliest assessments of strategy to the supply, operation, maintenance and disposal of individual items, facilities or assets. It has many applications, ranging from the evaluation of alternative activities for budgets and business plans to the management of cost overruns and delays in projects and programmes.

Risk management will also provide benefits in better accountability and justification of decisions, by providing a consistent and robust process that supports decision-making.

Risk and project management

Managing risk is an integral part of good management, and fundamental to achieving good business and project outcomes and the effective procurement of goods and services. It is something many managers do already in one form or another, whether it be sensitivity analysis of a financial projection, scenario planning for a project appraisal, assessing the contingency allowance in a cost estimate, negotiating contract conditions or developing contingency plans.

Although many managers do not use the term 'risk' when they undertake these activities, the concept of risk is central to what they are doing. Better management of risk and more successful activities are the outcomes.

Systematic identification, analysis and assessment of risk and dealing with the results contributes significantly to the success of projects. However, poorly managed project risks may have wide-ranging negative implications for the achievement of organizational objectives.

Risk should be considered at the earliest stages of project planning, and risk management activities should be continued throughout a project. Risk management plans and activities should be an integral part of an organization's management processes.

It is important for the project sponsor and the prime contractor, and the main sub-contractors where relevant, to use effective and consistent risk management processes. The processes should promote transparency and effective communication between the parties to facilitate effective and expeditious management of risks.

There are three keys to managing project and procurement risk effectively:

- identifying, analysing and assessing risks early and systematically, and developing plans for handling them;
- allocating responsibility to the party best placed to manage risks, which may involve implementing new practices, procedures or systems or negotiating suitable contractual arrangements; and
- ensuring that the costs incurred in reducing risks are commensurate with the importance of the project and the risks involved.

The scope of risk management for projects includes risks associated with the overall business approach and concept, the design and delivery of the project, transition into service, and the detailed operations and processing activities of the delivered asset or capability.

- Business risks include all those risks that might impact on the viability of the enterprise, including market, industry, technology, economic and financial factors, government and political influences.
- Project risk includes all those risks that might impact on the cost, schedule or quality of the project.
- Operations and processing risks include all those risks that might impact on the design, procurement, construction, commissioning, operations and maintenance activities, including major hazards and catastrophic events.

Definitions

Risk is exposure to the consequences of uncertainty. In a project context, it is the chance of something happening that will have an impact upon objectives. It includes the possibility of loss or gain, or variation from a desired or planned outcome, as a consequence of the uncertainty associated with following a particular course of action. Risk thus has two elements: the likelihood or probability of something happening, and the consequences or impacts if it does.

Risk management refers to the culture, processes and structures that are directed towards the effective management of potential opportunities and adverse effects.

The risk management process involves the systematic application of management policies, processes and procedures to the tasks of establishing the context, identifying, analysing, assessing, treating, monitoring and communicating risk.

Risk identification is the process of determining what, how and why things may happen.

Risk analysis is the systematic use of available information to determine how often specified events may occur and the magnitude of their consequences. It may use any of a wide variety of mathematical and other models and techniques.

Risk evaluation determines whether the risk is tolerable or not and identifies the risks that should be accorded the highest priority in developing responses for risk treatment.

Risk treatment establishes and implements management responses for dealing with risks, in ways appropriate to the significance of the risk and the importance of the project.

We usually think about risk in terms of potential problems or negative outcomes. However, under the definitions here, risk includes positive impacts or consequences as well, and risk management includes processes for identifying and taking advantage of opportunities and benefits.

For further definitions and a glossary of terms see the Glossary towards the end of this book.

When is project risk management used?

Risks arise because of uncertainty about the future. Risk exposure may arise from the possibility of economic, financial or social loss or gain, physical damage or injury, or delay. It may also be caused by changes in the relationships between the parties involved in the supply, ownership, operation and maintenance of assets for public or private purposes.

Risk management provides a structured way of assessing and dealing with future uncertainty. Traditionally, it has been concerned with the implications of events and changes in the future physical, social and economic environment. The term 'management' implies that risks are to be treated in an ordered fashion, rather than in a haphazard way.

The project risk management process applies across all project phases, and projects that arise at all phases of the asset life cycle, shown in outline in Figure I.1. There are different requirements for risk management at different stages in the life of a project proposal. For large projects, several risk analyses may be conducted, for example at the concept development and appraisal stages of a project proposal, to determine and evaluate alternative project strategies, for bidding and contract negotiation, for the construction of the approved project and for its operations.

Risk management processes are designed to assist planners and managers in identifying significant risks and developing measures to address them and their consequences. This leads to more effective and efficient decisions, greater certainty about outcomes and reduced risk exposure.

In the later stages of a project, the focus is on efficient and effective delivery. Risk management is directed towards ensuring more favourable and reliable outcomes are achieved in terms of the timeliness, cost and quality of the project and the services that are provided.

Many organizations undertake projects involving significant capital outlays, or groups of related projects that together make up large programmes. Three aspects of large projects or programmes make risk management desirable.

- Their size implies there may be large potential losses unless they are managed carefully, and conversely large potential gains if risks are managed well.

Figure I.1—Asset life cycle outline

- They often involve unbalanced cash flows, requiring large initial investments before meaningful returns are obtained. In these circumstances, and particularly for assets with potentially long lives, there may be significant uncertainty about future cash flows, due to changing economic conditions, advances in technology, changing patterns of demand for products or services, new competition, or varying operating requirements. For projects with significant social or environmental implications, the benefits may not all be readily measurable in cash terms and social values may change during the life of an asset. Factors like these must be assessed and managed to ensure the capital investment is worthwhile.
- Large public sector projects may involve a degree of private sector participation, either in the form of direct private sector investment or involvement in the through-life operations of a government-owned asset. This may require an additional focus on risk, particularly to identify and manage any residual risks for Government.

Size is not the only consideration, however. Some projects or programmes are inherently complex or risky, irrespective of their overall value, and particular attention to risk management is recommended. This might occur when projects involve the development or use of new technology, or when unusual legal or contractual arrangements are proposed. Specific risk management may also be required when there are important political, economic or financial aspects, sensitive environmental, social or safety issues, or stringent regulatory or licensing conditions to be met.

The approaches and techniques described in this book are not just for large or complex projects. They are applicable to all scales of projects, from the very large to the very small, and they will assist managers at all levels of project-related and asset-related activities. The framework for identifying, analysing and assessing risks and developing plans for dealing with them can be applied equally to smaller, simpler and routine projects and procurements, with significant benefits for the organizations involved.

Risk management provides useful inputs to the detailed activities within each of the broad life cycle stages in Figure I.1. For example, Figure I.2 shows the stages in the contracting process where a risk management approach can add value.

Similar processes apply for projects and activities that are not related to the acquisition of assets. Examples include:

- IT systems upgrades and implementations;
- organizational or procedural changes;
- business relocation;
- marketing initiatives;

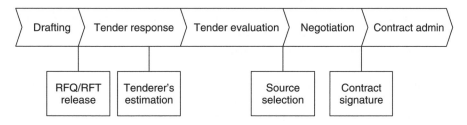

Figure I.2—Stages in contracting

- analysis of conditions for service-delivery contracts;
- environmental management.

Risk management can be applied usefully at all stages of a project or procurement. Table I.1 shows some examples. (Note that risk management processes have wide application in other stages in the life cycle of assets, omitted from this table, including operation, routine maintenance, major capital maintenance and refurbishment, and disposal.)

For some projects, risk management may be a formal requirement at specific stages of the project development. There may be many reasons for this:

- Economic viability assessment, for high-level strategic decision-making about whether or not to proceed with a project;
- Financial feasibility assessment, when a finance package is being assembled;
- Corporate governance and accountability, for managers, project staff, end-users and suppliers to demonstrate that they have fully assessed all the material risks, that the

Table I.1—Project stages and risk management application examples

Project stage	Application examples
Objectives and requirements analysis	Assessment of internal skills needed to assure the success of the process (for example, for procurement of services by outsourcing)
Formulation of procurement strategy	Incentive contract performance and fee modelling Development of equipment acquisition strategies
Capital evaluation	Capital evaluation of major spending initiatives (some examples from our recent experience include new mine development, IT systems acquisition, infrastructure provision, selection of capital equipment within major developments)
Analysis of options	Exploration of market testing strategies Quantitative analysis of strategic options, with cost and risk trade-offs Assessment of alternate technologies for major plant upgrades
Formulation of proposals for funding approval	Board, cabinet or ministerial submissions for approval of major projects Applications for additional funding
Preparation of procurement documents	Detailed development of requests for tender documents that address risks appropriately
Preparation of tender evaluation plans	Preparation and assessments of key delivery requirements for tender evaluation plans
Evaluation and selection of tenderers	Evaluation of tender submissions taking account of bidders' capacity to manage the risks involved
Negotiation and signature of contracts	Review of negotiation priorities ensuring effective risk allocation
Implementation and delivery	Implementation and delivery risks, including approvals, technical, construction, budgets, phasing, milestones
Commissioning and handover	Development and management of test and commissioning, transition, delivery

measures taken to control risk are appropriate, and that the economic reward for taking on the risk that remains is adequate;

- Contractual purposes, to assess alternative contractual and legal frameworks for the project, in the context of deciding who should bear what risks and determining an equitable allocation and sharing of risks and rewards between the parties involved;
- Tendering, when deciding whether or not to bid, or accept a bid, for a proposed project, and in what form;
- Regulatory purposes, for legislative, judicial or licensing agencies, or for public inquiries, to demonstrate accountability in a public or social context;
- Communication purposes, to provide information for owners, sponsors, users, contractors, joint venture partners or other stakeholders, or to demonstrate capability and competence in an area.

Within an organization, senior management needs to know and understand what risks and opportunities exist and how they are being managed, as a matter of good corporate governance. Management may have specific requirements for:

- Consistent reports of actual and emerging risks;
- Comparability across the organization;
- Consolidation of risks and opportunities across the organization;
- Effective mechanisms with which to direct priorities for risk management and to alert different parts of the organization to issues identified elsewhere that are relevant to them as well;
- Analysis of trends in risks across different activity types;
- Transparency and traceability of risk management decisions;
- Visibility of key risk treatment actions and their status;
- Timely requests for assistance, where necessary; and
- Plenty of warning, with no surprises!

The implementation of sound risk management practices enables senior managers to allocate resources more effectively to manage risks. They will be in a better position to be aware of the risks to the organization and put into place effective control measures to mitigate them. Where an adverse outcome does occur, those accountable will be able to demonstrate that they exercised an appropriate level of diligence, the basis for any decisions bearing on the risk and the organization's response to it.

A number of audits of private and public organizations have found that risk management is not always implemented effectively, and sometimes it is not addressed at all. Executives of these organizations are now requiring that risk management be implemented in an effective manner, to meet the management requirements of the organizations and to address the deficiencies identified through the audit activities.

Risk and government procurement

Recent changes in the nature of government procurement strategies in many countries have provided a new incentive for sound risk management. The emergence and increasing use of arrangements such as build-own-operate (BOO), build-own-operate-transfer (BOOT), public–private partnerships (PPP) and private finance initiatives (PFI) for asset and capability acquisition have changed the traditional procurement environment. These new structures require different kinds of contractual arrangements and new forms of control and accountability, all of which introduce new kinds of risks.

As part of the re-examination of how capabilities are provided by Government and the roles of public and private providers of services, many government agencies are contemplating or engaging in a range of new or different activities outside their traditional scope. Risk management is a critical element in strategic planning for all parties involved in the new relationships and patterns of service provision that are evolving.

Risk management is an important part of the drive to improve the overall quality and standard of government procurement activities. It is concerned with ensuring potential risks are identified early, the best options for managing them are selected and broad risk exposures are minimized. In this sense, government objectives are closely aligned with those of the private sector – achieving better project outcomes, more efficiently and more effectively, and with an appropriate structure of risk and reward.

In the government procurement arena, risk management is important in that it supports consistent and justifiable public decision-making, generating an audit trail of the available information and a documented method that demonstrates how this information was used to form effective decisions.

Approaches to project risk management

Project risk management is a topic of major current interest. It is being actively addressed by many government agencies and most of the professional project management associations around the world, and many relevant standards are extant or being developed. Some examples from the many approaches in use include:

- Project Management Institute (PMI), USA (2003), *Project Management Body of Knowledge*, Chapter 11 on risk management;
- Association for Project Management, UK (1997), *PRAM Guide*;
- AS/NZS 4360 (2004), *Risk Management*, Standards Association of Australia;
- IEC 62198 (2001), *Project Risk Management—Application Guidelines*;
- Office of Government Commerce (OGC), UK (2002), *Management of Risk*; and
- Treasury Board of Canada (2001), *Integrated Risk Management Framework*.

The standards and the guides from the professional associations provide only an outline of the topics that are essential for managing project risk, and they offer few insights into how the risk management process works in practice. This book provides a practical complement to these documents and publications.

The approach adopted here follows the structure of AS/NZS 4360, one of the first comprehensive risk management standards that could be applied readily to projects. Many of the other approaches have a similar structure and are directly comparable and compatible with this standard, albeit often using different terms. A brief comparison of some of them is provided in Chapter 12.

Overview of these project risk management guidelines

The first part of this book, Chapters 1 to 12, addresses the basics of project risk management. The focus is on simple processes, in the context of practical project management. Our recommended approach to project risk management is outlined, and each step is described in a detailed chapter. There is extensive case study material based on our risk management work with large projects in a variety of sectors and in different phases. The methods for risk assessment described in this part of the book are largely qualitative in nature.

Part II, Chapters 13 to 18, extends the risk management process into some specialized areas of projects and procurement, including tender evaluation, outsourcing and public–private partnerships, again with case material to illustrate the applications. Technical risk assessment tools are introduced, and environmental risk management processes are outlined.

Part III, Chapters 19 to 24, considers quantitative risk analysis methods and the way they can be used in large projects. Cost estimation case studies are used to introduce the concepts, which are then extended to capital evaluation and economic appraisal of projects under uncertainty.

The final part of the book, from Chapter 25, provides supporting information, including checklists, tables, a glossary and references.

Part I
The basics of project risk management

THE PROJECT RISK MANAGEMENT APPROACH

Chapter overview

- **Purpose**

The purpose of project risk management is to obtain better project outcomes, in terms of schedule, cost and operations performance.

- **Rationale**

The project risk management process is needed to ensure that:

- All significant risks to the success of the project are identified;
- Identified risks are understood, with both the range of potential consequences they represent and the likelihood of values in that range being determined as far as is necessary for decision-making;
- Assessment is undertaken of individual risks relative to the other risks to support priority setting and resource allocation;
- Strategies for treating the risks take account of opportunities to address more than one risk;
- The process itself and the risk treatment strategies are implemented cost-effectively.

- **Method**

The recommended approach to project risk management is consistent with the approach adopted for a wide range of other risk management processes. The application of those processes to projects requires integration of risk management with project management processes and activities.

Overview

The broad objectives of the project risk management process are to:

- enhance the capability of the organization;
- extend the organization's overall risk management processes to projects, and apply them in a consistent way; and
- enhance the management of projects across the organization and obtain better project outcomes, in terms of schedule, cost and operations performance, by reducing risks and capturing opportunities.

Good project risk management within an organization has the following characteristics:

- project risk management activities commence at the initiation of the project, risk management plans are developed and risk management continues throughout the project life cycle;
- project risk management is not a discrete stand-alone process, but is integrated with other project management functions; and
- the implementation of project risk management is the responsibility of all project stakeholders and they participate actively in the process.

This chapter provides a brief summary of the material that is developed in the following chapters.

Approach

The objective of risk management is to identify and manage significant risks. It involves several key phases, with feedback through a monitoring and review process.

In most projects, risk management overlaps with other management processes and procedures, in that many of the steps are undertaken as part of normal project management. This provides the basis for integrating risk management and project management activities.

The approach to project risk management adopted in this book is consistent with the Australian and New Zealand Standard on risk management, AS/NZS 4360 (Figure 1.1). This approach is consistent with similar approaches adopted by the major project management professional bodies and government agencies that have issued project risk guidelines. The steps in the process address important questions for the project manager (Table 1.1). Extensions to quantitative risk analysis are discussed in Chapters 19 to 23.

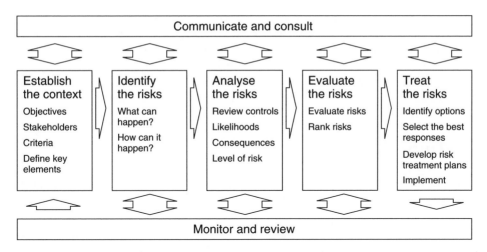

Figure 1.1—The project risk management process

Table 1.1—Questions for the project manager

Risk management process step	Management question
Establish the context	What are we trying to achieve?
Identify the risks	What might happen?
Analyse the risks	What might that mean for the project's key criteria?
Evaluate the risks	What are the most important things?
Treat the risks	What are we going to do about them?
Monitor and review	How do we keep them under control?
Communicate and consult	Who should be involved in the process?

Establish the context

Establishing the context is concerned with developing a structure for the risk identification and assessment tasks to follow. This step:

- establishes the organizational and project environment in which the risk assessment is taking place;
- specifies the main objectives and outcomes required;
- identifies a set of success criteria against which the consequences of identified risks can be measured; and
- defines a set of key elements for structuring the risk identification and assessment process.

Context inputs include key project documents, such as the project execution strategy, project charter, cost and schedule assumptions, scope definitions, engineering designs and studies, economic analyses, and any other relevant documentation about the project and its purpose.

The output from this stage is a concise statement of the project objectives and specific criteria for success, the objectives and scope for the risk assessment itself, and a set of key elements for structuring the risk identification process in the next stage.

Identify the risks

Risk identification determines what might happen that could affect the objectives of the project, and how those things might happen.

The risk identification process must be comprehensive, as risks that have not been identified cannot be assessed, and their emergence at a later time may threaten the success of the project and cause unpleasant surprises. The process should be structured using the key elements to examine risks systematically, in each area of the project to be addressed.

A number of techniques can be used for risk identification, but brainstorming is a preferred method because of its flexibility and capability, when appropriately structured, of generating a wide and diverse range of risks.

Information used in the risk identification process may include historical data, theoretical analysis, empirical data and analysis, informed opinions of the project team and other experts, and the concerns of stakeholders.

The output is a comprehensive list of possible risks to the successful outcome of the project, usually in the form of a risk register, with management responsibilities (risk owners) allocated to them.

Analyse and evaluate the risks

Risk assessment is the overall process of risk analysis and risk evaluation. Its purpose is to develop agreed priorities for the identified risks.

- Risk analysis is the systematic use of available information to determine how often specified events may occur and the magnitude of their consequences.
- Risk evaluation is the process of comparing the estimated risk against given risk criteria to determine the significance of the risk.

The assessment process:

- determines the consequences of each risk, should it arise;
- assesses the likelihood of those consequences occurring;
- converts the consequence and likelihood ratings to an initial priority for the risk; and
- develops agreed risk priorities and inherent risk levels.

The agreed priorities are used to determine where the greatest effort should be focused in treating identified risks. They facilitate structured action planning and resource allocation.

This stage of the risk management process generates a prioritized list of risks and a detailed understanding of their impacts upon the success of the project should they occur. The consequence and likelihood ratings and the agreed risk priorities are all recorded in the risk register.

Treat the risks

The purpose of risk treatment is to determine what will be done in response to the risks that have been identified, in order to reduce the overall risk exposure. Unless action is taken, the risk identification and assessment process has been wasted. Risk treatment converts the earlier analyses into substantive actions to reduce risks.

The primary inputs to this step are the lists of risks and their agreed priorities from the previous step and the current project plans and budgets.

Risk treatment involves:

- identifying the options for reducing the likelihood or consequences of each Extreme, High or Medium risk;
- determining the potential benefits and costs of the options;
- selecting the best options for the project; and
- developing and implementing detailed Risk Action Plans.

Risk Action Plan Summaries are usually required for each risk classified as Extreme or High on the agreed risk priority scale.

Monitor and review

Continuous monitoring and review of risks ensures new risks are detected and managed, and that action plans are implemented and progressed effectively. Review processes are often implemented as part of the regular management meeting cycle, supplemented by major reviews at significant project phases and milestones.

Monitoring and review activities link risk management to other management processes. They also facilitate better risk management and continuous improvement.

The main input to this step is the risk watch list of the major risks that have been identified for risk treatment action. The outcomes are in the form of revisions to the risk register, and a list of new action items for risk treatment.

Communicate and consult

Communication and consultation with project stakeholders may be a critical factor in undertaking good risk management and achieving project outcomes that are broadly accepted. They help owners, clients and end users understand the risks and trade-offs that must be made in a large project. This ensures all parties are fully informed, and thus avoids unpleasant surprises. Within the project management team, they help maintain the consistency and 'reasonableness' of risk assessments and their underlying assumptions.

In practice, regular reporting is an important component of communication. Managers report on the current status of risks and risk management as required by sponsors and company policy. Senior managers need to understand the risks they face, and risk reports provide a complement to other management reports in developing this understanding.

The risk register and the supporting action plans provide the basis for most risk reporting. Reports provide a summary of project risks, the status of treatment actions and an indication of trends in the incidence of risks. They are usually submitted on a regular basis or as required, as part of standard management reporting. Major projects may require more extensive reporting on a periodic basis or at key milestones.

ESTABLISH THE CONTEXT

Chapter overview

- ### Purpose

  Establishing the context is concerned with developing a structure for the risk identification and assessment tasks to follow.

- ### Rationale

  This step is needed:

  - to establish the organizational and project environment in which the risk assessment is taking place;
  - to specify the main objectives and outcomes required;
  - to identify a set of success criteria against which the consequences of identified risks can be measured; and
  - to define a set of key elements for structuring the risk identification and assessment process.

- ### Inputs

  Context inputs include key project documents, such as the project execution strategy, project charter, cost and schedule assumptions, scope definitions, engineering designs and studies, economic analyses, and any other relevant documentation about the project and its purpose.

- ### Method

  - Review organizational and project documentation.
  - Perform stakeholder analysis.
  - Develop criteria for success.
  - Develop a set of key elements.

- **Outputs**

  The output from this stage is a concise statement of the organizational and project objectives and specific criteria for success, the objectives and scope for the risk assessment, and a set of key elements for structuring the risk identification workshop in the next stage.

- **Documentation**

  - Stakeholder analysis (format as in Figure 2.1)
  - Project context review summary (format as in Figure 2.2)
  - Key elements (format as in Figure 2.4 and Figure 2.5)

Objectives and criteria

To ensure that all significant risks are captured, it is necessary to know the objectives of the organization and the project. Objectives lie at the heart of the context definition, and they are linked into the risk management process via criteria for measuring success. Success criteria are the basis for measuring the achievement of objectives, and so are used to measure the impacts or consequences of risks that might jeopardize those objectives.

The first step identifies the scope of the project, the main questions and issues of concern to the organization, and the relationship between the project and the organization's strategy and business objectives.

General requirements for the organization that is buying or procuring the project are often specified in the form of policy objectives. They are usually applicable to all purchases, and so are often elaborated in procurement specifications and contracting procedures, often with specific additional approval and other requirements to be applied for large projects.

An example of general project procurement objectives from a private sector commercial organization is shown in Table 2.1. In practice, these project policy guidelines are complemented by a set of contracting rules and processes.

Table 2.1—Private sector procurement policy example

The company's policy is to develop a clear and definite project execution strategy that will:

- adopt the most cost effective strategy by making use, to the extent available, of resources, expertise and experience within the engineering department and the company as a whole;
- ensure the user business units are involved in developing the strategy;
- optimize project schedule to ensure timely implementation and operation of project facilities within the framework of the company's overall operational plan;
- minimize disruption to any current operations at any company site or facility;
- minimize health, safety and environmental risks during construction.

For a government procurement, there are likely to be additional requirements that must be addressed and demonstrated explicitly, and may be subject to external audit and oversight. They include:

- value for money;
- open and effective competition;
- ethical behaviour and fair dealing;
- maximizing opportunities for local industry to compete;
- environmental aspects;
- quality assurance;
- government sanctions against specified countries;
- social justice policies.

The requirements may have different interpretations, depending on the organization's business objectives and the phase of the procurement cycle.

- In the planning stages of a project, requirements are often related to broad policy and performance aspects, expressed in general terms. They may also include some or all of the benefit and cost criteria used in the economic appraisal process. Risk analysis and risk management planning are often undertaken at the same time as an economic appraisal; see Chapter 23.
- In the bidding stages, value for money is critical, and ethical behaviour and probity may be important considerations, particularly for a public-sector entity.
- Later, in the delivery, operation and maintenance stages, criteria are likely to be more specific and concerned with the most efficient completion of the project, the optimum provision of products and services and the satisfaction of users' needs. In this case, demand levels, revenues and expenses, schedule delays, and the quality of the product or service may be appropriate measures. Although these criteria are used during the later stages of the project, they are developed much earlier. They should be specified in the initial brief and user needs analysis in the first stages of the requirements planning process.

Specific requirements are typically related directly to the project itself. They include such objectives as:

- cost control, ensuring the project is conducted within the available budget;
- schedule control, ensuring the project is completed within the time frame allowed;
- performance quality control, ensuring the project and its outcomes are suitable for their intended purpose.

Specific objectives and criteria are developed by reviewing key project documents, such as the project execution strategy, project charter, cost and schedule assumptions, scope definitions, engineering studies and designs, economic analyses, and any other relevant documentation about the project and its purpose.

Stakeholder identification and analysis

Stakeholder analysis is important in risk assessments for most activities. It is usually undertaken at an early stage of planning.

All projects and procurements involve at least two stakeholders: the procuring entity (the buyer) and the supplier of goods or services (the seller). The differing objectives of these two parties, and the contractual relationship between them, are key determinants in the allocation and management of risk in the procurement process.

In most projects, though, there is a wider set of stakeholders as well, whose desired outcomes must be considered when planning a project. For example, other stakeholders who may have to be considered include:

- in a corporate business, the board and controlling shareholders, senior executives and the managers of other business units who may be affected by the project;
- in a government procurement, the portfolio minister, other ministers and local members whose electorates may be affected by procurement activities or associated employment or other opportunities;
- the customer business unit or agency, where the procuring entity is acting on behalf of an end-user;
- the user community, including the management, staff and clients of the customer business unit;
- regulators who must approve the project and the project delivery process;
- people who may be affected by the project or the project delivery process, such as those living near a new plant or building;
- the environment, as a general proxy stakeholder;
- special interest groups, such as environmental lobby groups;
- sub-contractors to the main supplier;
- financial institutions and other providers of private-sector funding; and
- the media.

Stakeholder analysis provides decision-makers with a documented profile of stakeholders so as to better understand their needs and concerns. It involves considering the objectives of each stakeholder in relation to the requirement. Such analysis plays an important part in demonstrating the integrity of the process and in ensuring the objectives of the risk assessment encompass all legitimate stakeholders' objectives and expectations. Involving stakeholders builds acceptance and can generate constructive solutions. Failure to identify and include the stakeholders may lead to failure in the acceptance of the proposal and its strategy by management, customers, staff, regulators and the community.

Examples of stakeholders for a government project are shown in Table 2.2. Table 2.3 lists stakeholders in a private sector project.

The main aims and objectives of relevant stakeholders should be considered explicitly. This may take a very simple form, such as the stakeholder and issues list in Figure 2.1. An example of stakeholder analysis for a public-sector project is shown in Table 2.4. More sophisticated analyses may be appropriate where major social and community risks are anticipated.

Table 2.2—Stakeholders in a procurement project for a government agency

Group	Stakeholders
Government agency	Executive management
	Agency business units involved in the procurement process
	Agency users
Governments and their ministers	National Government
	Portfolio minister
	State and local governments
Other government departments	Central funding agencies
Finance providers	Financial institutions and their depositors
Industry	Suppliers of capability
Communities	Local businesses who benefit directly
	Local businesses who benefit indirectly
	Local communities and neighbours of a project site

Table 2.3—Stakeholders in a private sector project

Group	Stakeholders
Senior management	Major shareholders
	The board
	Executive management team
Business units with an interest in the project	Sponsoring business units, including users
	Engineering function
	Maintenance function
	Other users
	Administrative and support functions
Staff	Operators
	Maintainers
Industry	Contractors
	Suppliers and service providers
Commercial counterparts	Purchasers and users of products
	Shippers
Regulators	Construction and building approvals regulators
	Occupational health and safety regulators
	Environmental protection agencies
Community	Public in the local area
	Wider community outside the local area

Criteria

The requirements of the organization and the key stakeholders are used to derive a set of criteria for the project. These will be used to determine the specific scales against which the consequences

Project:		Reference:
Stakeholder	**Key issues and objectives**	
Compiler:	Date:	Reviewer:	Date:

Figure 2.1—Stakeholder and issues summary

of risks will be assessed in the following stages of the risk analysis, discussed in detail in Chapter 4. They may also form the basis of project evaluation at the end of the acquisition.

The range of criteria may be wide. Table 2.5 shows an example from a medium-scale project where community acceptance was important. This list of criteria was a valuable guide for the project manager through the initial planning and design stages of the project.

Table 2.4—Stakeholder analysis worksheet, public-sector project

Stakeholder	Desired outcomes
Executive managers	A capability delivered on schedule, within approved project costs and annual expenditure levels, that meets the endorsed requirements A selected capability acquisition option that demonstrably provides the best value for money
Business units involved in the procurement	A well structured and efficient procurement strategy Open and effective competition A selected capability acquisition option that demonstrably provides the best value for money
Agency users	A delivered capability that meets the endorsed requirements and the needs of users
Government and ministers	An effective capability for the nation A selected capability acquisition option that demonstrably provides the best value for money Benefits for business and the economy
State and local governments and their ministers	Enhanced opportunities for their local business communities and economies

(Continued opposite)

Central funding agencies	Cost-efficient acquisition of endorsed capabilities
	An open and accountable acquisition process
	Budget allocations that are managed efficiently and effectively
Financial institutions	Enhanced business opportunities
	Effective management of risks associated with the provision of capital investment
	A reasonable profit on business investments
Industry	Enhanced business opportunities, sustainable on a long-term basis
	A delivered capability that meets the needs of users
	Effective management of risks associated with the provision of the capability requirement
	A reasonable profit on the supply and operation of the capability
Local businesses	Enhanced business opportunities, whether as a prime contractor or sub-contractor
	A reasonable profit on business activities

Table 2.5—Criteria for a medium-scale project (case example)

Criterion	Notes
Availability	The availability of existing facilities must be maximized by reducing the disruption to current business operations as far as possible
Community relations	The highest standards of community consultation and liaison must be maintained
Economics	The project must be clearly justifiable in economic terms, measured by profitability and rate of return
Environment	The solutions to the technical issues must be environmentally sound; an alternative solution should be available
Funding	Avoid expenditure outside allocated budgets; maximize the use of special purpose grant funds
Industrial relations	Optimize industrial relations by negotiation with staff representatives and use of appropriate enterprise agreements
Quality	The client requires equipment that is properly engineered and reliable
Safety	Project delivery processes must ensure the highest standards of safety; contract conditions must contain appropriate clauses
Staff development	The project delivery method and outcomes should enhance the core skills of the organization and the abilities of the staff involved
Timing	The project must be completed by the specified date to meet user obligations

Table 2.6 lists critical success factors for a simple project activity involving the purchase and installation of replacement equipment, with the relevant measures used for each factor.

Table 2.7 shows criteria for a high-technology defence project, related to the objectives of the stakeholders.

The criteria and the associated objectives for an oil production business are shown in Table 2.8.

Table 2.6—Criteria and measures for a small-scale project (case example)

Criterion	Notes	Measure
Cost	The installation and testing must be completed within allocated budgets	Budget $$, plus 30 hours of internal management time
Disruption	The disruption to current operations must be minimized	Lost processing time less than 40 terminal hours
Functionality	The new equipment should have comparable functionality and operator interfaces	New equipment to pass standard Benchmark Tests 1 (100%) and 2 (98%)
Quality	The operators and the user agency require reliable equipment	Down time less than 5 minutes per month over the first six months' operation
Timing	The products must be delivered and commissioned by the specified date to meet the purchaser's business obligations	Phase 1 equipment commissioned by 7 April; phase 2 by 14 May; system test completed by 21 May
Training	All staff must be trained on the new equipment	All operator conversion training completed by 3 April

Table 2.7—Criteria related to objectives for a defence project

Criterion	Objectives
Performance	The acquired capability meets the requirements of the endorsed concepts of operations and the needs of defence users
Cost	The capability is delivered within approved project costs and annual expenditure levels Budget allocations are managed efficiently and effectively Defence is cost-efficient in acquiring its endorsed capabilities
Schedule	Critical milestones are met and the capability is delivered on schedule
Supportability and sustainability	The acquired capability can be maintained and supported throughout its life
Political	The acquisition process is fully visible and accountable, and is seen to provide best value for money The country has an effective and sustainable defence capability The benefits of defence business to the economy are maximized
Community	Industry business opportunities are maximized, and are sustainable on a long-term basis Industry and finance entities associated with the project make a reasonable commercial profit Adverse community impacts are minimized

Context review summary

Summarize the review of project documents in a context summary table, like that shown in Figure 2.2. Some organizations adopt generic criteria for project evaluation and risk assessment, such as those in Table 2.5 or Table 2.7. If your organization has done this, note any essential modifications to general criteria under the heading 'Specific changes to criteria'. Where possible, try to minimize the changes to these tables, to maintain consistency

Table 2.8—Criteria related to objectives for an oil production business

Criterion	Objectives
Production loss or restriction	Maximize the value of hydrocarbon resources Increase sustainable production Annual production targets and costs
Facility damage	Minimize disruption to operations; no damage to plant or equipment
Facility integrity	Minimize disruption to operations Maintain asset or system condition and performance
Project performance	Cost-effective strategy Operating entities are involved Timely implementation and operation of project facilities Time, cost and performance related to budget
Financial impacts	Supply costs reduced by 10% Capital costs optimized Operating costs improved No losses, no increased or additional costs
Employees	Low turnover, grow skills and experience Health, safety and environmental performance Minimize health, safety and environmental (HSE) risks during construction
Health and safety	Health and safety performance Minimize health and safety risks during construction No injuries, fatalities or long-term health problems
Environment and community	Environment and community performance Minimize environmental and community risks during construction No releases to the environment or public outrage
Image and reputation	Exceptional high performance Shareholder and public support and trust

between project risk assessments. The heading 'Reference documents' in Figure 2.2 refers to the key project documents that were used as inputs to the context stage.

Sometimes more detail is needed and it is useful to expand the criterion definitions and methods of measuring their achievement. In this case a list like that in Figure 2.3 may be appropriate (and see also Table 2.6).

Key elements

Except for very small projects, risk identification will generally be unproductive if an attempt is made to consider the project as a whole. It is much more effective to disaggregate the project into sections or key elements for risk identification.

Key elements are a set of topics to be considered one by one during risk identification. Each topic is somewhat narrower than the project as a whole, allowing those performing the identification to focus their thoughts and go into more depth than they would if they tried to deal with the whole project at once. A well-designed set of key elements will stimulate

Project name:		Reference:
Project description:		
Objectives for the project: Organizational objectives: Business unit objectives: Project objectives:		
Objectives for the risk assessment:		
Specific changes to criteria (if any):		
Reference documents:		
Compiled by:	Date:	Reviewed by:	Date:

Figure 2.2—Context review summary

creative thought, and ensure that all important issues are put before those responsible for identifying risks. When a brainstorming meeting is used to identify risks, the key elements form the agenda and the basis of the timetable for that meeting.

The set of key elements must be complete, in that it covers all significant issues. However, as the number of key elements tends to drive the duration of the risk identification activity, it must also be contained to an appropriate scale. It must balance sufficient specific language to stimulate the identification of risks against enough generality to avoid prejudging the identification process.

Project:		Reference:	
Criterion	**Definition**	**Measurement method**	
Compiler:	Date:	Reviewer:	Date:

Figure 2.3—Criteria summary

The key elements may be based on different aspects of the project, depending on the objectives and key issues of concern to the organization and the other stakeholders. Table 2.9 indicates some of the ways of structuring the elements for different purposes.

In many cases, there is considerable overlap between the categories of elements noted in Table 2.9. For example, in many projects the cost items are the major activities, or they are associated directly with physical components. Often, the Work Breakdown Structure (WBS) for the project is the best starting point, with its companion WBS Dictionary that describes in words the content of each work element. This is particularly convenient, as

Table 2.9—Elements for structuring the risk assessment

Purpose, objectives, relevant issues	*Basis for selecting the elements*
Business planning and strategic procurement	Business activities
Budget constraints; external financing	Cost items
Operating issues; fitness for purpose; value for money	Functions of the supplied product or service
Technical and environmental issues; reliability; allocation of engineering and management effort	Physical components
Environmental aspects; effect of the environment on the outcomes (e.g. access, weather)	Physical locations
Timing and schedule; industrial relations aspects; construction risks	Project activities
General project risks, undertaken early in the planning stage; stop/go decisions; commercial structuring; overall procurement approach and strategy	Project phases
Programme risks; programme funding; strategic planning	Projects and sub-projects in the programme
Environmental and community issues; approval processes; financing aspects	Stakeholders

then the risk analysis is aligned with the other important aspects of the project, including responsibility structures, design and planning structures, and costs and schedules.

Although the WBS provides a good starting point for a set of key elements for many projects, there are usually other related topics that need to be added. A generic set of key elements is shown in Table 2.10 for a facility construction project for a resource business;

Table 2.10—Generic key elements for a facility construction

Element	Notes
1 Technical	
Design basis	Input resource quality, variability, related projects
Process	System performance
Mechanical and materials	Equipment performance, corrosion
Piping and layout	—
Electrical	—
Instrumentation and control	—
Loss prevention and HSE	Hazards, protection systems, safety, emergency planning, environmental constraints
Civil and structural	—
Plant interfaces	Capacity of plant interface equipment, consistency of standards
2 Estimates	
Capital cost	Initial capital, sustaining capital
Operating costs	Operations, maintenance
Schedule	Milestones
3 Delivery	
Project management	Process, people, systems, planning
Engineering	Documentation, manuals, quality, completeness
Procurement	Tender process, selection, negotiation, contract terms
Contract management	Performance monitoring, variations, guarantees
Construction	Mobilization, nearby live plant, permits to work, contractors
Interfaces	Tie-ins with existing plant and services, shutdowns
Commissioning	Testing, performance trials, start-up
Resources	People, equipment, materials, services
4 Operations	
Operations	Normal conditions, abnormal conditions
Maintenance	Availability, reliability, testing, spares; future inspection, maintenance and monitoring
Resources	Personnel (number, training, skills), service
5 Other	
Internal relationships	Internal stakeholders, users, other projects
Commercial relationships	—
External factors	External stakeholders, natural events
Legal issues	Liabilities
Regulatory aspects	Relevant regulators, legislative or regulatory constraints
Other matters	Other risks not included elsewhere

Note: HSE denotes health, safety and the environment.

these could be used as a starting point for developing specific key elements for particular projects in the business.

Table 2.11 shows a similar generic set of key elements for a technical project involving acquisition of an asset with associated through-life support.

Table 2.12 shows a simple set of key elements based on system components for a project to build an electricity sub-station to a standard design. These elements were all at Level 3

Table 2.11—Generic key elements for a technical project

Element	Notes
Technical operation and performance	Capability, specification compliance, technical issues
Integration	System integration, external interfaces and users, interoperability
Test and evaluation (T&E)	Varying levels of T&E throughout the acquisition process
Completion, acceptance and commissioning	Resolution of changes and defects, transition, end-users, workforce postings and training
Integrated logistics support (ILS)	All major elements of ILS that impact on the acquisition
Project management	Monitoring and control mechanisms
Resources	Business units involved in the procurement process, contractors and sub-contractors, end-users
Financial	Includes budget allocations, project cost approvals, through-life budgeting requirements, financial structures, financial institution supportability
Contractor relations	Contractual and business issues
Stakeholder relations	Relationships with users, expectations management, public and community relations, political issues (internal and external)

Table 2.12—Key elements based on system components for an electricity sub-station

Management	Transformer	Switchyard	Controls	Protection	Miscellaneous items	Works
Project management	Transformer	Switchgear	Controls	Earth grid	Auxiliary equipment	Civil works and building
Design management	Transformer footing	Switchgear 132 kV	1050 Hz	Lightning mast	Conduit	Site works
Procurement management		Switchgear 22 kV		Protection HVDFR		
Construction management		Strain tower		Protection transformer		
Contract admin.				Circuit breaker 22 kV		
				Circuit breaker 132 kV		

of the associated WBS, providing a uniform level of detail across the project for the risk assessment, although detail at WBS Level 4 was available to support the assessment team.

It is sometimes appropriate to use different levels in the WBS according to the cost and risk structure. Project management and administrative elements might be treated at a high WBS level (i.e. at a low level of detail), but major equipment items might appear at lower WBS levels (i.e. in finer detail).

For example, Table 2.13 shows the WBS at Levels 2 and 3 for a surveillance aircraft upgrade. This structure was also used for risk assessment in this project. Where it was appropriate, technical equipment elements were considered in more detail in the assessment process, although no Level 4 elements were identified explicitly.

Table 2.13—WBS for an aircraft upgrade

Level 1	Level 2	Level 3
Aircraft system	Aircraft	Airframe
		Communications
		Navigation
		Radar
		Acoustics
		Data management system
		Armament/ordnance
		Other sensors
	Operational mission simulator (OMS)	
	Systems engineering laboratory (SEL)	Aircraft support
		OMS and SEL support
		Test software support
	Training	Training equipment/material
		Training services
	Support and test equipment	Operational mission support equipment
		Special-purpose support equipment
		Common support and test equipment
	System test and evaluation	Ground test and evaluation
		Flight test and evaluation
		Test and evaluation support
	Management	System engineering
		Project management
		ILS management
	Data	Technical publications
		Engineering data
		Management data
		Support data
		Data depository
	Aircraft modification	
	Interim support	

It may also be necessary to adjust the WBS structure for risk analysis purposes. For example, consider the procurement of technical items to be installed in several locations that are geographically dispersed, such as communications facilities, computing equipment or customer service centres. The cost structures for procurements like these are frequently based on the physical location, as activities occur in different places and contract payments are geared to successful site-by-site installation and acceptance testing. However, if the main risks are technical in nature, or related directly to the different kinds of equipment to be installed, a structure based on different kinds of components may be more useful for risk analysis.

For example, Table 2.14 shows a contract WBS adapted from the request for tender documents for a communications system project, with the WBS used in the risk assessment. The contract WBS was structured at Level 3 by geographical location, as this was used in the contract payment and delivery schedule, with equipment items at Levels 4 and 5. The risk WBS used equipment items at Level 3, as the main problems were more likely to be

Table 2.14—Contract WBS and risk WBS for a communications system

Contract WBS			Risk WBS	
Level 2	Level 3	Level 4	Level 2	Level 3
Prime Equipment			Prime Equipment	
	North			Radios, Type A
		Radios, Type A		Radios, Type B
		Radios, Type B		Switches
		Switches		Power Supplies
		Power supplies		Other equipment
		Other equipment		Integration
		Integration and test		Installation
	South	As above …		Testing
	Central	As above …		
Site Activation			Site Activation	
	North			Preparation
	South			Activation
	Central			Refurbishment
Logistic support			Logistic support	
	Data			Data
	Spares			Spares
	Training			Training
Management			Management	
	Project management			Project management
	Engineering management			Engineering management
	Logistics management			Logistics management

Note: Level 1, the communications system project, has been omitted in each case.

related to equipment functionality and integration than specific sites. (Note that the risk WBS here is more specific than the general risk breakdown structure advocated by Hillson, 2004.)

Examples of key elements for environmental risk assessment are provided in Chapter 18.

Structuring key elements requires judgement from the responsible manager. There will be a trade-off between the effectiveness of the risk analysis process and the integration of its outcomes with other aspects of analysis and project planning. In most circumstances, it is recommended that the structure that is most effective for the risk analysis be chosen. Using an inappropriate structure can lead to significant items being omitted inadvertently, with potentially serious consequences, as well as making the process very inefficient.

For many risk analysis purposes, a broad view of a project may be more appropriate than a detailed one, to facilitate a wide review of the risks that might impact on it. A target structure in the range from 20 to 50 elements is often sought. (Compare this with the high level of detail contained in project evaluation and review technique (PERT) or hazard and operability (Hazop) analyses, that may contain hundreds or even thousands of activities or components.)

The elements should be numbered consecutively. Later steps will extend the numbering scheme: for this reason, this numbering may be different from the WBS numbering, and it is important that it not be confused with it. The key element summary (Figure 2.4) can be used to summarize the elements, the numbering scheme and cross-references to the WBS.

For each element, use the key element description (Figure 2.5) to expand on the definition. Define each element in terms of what is involved (supply items, construction, installation

Project:		Reference no:
Element number	**Name and description**	**WBS references**
Compiler:	Date:	Reviewer:	Date:

Figure 2.4—Key element summary table

Project:	Reference no:
Element:	
Description:	
Assumptions:	
Source material:	

Compiler:	Date:	Reviewer:	Date:

Figure 2.5—Key element description

or management tasks), timings (start and end dates, critical linkages), measurements available, drawing references, equipment lists and data sources considered and accepted or rejected. Attach other material and supporting documentation, including system diagrams or component lists, as appropriate. The reference number is the element number from the key element summary. If the project is using a formal WBS on which the key elements are based, much of this information may be contained in the WBS Dictionary.

The main assumptions about the element should be stated explicitly, particularly if different people are involved in different parts of the risk identification and assessment process, as may occur in a large project. This is necessary to ensure compatible and consistent assumptions are made throughout the assessment and to facilitate subsequent review. Clearly stated assumptions are particularly important in the early stages of a project, before everything has been fully defined, when analysis and assessment must be undertaken on the basis of reasoned professional judgements about how the later stages of project will proceed.

Start a risk analysis project file, with one section for each element. So far, each section will contain only the key element description. Later tasks will add risk and response material to this. The file will become an important database of information about the project, the risks that might impact on it, and the management responses and action plans for dealing with them.

RISK IDENTIFICATION

3

Chapter overview

- ## Purpose

  Risk identification determines what might happen that could affect the objectives of the project, and how those things might happen.

- ## Rationale

  The risk identification process must be comprehensive, as risks that have not been identified cannot be assessed, and their emergence at a later time may threaten the success of the project and cause unpleasant surprises. The process should be structured using the key elements to examine risks systematically, in each area of the project to be addressed.

- ## Inputs

  Information used in the risk identification process may include historical data, theoretical analysis, empirical data and analysis, informed opinions of the project team and other experts, and the concerns of stakeholders.

- ## Method

  Risk identification techniques may include:

  - brainstorming;
  - checklists;
  - questionnaires circulated to a range of personnel;
  - examination of previous similar projects; and
  - specialist techniques.

> **● Outputs**
>
> The output is a comprehensive list of possible risks to the successful outcome
> of the project. (Subsequent steps in the process will develop priorities for
> dealing with them.)
>
> **● Documentation**
>
> Risk description (format as in Figure 3.1)
> Risk register (format as in Figure 4.1)

Introduction

This step involves identification of risks that arise from all aspects of the context
described in the previous step. The process may concentrate on one or many possible
areas of impact relevant to the project, but a standard methodology should be
applied across all functions. It is important to ensure that the widest range of risks is
identified, as risks that are omitted at this step may not be analysed and treated in
subsequent steps.

Valid information is important in identifying risks and in understanding the likelihood
and the consequences of each risk. Existing information sources need to be accessed and,
where necessary, new data sources developed. Although it is not always possible to have the
best or all information, it should be as relevant, comprehensive, accurate and timely as
resources will permit. This means that it is critical to have specialist and experienced staff
assist in the risk identification activity.

Tools and techniques for risk identification

There are many tools and techniques for identifying the risks associated with projects.
These include:

- brainstorming;
- examination of local or overseas experience with similar activities and projects, including
  analysis of post-project completion reports and audits;
- checklists;
- interviews and focus group discussions;
- scenario analyses;
- surveys and questionnaires; and
- Work Breakdown Structure analysis.

Brainstorming

The preferred approach to identifying risks is brainstorming in a group workshop. This is a little more demanding on the participants than the use of superficially attractive mechanisms such as checklists, but it is significantly more effective. Brainstorming allows the identification process to draw on the creative capacity of the participants, reducing the danger of overlooking new and emerging issues, as can happen with checklists.

Brainstorming is a very useful technique for the initial identification of a wide range of risks, particularly for large or unique projects. It is an interactive, team-based approach, depending for its success on the breadth of experience and skills present in the brainstorming group and the skills of the facilitator. It usually involves the key members of the project team, together with any specialists who can bring additional necessary expertise to the process.

The aim of the brainstorming session is to cover all potential risks, without making judgements about their importance in the initial stages.

A structured brainstorming session often follows a well-defined sequence of steps. A facilitator must be appointed and the brainstorming team selected and briefed on the purpose of the exercise and the outcomes desired. The group should meet in a room away from disturbances, preferably equipped with an electronic whiteboard.

The facilitator should then review the procurement, the purpose of the workshop and its structure. Next, each element of the procurement is assessed in detail. For each element, these steps are often followed:

- The element is defined, by someone familiar with it, so that everyone understands what is being considered.
- The team spends a few moments thinking about the possible risks and noting them on rough paper.
- The member most familiar with the element writes the initial risk list on the whiteboard, without comments from the other participants.
- The other participants then make their contributions to the list. Typically, the list may double in size in this step. No judgements should be made up to this point.
- The team reviews the list, classifying and grouping similar risks where appropriate, and adding new ones as ideas are generated. The list can then be simplified if necessary. The aim is usually to generate a list of about ten risks for each item, although this will vary widely depending on the element being considered.

Ten is a purely practical limit to the size of the list of risks, to avoid excess effort being spent on very minor items, but ten should not be considered as a firm constraint. Generally, it is better to have too many risks than too few, and nothing important should be omitted just to keep the list short. It is also important to document those risks that are discarded, to maintain an audit trail and to facilitate later review if necessary.

Where appropriate, a category 'Minor risks' may be included in the list as a summary and reminder of the risks omitted in the simplification process.

A similar process is followed for each key element.

A structured workshop is the most effective format for brainstorming. If this is impractical, structured interviews by skilled consultants, questionnaires or written surveys can be used, although these are likely to be less cost-effective than the preferred workshop approach.

Whatever form of brainstorming is adopted, it is imperative that any checklists, or other predetermined views of the risks that might arise, be excluded from consideration until after the brainstorming, or at least that attention should not be drawn to them in advance. Experience and knowledge will always form a valuable part of the risk identification process. The way the process is managed must ensure that this historical information does not block a creative assessment of the future, where matters that have never been seen before might arise, and the balance between familiar risks might shift dramatically.

Brainstorming is valuable when considering new or non-standard procurement activities, as it promotes variety and innovative thinking. For routine procurements, checklists may be faster and more efficient.

Workshop participants

The selection of participants for a brainstorming workshop is very important. They should be chosen to include expertise from a cross section of disciplines and stakeholders that covers all areas of interest in the project. This may require people external to the project team to be included.

Where time and resources permit, all members of the project team should attend the brainstorming session, including functional unit members assigned to the project on a part-time basis. People who might be included in a brainstorming group are:

- the project manager and the project team;
- project sponsors and site representatives;
- discipline engineers;
- experts with specific knowledge in particular areas of concern, where there may be insufficient expertise in the project team;
- commercial specialists;
- health, safety and environmental specialists;
- people with experience in similar previous or current projects;
- users of the project outcomes;
- key stakeholders who need to be confident in the project and the project management process before approvals are granted.

As well as specialists and stakeholders, there are often advantages to including a 'creative outsider' in a brainstorming workshop. This may be an 'intelligent layperson' who can ask questions and make suggestions that are outside the standard ways of thinking about the problem, thus stimulating different approaches and ideas.

There are often benefits in conducting joint workshops early in the life of a project, involving the sponsor, the project team and, if appropriate, the contractor's management team. This builds understanding of the priorities and issues of concern to all those involved in the project, aids communication, and can provide significant assistance to managers from all parties in allocating and managing risks most effectively.

Experience with similar projects

The brainstorming process can be aided by using information about similar projects in the past, the problems that were encountered or considered, and the problems that were avoided. Where available, the risk assessments from previous projects may be an ideal guide. However, information from previous projects does have limitations, similar in nature to those associated with checklists discussed below.

Including people with wide experience in similar activities in the brainstorming session is often beneficial, and one way of capturing the lessons from other projects. However, care must be taken that undue emphasis is not placed on unusual events that have a high profile for participants because of their personal involvement.

Checklists

Efforts to simplify the identification of risks and minimize the demands on those who perform this function often lead to the use of checklists of standard risks from previous projects or that are known to arise in a particular context.

Checklists are quick to use, and they provide useful guides for areas in which the organization has a depth of experience, particularly for projects that are standard or routine in nature. Sometimes these take the form of standard procedures that have a similar effect. For example, many organizations have checklists for such frequent activities as tendering or contract negotiations, designed to avoid or minimize the risks in those activities. Often, the checklists are part of the organization's quality assurance procedures and documentation.

While checklists can be valuable for routine activities, they can be a major handicap for non-standard or unique projects. When a project is not the same as anything the organization has dealt with before, then a checklist can provide a constraint on creative thought by preconditioning the expectations of those involved and blocking the identification of risks that go beyond those in the list, so that the unique aspects are not assessed as fully as necessary. For projects that involve new features, a brainstorming approach is recommended initially, with checklists reserved for stimulating brainstorming sessions, reviewing the identification process and ensuring that no known issues have been left out. Similar comments apply to the use of previous project experience as a guide for generating lists of risks.

Chapter 27 contains checklists of risks from a variety of sources, including lists developed for recent procurements through structured brainstorming. Additional examples relating to specific forms of procurement are provided in Chapters 15 and 16. Individual organizations should extend these checklists as they gain more experience with specific projects.

Other identification techniques

In some circumstances, special techniques may be appropriate for risk identification. Many of them are standard engineering analysis and design tools. They include:

- hazard and operability studies – a Hazop is a structured approach that systematically analyses every part of a process to identify how hazards, operability problems and deviations from design intent may arise;
- quantitative analysis of safety risks and their impacts (QRA);
- fault tree analyses – fault tree analysis is a systems engineering method for representing the logical combinations of the system states and possible causes that can contribute to a specified event (called the top event);
- event tree analyses – an event tree describes the possible range and sequence of outcomes that may arise from the initiating event;
- other systems engineering techniques.

The details of these methods are generally outside the scope of this book, although descriptions and examples of some of the more important techniques are provided in Chapter 17. If you think you need to use them, you should seek specialist assistance.

Documenting risks

Each element and each risk should be numbered, to facilitate storage and retrieval of information. Often the risk numbers are nested within the element number, and the nested numbering is extended as necessary as the analysis progresses.

Each risk should be described. The risk description work sheet in Figure 3.1 provides one way of recording this. In practice, such sheets are used as summaries, supported by additional detailed or technical information.

The description of the risk should include the main assumptions and mechanisms leading to the risk arising, the criteria likely to be affected, the phases of the project in which it is most likely to occur and notes on the consequences if it does arise. Sources of information should also be noted.

Responsibility for risks

Management responsibility for dealing with each specified risk and ensuring effective treatment plans are developed and implemented should be assigned and recorded. The responsible manager is sometimes called the risk owner.

Project: Element: Risk: Manager (risk owner):	Reference:
Description and mechanisms:	
Key assumptions:	
Sources of information:	
List of attachments:	

Compiler:	Date:	Reviewer:	Date:

Figure 3.1—Risk description work sheet

Sources of information

Very often, the best sources of information for assessing risks and their consequences are the members of the project team. However, for particularly large or risky elements, additional information will almost certainly be required.

As a general rule, all available data sources should be used when assessing high-priority elements and risks, and evaluating ways of managing them. Information sources may include:

- historical records, often for similar or related projects;
- project experience, either specific to the kind of project being assessed or more general experience with large or complex activities or with similar kinds of contractors or suppliers;
- industry best practice and user experience, including relevant benchmarks and standards;
- relevant published literature and research reports, including appropriate theory, for example relating to failure modes or equipment reliability;

- product brochures, technical manuals and audit reports;
- test marketing and market research, where there is benefit in seeking or creating new information relating to specific aspects of the project, and particularly its acceptability to its intended end-users or customers;
- experiments and prototypes, where there may be technical risks or areas in which more empirical rather than theoretical information may be useful;
- economic or other models, to provide the necessary theoretical foundations for specific and general risk assessments, including traditional cash-flow and sensitivity models where appropriate;
- expert commercial and technical judgement, including that of the project team and appropriate external advisers where necessary.

Expert judgement cannot be avoided in project risk management. Relevant historical and other information must be used where appropriate, but **this** project has not taken place yet, and so the information must be interpreted in the context of the specific application being considered. There is no guarantee that the future will be the same as the past!

Project conditions

Project conditions are those aspects of risks, responses or controls that are specified only loosely, involve high consequences with low probability of occurrence, or have implications which are beyond the responsibility of those interested in the analysis. The results of the risk assessment are conditional on the risks not arising, or the responses or controls working as intended.

Project conditions might include risks like a general strike, major fires, sabotage, external conflict or a major change of government policy. Risks of this kind should not be ignored, but other forms of risk analysis may be more appropriate. For example, detailed security analyses or safety studies might be undertaken, using approaches and techniques that are specific to the security or safety risks being considered.

It is important to identify project conditions and to document them as far as possible. Documentation should include the reasons for treating the risk as a condition, an indication of what further analysis should be done on it and the management responsibility for action. This should be included on the risk description sheet.

Risk lists

Chapter 27 contains lists of generic risks based on recent project experience from a variety of sources. They may provide a starting point for the identification of risks described in this chapter. However, remember the limitations of checklists discussed earlier.

QUALITATIVE RISK ASSESSMENT

Chapter overview

- ## Purpose

Risk assessment is the overall process of risk analysis and risk evaluation. Its purpose is to develop agreed priorities for the identified risks.

- **Risk analysis** is the systematic use of available information to determine how often specified events may occur and the magnitude of their consequences.
- **Risk evaluation** is the process of comparing the estimated risk against given risk criteria to determine the significance of the risk.

- ## Rationale

Agreed priorities are used to determine where the greatest effort should be focused in treating identified risks. They facilitate structured action planning and resource allocation.

- ## Inputs

Information used in the risk assessment process may include historical data, theoretical analysis, empirical data and analysis, informed opinions of experts and the concerns of stakeholders.

- ## Method

- Determine the consequences of each risk, should it arise.
- Assess the likelihood of those consequences occurring.
- Convert the consequence and likelihood ratings to an initial priority for the risk.
- Agree risk priorities and inherent risk levels.

- ● **Outputs**

  Outputs comprise:

  - ● a prioritized list of risks and a detailed understanding of the impact upon the success of the project should they occur; and
  - ● consequence and likelihood ratings, agreed risk priorities and inherent risk levels.

- ● **Documentation**

  Record ratings, priorities and risk levels in the risk register.

Introduction

Risk identification generates a list of the risks that might impact on the project. Often the list will be extensive, and it is necessary to separate the important items from the less important ones. This process is called risk assessment.

Risk assessment has several objectives:

- ● it gives an overview of the general level and pattern of risk facing the project;
- ● it focuses management attention on the high-risk items in the list;
- ● it helps to decide where action is needed immediately, and where action plans should be developed for future activities; and
- ● it facilitates the allocation of resources to support management's action decisions.

Qualitative risk analysis

The risk analysis step assigns each risk a priority rating, taking into account existing activities, processes or plans that operate to reduce or control the risk. It may use forms of analysis that range from simple qualitative methods to more sophisticated quantitative approaches.

- ● Qualitative analysis is based on nominal or descriptive scales for describing the likelihoods and consequences of risks. This is particularly useful for an initial review or screening or when a quick assessment is required.
- ● Semi-quantitative analysis extends the qualitative analysis process by allocating numerical values to the descriptive scales. The numbers are then used to derive quantitative risk factors.
- ● Quantitative analysis uses numerical ratio scales for likelihoods and consequences, rather than descriptive scales.

This chapter addresses the qualitative approach, which is simple, easy to use and sufficient for many purposes in a wide range of projects. Semi-quantitative analysis is discussed in detail in Chapter 5, and an extended example of its use in tender evaluation is provided in Chapter 13. Quantitative analysis requires different and more advanced skills; Chapters 19 to 23 describe its use in projects.

The analysis stage assigns each risk a priority rating, taking into account existing activities, processes or plans that operate to reduce or control the risk.

The significance of a risk can be expressed as a combination of its consequences or impacts on project objectives, and the likelihood of those consequences arising. This can be accomplished with qualitative consequence and likelihood scales and a matrix defining the significance of various combinations of these. Table 4.1 illustrates the general principle contained in most priority-setting processes: risks are high-priority if problems are likely to arise and if they have large potential consequences.

This is a very simple structure. In practice, it is often too simple, because the two-way distinctions between high and low likelihood and high and low consequence produce only four combinations. This is rarely enough discrimination for effective decision making. Table 4.2 shows an extension of the structure to a five-by-five matrix. This provides greater discrimination, and allows more classifications of priority. (A further example is provided in Table 4.9.)

A matrix like Table 4.2 can be structured according to the kinds of risks involved in the project and the organization's objectives, criteria and attitudes to risk. For example, the specific example in Table 4.2 is not symmetric, indicating that the organization is concerned about most catastrophic events, even if they are rare. This might be appropriate where human safety is threatened and the organization needs to ensure the associated risks are being managed whatever the likelihood of their occurrence. Where the impacts of potential risks are purely

Table 4.1—Basic priority-setting matrix

	Consequence	
Likelihood ⩔	*Low*	*High*
High	Medium risk	High risk
Low	Low risk	Medium risk

Table 4.2—More detailed priority-setting matrix

	Consequences				
Likelihood	*Insignificant*	*Minor*	*Moderate*	*Major*	*Catastrophic*
Almost certain	Medium	Medium	High	High	High
Likely	Low	Medium	Medium	High	High
Possible	Low	Medium	Medium	Medium	High
Unlikely	Low	Low	Medium	Medium	High
Rare	Low	Low	Low	Medium	Medium

economic, and particularly where there may be a 'cap' or limit to the potential exposure, catastrophic but rare events may be viewed as moderate risks and not treated in such detail.

To implement a structure like this, it is important that clear and consistent definitions of the consequence and likelihood scales are used. These are likely to depend on the nature of the project, its objectives and criteria, and the kinds of risks anticipated.

Consequences of risks

Consequences are rated in terms of the potential impact on the criteria, often on five-point descriptive scales linked to the criteria identified in the context step. Table 4.3 provides an example of consequence scales for a recent acquisition of a technical defence system. Table 4.4 shows similar scales for an industrial project.

Where a risk has several consequences on different parts of the scale, the highest consequence is used to generate the rating. This generates a conservative view of the overall consequences of the risk.

Scales like these often generate considerable discussion amongst senior managers and the project team.

- The numerical limits in a financial impacts scale are often linked to the size of the project, the size of the organization undertaking it, or the amount it can afford to lose. There is often a trade-off between risk and opportunity, the resolution to which must usually take place at managerial levels well above that of the project.
- In some organizations, the health and safety scale is adjusted so that a single fatality falls in the most severe consequence category. This reflects the organization's attention to employee safety as a core part of its vision and duty of care.

Generally, you should review carefully the consequence scales you intend to use for each project, to ensure they reflect the organization's objectives and criteria for success. By all means use the examples in this chapter as a guide, but remember they are only examples, and if they are not agreed and accepted by senior management the outcomes from the risk assessment may not be accepted readily.

For smaller, less complex or routine projects or procurement activities, a simpler consequence scale like Table 4.5 might be appropriate. It is important to remember that the scales are to be used for assessing priorities, so comparability and consistency are often more important than absolute numbers.

Likelihoods

Likelihoods are rated in terms of annual occurrence on a five-point descriptive scale, showing the likelihoods of specific risks arising and leading to the assessed levels of consequences. Table 4.6 shows an example of a scale suitable for a major asset procurement, where the time span of the scale is linked loosely to the 40-year nominal life of the asset.

Table 4.3—Consequence ratings for a technical systems acquisition

	Performance	Cost	Schedule	Supportability and sustainability	Political	Community
A	Performance degradation is such that the system or facility is unusable. Significant re-design is required. Sponsor definitely will not consider a specification change.	Budgeted cost estimates increased by more than 50%. Major cost overrun. Additional budget is needed.	Schedule is hopelessly lost with no chance of recovery. Contract cancellation probable or will be seriously considered.	System, infrastructure or segment severely compromised. Mission generation curtailed due to poor system or facility supportability. System or facility essentially unsupportable as proposed and requires significant resources to meet mission requirements.	Leads to major political embarrassment. Senior staff held accountable or released from service. Major organization restructure.	Community reaction and concern is overwhelming, causing major changes or cancellation. Issues are substantial and require major diversion of project resources to resolve.
B	Performance degradation has substantial impact on mission performance and will severely degrade capability if not corrected. Sponsor unwilling to approve a specification change.	Budgeted cost estimates increased by 20–50% and not manageable within current contingency.	Major slippage to system, infrastructure or segment milestones. Reprogramming of the baseline schedule definitely required. Acquisition subject to sponsor review.	System, infrastructure or segment availability is significantly compromised. Missions, maintenance planning, engineering support, logistics support or training are significantly impacted.	Minister initiates a review into the requirement or branch as a whole.	Community reaction and concern is significant and may impact on the success of the initiative. Issues are substantial and require dedication of significant project resources to resolve.
C	Performance degradation has noticeable effect on mission performance and may be on the limits of acceptability. Sponsor	Budgeted cost estimates increased by 5–20% and may be manageable within current contingency.	Some slippage to system, infrastructure or segment delivery dates. Major milestones impacted. May require	System infrastructure or segment availability is noticeably compromised. Missions, planning, maintenance	Issue will be in ministerial brief and may initiate enquiries or a review of the issue.	Community reaction and concern is evident. All or most concerns are capable of

(Continued over leaf)

Table 4.3—(Continued)

	Performance	Cost	Schedule	Supportability and sustainability	Political	Community
	hesitant but willing to approve a specification change if no other option is available.		baseline schedule reprogramming.	support, engineering support, logistics support or training are impacted. Consumption of logistics resources and availability is outside limits of acceptability.		management by actions.
D	Minor reduction in performance, but tolerable. Specification change likely to be approved.	Budgeted cost estimates increased by less than 5% but manageable within current contingency.	Minor slippage to system infrastructure or segment delivery milestones. Internal milestones require reprogramming.	Minor impact on system, infrastructure or segment availability.	Issue may be in ministerial brief but would not be expected to draw attention.	Community recognizes issues but does not react.
E	Negligible impact on performance anticipated.	Budgeted cost estimates not exceeded. Some transfer of money.	Some reprogramming of internal milestones but no overall change to acquisition schedule. Acceptance dates for major segments not affected.	Negligible impact on system, infrastructure or segment.	Issue would not be included in ministerial brief.	Little or no community reaction or recognition.
Notes	This criterion includes equipment, facilities, mission systems and support segment performance, as well as safety.	This criterion includes acquisition costs and through-life costs.	This criterion refers to milestones for all segments of the acquisition.	This criterion includes reliability, availability, maintainability, ILS and support processes.		

Table 4.4—Consequence ratings for an industrial project

Rating	Financial impacts	Facility integrity	Project performance	Employees	Health and safety	Environment	Regulatory	Image and reputation
A Catastrophic	Direct loss or increased cost > $20 million Estimating error or capital loss > $20 million Fraud > $1 million	Major unacceptable system, asset, integrity or condition problem Failure to achieve critical system, asset or performance goals	Time-critical project misses major milestone or deadline > 6 months Failure to achieve critical system, asset or performance goals	A large number of senior managers or experienced employees leave the company	Multiple fatalities of staff, contractors or the public	Long-term environmental damage (5 years or longer), requiring > $5 million to study or correct or in penalties	Regulatory intervention and prosecution possible	Damage to corporate reputation at international level; raised in international media Major loss of shareholder or community support
B Major	Direct loss or increased cost of $5–20 million Estimating error or capital loss of $5–20 million Fraud $0.5–1 million	Failure to achieve some system, asset, integrity or condition targets Failure to achieve some performance targets	Time-critical project misses major milestone or deadline by 3–6 months Failure to achieve some performance targets	Some senior managers or experienced employees leave High turnover of experienced employees Company not perceived as an employer of choice	Single fatality; serious injury or occupational illness (non-recoverable) or permanent major disabilities (acute or chronic)	Medium-term (1–5 years) environmental damage, requiring $1–5 million to study or correct	Breach of licenses, legislation, regulation or corporate-mandated standards	Damage to corporate reputation at national level; raised in national media Significant decrease in shareholder or community support

(Continued over leaf)

Table 4.4—(Continued)

Rating	Financial impacts	Facility integrity	Project performance	Employees	Health and safety	Environment	Regulatory	Image and reputation
C Moderate	Direct loss or increased cost of $1–5 million Estimating error or capital loss of $1–5 million Fraud $0.25–0.5 million	Some reduction in system, asset, integrity or condition Some reduction in performance	Time-critical project misses major milestone or deadline by 1–3 months Some reduction in performance	Poor reputation as an employer Widespread employee attitude problems High employee turnover	Lost time or restricted injury or occupational illness (recoverable)	Short-term (< 1 year) environmental damage, requiring up to $1 million to correct	Breach of standards, guidelines or impending legislation, or subject raised as a corporate concern through audit findings or voluntary agreements	Adverse news in state or regional media Decrease in shareholder or community support
D Minor	Direct loss or increased cost of $0.25–1 million Estimating error or capital loss of $0.25–1 million Fraud $0.1–0.25 million	Minor system, asset, integrity or condition degradation Minor performance degradation	Time-critical project misses major milestone or deadline by < 1 month Minor performance degradation	General employee morale and attitude problems Increase in employee turnover	Medical treatment required	Environmental damage, requiring up to $250,000 to study or correct	Exceedance of internal procedures or guidelines	Adverse news in local media Concerns on performance raised by shareholders or the community
E Insignificant	Direct loss or increased cost below $250,000 Negligible estimating error or capital loss Negligible fraud	Negligible system, asset, integrity or condition impact Negligible performance impact	Negligible milestone or deadline delay Negligible performance impact	Negligible or isolated employee dissatisfaction	On-site first aid required No lost time or occupational illness	Negligible environmental impact, managed within operating budgets	No breach of licenses, standards, guidelines or related audit findings	Reference to community consultation group Public awareness may exist, but there is no public concern

Table 4.5—Consequence scale for a repetitive procurement

	Rating	Consequence description
A	Catastrophic	Extreme event, potential for large financial costs or delays, or damage to the organization's reputation
B	Major	Critical event, potential for major costs or delays, or inappropriate products
C	Moderate	Large impact, but can be managed with effort using standard procedures
D	Minor	Impact minor with routine management procedures
E	Insignificant	Impact may be safely ignored

Table 4.6—Likelihood ratings

Rating		Likelihood description		
		The potential for problems to occur and lead to the assessed consequences		
A	Almost certain	Very high, may occur at least several times per year	Probability over 0.8	A similar outcome has arisen several times per year in the same location, operation or activity
B	Likely	High, may arise about once per year	Probability 0.5–0.8	A similar outcome has arisen several times per year in this organization
C	Possible	Possible, may arise at least once in a 1–10-year period	Probability 0.1–0.5	A similar outcome has arisen at some time previously in this organization
D	Unlikely	Not impossible, likely to occur during the next 10 to 40 years	Probability 0.02–0.1	A similar outcome has arisen at some time previously in a similar organization
E	Rare	Very low, very unlikely during the next 40 years	Probability less than 0.02	A similar outcome has arisen in the world-wide industry, but not in this organization

Table 4.7 shows an extended likelihood scale that was developed for a multi-purpose set of assessments. The high-frequency levels were needed to assess strategic risks with project-wide effects; the low-frequency levels were needed to assess rare technical risks that were to be included in regulatory submissions; and there was some overlap. A combined likelihood scale, with a correspondingly extended priority-setting matrix, was used to ensure comparability of outcomes across the different areas in the project where major risk assessments were being undertaken, and to enhance consistent reporting to the board.

The scale in Table 4.6 has been used successfully in risk analyses for large projects. However, it can be adapted easily to smaller and less complex procurements. For example, for routine procurements that take place several times per year, the scale in Table 4.8 might be appropriate. As was the case for the consequence scales, comparability and consistency are important.

Table 4.7—Extended likelihood ratings

Level	Descriptor	Description	Frequency	Probability
A	Almost certain	Very high, may occur at least once per year	1 per year	0.8–1
B	Likely	Likely to arise at least once in a 1–5-year period	1 per 5 years	0.2–0.8
C	Possible	Possible, may arise at least once in a 1–10-year period	1 per 10 years	0.1–0.2
D	Unlikely	Not impossible, could occur at some time during the life of the facility	1 per 25 years	0.04–0.1
E	Very unlikely	May occur only in exceptional circumstances	1 per 100 years	0.01–0.04
F	Rare		1 per 1,000 years	0.001–0.01
G	Very rare		1 per 10,000 years	0.0001–0.001

Table 4.8—Likelihood scale for a repetitive procurement

	Rating	Description
A	Almost certain	Likely to occur during the next procurement
B	Likely	Likely to occur in the next few procurements
C	Possible	Likely in the next 10 procurements
D	Unlikely	Possible, but unlikely in the next 10 procurements
E	Rare	Highly unlikely in the next 20 procurements

Events that are more than likely to arise – those with a probability greater than 0.8 over the life of a project – should be distinguished from other less likely events. Any events considered more likely than not to occur should be accommodated within the project plans.

Initial risk priorities

A simple matrix is used to combine the likelihood and consequence ratings to generate initial priorities for the risks. An example with four priority levels is shown in Table 4.9; a slightly different example was shown in Table 4.2.

The outcome of this stage of the risk analysis is an initial view of the significance of the identified risks. In some circumstances, particularly with simple scoring schemes, risks can be honestly assigned too high or too low a significance on the first pass. The next stage is designed to review this assignment and adjust it where necessary.

A note on scales and terminology

There are many different words used for describing likelihoods, impacts and risk priorities in different books and references on risk management. In our work, as in this book, we have

Table 4.9—Risk priority rating

| Likelihood | Consequences | | | | |
| | *Insignificant* | *Minor* | *Moderate* | *Major* | *Catastrophic* |
	E	D	C	B	A
A Almost certain	Medium	Medium	High	High	Extreme
B Likely	Medium	Medium	Medium	High	Extreme
C Possible	Low	Medium	Medium	High	High
D Unlikely	Low	Low	Medium	Medium	High
E Rare	Low	Low	Medium	Medium	Medium

Table 4.10—Scale point descriptions

Scale point	Consequences	Likelihoods	Risk priorities
A	Catastrophic or severe for risks Outstanding for opportunities	Almost certain	Extreme
B	Major	Likely	High
C	Moderate	Possible	Medium
D	Minor	Unlikely	Low
E	Insignificant or negligible	Rare	

tried to standardize the terminology and scale points we use for risk assessments, although other terms are used occasionally in some of the case material that is presented.

We use five-point scales for consequences and likelihoods in most circumstances. They are simple to comprehend, easy to use in a workshop environment, and provide adequate discrimination. We find that three-point and four-point scales do not always allow critical distinctions to be made, and scales with more than five points are often cumbersome to use in practice.

We label scale points from A to E, with A at the 'high' end. We avoid numbers as labels, because we find some people use them as numbers instead of labels, and then try to perform arithmetic calculations with them. The scales are ordinal or ranking scales, not ratio scales, so arithmetic manipulations are quite inappropriate, although the semi-quantitative assessments described in Chapter 5 use a similar approach.

We try to use consistent names for describing each scale point, summarized in Table 4.10. This gives each word a unique meaning as a description of a consequence, a likelihood or a risk priority, avoiding confusion.

Risk evaluation

Risk evaluation is about deciding whether risks are tolerable or not to the project, taking into account:

- the controls already in place or included in project plans;
- the likely effectiveness of those controls;

- the cost impact of managing the risks or leaving them untreated;
- benefits and opportunities presented by the risks; and
- the risks borne by other stakeholders.

The evaluation step compares risk priorities from the initial analysis against all the other risks and the organization's known priorities and requirements. Any risks that have been accorded too high or too low a rating are adjusted, with a record of the adjustment being retained for tracking purposes. The outcome is a list of risks with agreed priority ratings.

Adjustments to the initial priorities may be made for several reasons.

- Risks may be moved down. Typically these will be routine, well-anticipated risks that are highly likely to occur, but with few adverse consequences, and for which standard responses exist.
- Risks may be moved up. Typically there will be two categories of risks like this: those risks that the project team feel are more important than the initial classification indicates; and those risks that are similar to other high-priority risks to the project and hence should be considered jointly with them.
- Some risks may be moved up to provide additional visibility if the project team feels they should be dealt with explicitly.

The two-stage process of assessment followed by evaluation makes best use of the specialized knowledge of the team dealing with the project. It also avoids errors associated with risks or elements that do not fit exactly into the indicators and scales used for the initial ranking.

For each risk, the name of the manager responsible for the development of treatment options should be recorded. The project manager has overall responsibility for ensuring all risks are managed; the intent here is to specify to whom each risk treatment task has been delegated.

Inherent risks

As an extension of the evaluation process, the inherent risk level for each risk may be considered, using the four-point scale in Table 4.11. The inherent level of risk is the level that would exist if the controls did not work as intended, or if there were a credible failure

Table 4.11—Inherent risk rating

	Inherent risk
A	Extreme inherent risk
B	High inherent risk
C	Medium inherent risk
D	Low inherent risk

of controls. This provides an indication of the importance of the existing controls and a pointer to those areas where monitoring of controls may be important. Chapter 6 provides additional guidance on this aspect.

The risk register

The risk register for a project provides a repository for current information about the risks and the treatment actions relating to them. As will be discussed in Chapter 7, this is a living database that is updated as the project progresses and risks change.

A typical format for a project Risk Register is shown in Figure 4.1. The contents of the columns are described in Table 4.12.

Table 4.12—Risk register columns and their contents

Column heading	Content and notes
E	The reference number of the key element (Chapter 2)
Element	A brief description of the key element (Chapter 2)
Group	This column is used for grouping similar risks as an aid to developing treatment options and action plans
R	A unique identifying number for the risk. This often has the form E.xx, where E is the element number from the first column and xx is a two-digit identifying number
Risk	A brief description of the risk, its causes and its impacts
Existing controls	A brief description of the controls that are currently in place for the risk. At an early stage in the life of a project, the controls may be those that are expected to be in place if normal project management processes are followed.
C	The consequence rating for the risk, with the controls in place, using scales like those in Table 4.3, Table 4.4 or Table 4.5.
L	The likelihood rating for the risk, using scales like those in Table 4.6, Table 4.7 or Table 4.8.
Agreed priority	The agreed priority for the risk, based on an initial priority determined from a matrix like Table 4.2, Table 4.9, Figure 11.1 or Figure 11.2, adjusted to reflect the views of the project team in the risk assessment workshop.
Inherent risk	The inherent risk rating for the risk, if there were a credible failure of controls or they failed to work as intended, using the scale in Table 4.11.
Action sheet	A cross-reference to the action summary for the risk, in one of the forms shown in Chapter 6.
Responsibility	The name of the individual responsible for managing the risk.

E	Element	Group	R	Risk	Existing controls	C	L	Agreed priority	Inherent risk	Action sheet	Responsibility

Figure 4.1—Format of a typical risk register

Semi-Quantitative Risk Assessment

5

Chapter overview

- ### Purpose

  The processes described in this chapter assist in identifying potentially high-risk systems, sub-systems, elements or stages of a project, without identifying the underlying risks explicitly. They may also be used for regular surveys of the 'riskiness' of project elements.

- ### Rationale

  Agreed priorities are used to determine where the greatest attention, planning and detailed risk assessment effort should be focused in the project.

- ### Inputs

  Information used in the assessment process may include key project documents, such as the project Work Breakdown Structure (WBS), project execution strategy, project charter, cost and schedule assumptions, scope definitions, engineering designs and studies, economic analyses and any other relevant documentation about the project and its purpose. Other information such as historical data, theoretical analysis, empirical data and analysis, informed opinions of experts and the concerns of stakeholders may also be useful.

- ### Method

  - Develop an appropriate system or element structure for examining the project.
  - Use a semi-quantitative approach to assess the likelihood of risks arising in each element, and their consequences.
  - Convert the consequence and likelihood ratings to an initial priority for the element.

- ## Outputs

  - A list of elements prioritized by 'riskiness'.
  - Consequence and likelihood ratings, and agreed priorities for the elements.

- ## Documentation

  - Assessment sheets like Figure 5.1 or Figure 5.2.
  - Diagrammatic representations like Figure 5.3.

Introduction

Priorities may be set in different ways in the project management process. The previous chapter dealt with the allocation of priorities to individual risks that require specific remedial actions. This chapter addresses the allocation of priorities to systems, sub-systems, elements or stages of the project where management attention is recommended, without identifying any individual risks explicitly. Such priority-setting may be used to determine where the greatest attention, planning and detailed risk assessment effort should be focused in the project, or as part of a regular risk survey of a project's risk management progress.

The chapter illustrates an application of a semi-quantitative risk analysis approach. The previous chapter described simple qualitative approaches for risk assessment. More complex quantitative methods require specific numerical estimates of probabilities and distributions of impacts, but probabilities are difficult for many people to estimate, since few use them in their everyday activities, and impacts may not be easily quantified in absolute terms at the early stages of a project. Semi-quantitative approaches to risk prioritization sit between the qualitative and quantitative approaches in terms of complexity. They do not use direct likelihood or impact estimates – they begin with qualitative scales, then transform these into numerical values for use as indicators or indirect measures of likelihoods, impacts and priorities.

Such indirect or semi-quantitative indicators are adequate when comparative results are required. In particular, when a quick survey of the elements of a project is needed to determine where management attention should be focused, the objective is to rank the elements from 'most risky' to 'least risky', and absolute measures are not necessary.

Chapter 13 illustrates how the processes described here can be extended to provide a basis for the comparison of risks associated with different tenderers' approaches to project delivery as part of project tender evaluation.

Key elements

The first step in the assessment process is to determine the project level at which the survey is to be conducted and hence develop a list of key elements. The most appropriate project level usually depends on its size – Levels 3, 4 or 5 of the WBS are often suitable. The aim is to examine the project in sufficient detail to identify high-risk areas relatively precisely, without having to examine everything in great depth.

The key WBS elements are identified and described, according to the level of detail chosen. This process was described at length in Chapter 2.

Likelihood and impact assessment

The likelihood of risks arising in an element of a project can be estimated by identifying the major drivers of risk in that element. For example, attributes of maturity, complexity and dependency have been identified as key risk drivers in technical projects involving a substantial mix of hardware and software: risks are more likely to arise if the hardware and software is immature, complex or highly interdependent with other systems or projects.

An assessment form for technical procurement projects is shown in Figure 5.1, based on scales developed at the US Defense Systems Management College at Fort Belvoir. An

Project:		Reference:
Element:		
Hardware maturity	**Software maturity**	**Dependency**
Existing technology	Existing technology	Independent of existing system, facility, associate contractor
Minor redesign	Minor redesign	Schedule dependent on existing system schedule, facility, contractor
Major change feasible	Major change feasible	Performance dependent on existing system performance, facility
Technology available, complex design	New software, similar to existing	Schedule dependent on new system schedule, facility, contractor, etc.
State of the art, some research complete	State of the art, never done before	Performance dependent on new system performance, facility, contractor
Other more substantial maturity risk	Other more substantial maturity risk	Other more substantial dependency risk

Figure 5.1—(Continued over leaf)

Hardware complexity	Software complexity	Commercial risk
Simple design	Simple design	No sub-contract element
Minor increase in complexity	Minor increase in complexity	Minor sub-contracting of non-critical elements
Moderate increase in complexity	Moderate increase in complexity	Minor sub-contracting of critical elements
Significant increase in complexity	Significant major increase in number of modules	Significant sub-contracting to accredited supplier, not single source
Extremely complex	Highly complex, very large data bases, complex operating executive	Single-source accredited supplier of critical elements
Other more substantial complexity risk	Other more substantial complexity risk	Other more substantial commercial risk
Technical factor	**Cost factor**	**Schedule factor**
Minimal consequences	Budget estimates not exceeded	Negligible schedule impact
Small performance reduction	Over budget by 1–5%	Minor slip (less than 1 month)
Some performance reduction	Over budget by 5–20%	Small slip in schedule
Significant degradation in technical performance	Over budget by 20–50%	Schedule slip more than 3 months
Technical goals cannot be achieved	Over budget by more than 50%	Large slip, affects segment milestones

Compiler:	Date:	Reviewer:	Date:

Figure 5.1—Assessment form for technical projects

additional commercial risk factor has been added to those developed at Fort Belvoir, to cover more explicitly the sub-contracting arrangements that are common in many large projects.

This framework has been extended to many other kinds of projects and procurements other than large technical ones, using indicators that are specific to the project and the critical success factors of interest. Examples of the kinds of indicators that have been used for this purpose are shown in Table 5.1 and Table 5.2. Details of the scales that may be used are provided below.

Figure 5.2 shows an alternative assessment sheet, in which different risk and consequence indicators can be used in a very flexible manner. This sheet also allows assumptions and other notes on responses to be recorded.

Practical experience suggests that numerical scales are often confusing, and that simple descriptive scales are adequate initially. That is why the survey form in Figure 5.1 contains no numerical information. The descriptive assessments are converted to numerical measures as

Table 5.1—Likelihood indicators

Focus	Indicator	Low risk	High risk	Detail
Technical	Hardware maturity	Off the shelf	State of the art	Table 5.3
	Hardware complexity	Simple	Many components	Table 5.4
	Software maturity	Well proven	New code required	Table 5.3
	Software complexity	Few modules	Many modules	Table 5.4
	Integration and interfacing	None required	Major integration with R&D	Table 5.5
Requirement	User specification complexity	Very simple	Highly complex	
Linkages	Dependence	Stand alone	Highly linked	Table 5.5
Commercial	Commercial	Own resources	Many sub-contractors	Table 5.6
	Contract	Standard contract	Complex structure	
Capability	Ability to perform	Skilled resources available	No in-house capability	
	Management processes	Existing systems are adequate	New systems needed	Table 5.6
Location	Location	Home region	Remote or overseas	

Table 5.2—Consequence indicators

Focus	Indicator	Low impact	High impact	Detail
Cost	Cost increase	No budget impact	Very large potential overrun	Table 5.7
Schedule	Schedule delay	On time	Key milestones not achieved	Table 5.7
Quality	Performance	User criteria exceeded	Key criteria not met	Table 5.7
	User satisfaction and relationship	Users very happy	Major dispute with users	
	User's business	User's business enhanced	User's business impaired	
Reputation	Reputation	Reputation enhanced	Highly adverse publicity	

Project: Element:							Reference:	
Likelihood indicators	**Rating** **(High–Low)**						**Discussion, key assumptions** **and responses**	**Score**
	A	B	C	D	E	F		
	A	B	C	D	E	F		
	A	B	C	D	E	F		
	A	B	C	D	E	F		
	A	B	C	D	E	F		
	A	B	C	D	E	F		
					Average likelihood score:			
Consequence indicators	**Rating** **(High–Low)**						**Discussion, key assumptions** **and responses**	**Score**
	A	B	C	D	E	F		
	A	B	C	D	E	F		
	A	B	C	D	E	F		
	A	B	C	D	E	F		
	A	B	C	D	E	F		
	A	B	C	D	E	F		
					Average consequence score:			

	Scoring:	A	B	C	D	E	F
		0.9	0.8	0.7	0.5	0.3	0.1

Risk factor:

Likelihood score + Consequence score − Product of scores

Compiler:	Date:	Reviewer:	Date:

Figure 5.2—An alternative assessment sheet

a separate step, using the tables contained in later sections in this chapter. (More formal quantitative analyses can be developed later if necessary.)

Risk factors and priorities

To calculate risk factors or levels, the descriptive likelihood assessments are converted to numerical measures, for example using the Tables 5.3 to 5.6 or the scoring factors in Figure 5.2. The numerical measures are averaged, to give a risk likelihood measure P. A similar process is followed for the consequence assessments, using Table 5.7, to give an average consequence measure C. A risk factor RF or combined risk measure is then calculated for each risk.

$$P = \text{risk likelihood measure, on a scale 0 to 1}$$
$$= \text{average of likelihood factors;}$$

$$C = \text{consequence measure, on a scale 0 to 1}$$
$$= \text{average of consequence factors;}$$

Table 5.3—Maturity factors

Measure		Hardware maturity	Software maturity
0.1	Rare	Existing	Existing
0.3	Unlikely	Minor redesign; modifications to circuit cards and racks	Minor redesign; modifications to computer software configuration items (CSCIs) and software patches
0.5	Possible	Major changes feasible; new line replaceable units and changes to secondary structures	Major changes feasible; significant changes to CSCIs
0.7	Likely	Technology available; substantial design effort required	New CSCI within the software environment
0.8	Highly likely	State of the art; some research complete	New CSCI outside existing software environment
0.9	Almost certain	Other more substantial maturity risk	Other more substantial maturity risk

Table 5.4—Complexity factors

Measure		Hardware complexity	Software complexity
0.1	Rare	Simple or existing design	Simple or existing design
0.3	Unlikely	Minor increase in complexity	Minor increase in complexity
0.5	Possible	Moderate increase in complexity	Moderate increase in complexity
0.7	Likely	Significant increase in complexity	Significant increase in number of modules
0.8	Highly likely	Extremely complex, new design	Highly complex, new design, very large databases, complex operating executive
0.9	Almost certain	Other more substantial complexity risk	Other more substantial complexity risk

Table 5.5—Integration and interfacing and dependency factors

Measure		Integration and interfacing	Dependency
0.1	Rare	None required	Independent of existing system, facility or associate contractor
0.3	Unlikely	Minor integration and interfacing required	Schedule dependent on existing system schedule, facility or associate contractor
0.5	Possible	Major integration and interfacing required, but done before	Performance dependent on existing system performance, facility or associate contractor
0.7	Likely	Major integration and interfacing required, never done before	Schedule dependent on new system schedule, facility or associate contractor
0.8	Highly likely	Major integration and interfacing required, R&D effort required	Performance dependent on new system performance, facility or associate contractor
0.9	Almost certain	Other more substantial integration and interfacing risk	Other more substantial dependency risk

Table 5.6—Commercial risk and management process factors

Measure		Commercial risk	Management process
0.1	Rare	No sub-contract element	Existing management processes adequate
0.3	Unlikely	Minor sub-contracting of non-critical elements	Minor modifications needed to existing management systems and procedures
0.5	Possible	Minor sub-contracting of critical elements	Major modifications needed to existing management systems and procedures
0.7	Likely	Significant sub-contracting to accredited supplier, not single source	Sophisticated management systems required
0.8	Highly likely	Single-source accredited supplier of critical elements	New or complex management systems required to be developed
0.9	Almost certain	Other more substantial commercial risk	Other more substantial management process risk

Table 5.7—Cost increase, schedule delay and performance degradation factors

Measure		Cost factor	Schedule factor	Performance factor
0.1	Insignificant	Budget estimates not exceeded, some transfer of money	Negligible impact, slight schedule change compensated by available schedule slack	Minimal or unimportant performance impacts
0.3	Low	Project cost estimates exceed budget by 1–5%	Minor slip in project schedule, less than 1 month	Small reduction in performance
0.5	Moderate	Project cost estimates increased by 5–10%	Small slip in project schedule, from 1 to 3 months	Some reduction in performance
0.7	Very high	Project cost estimates increased by 10–20%	Project schedule slip from 3 to 6 months	Significant reduction in performance
0.9	Catastrophic	Project cost estimates increased by more than 20%	Large project schedule slip, key milestones not achieved	Key performance criteria cannot be achieved

$$RF = \text{risk factor}$$
$$= P + C - (P*C).$$

The risk factor RF, from 0 (low) to 1 (high), reflects the likelihood of a risk arising and the severity of its impact. The risk factor will be high if the likelihood P is high, or the consequence C is high, or both.

Note that the formula only works if P and C are on scales from 0 to 1. Mathematically, it derives from the probability calculation for disjunctive events: prob(A or B)= prob(A)+ prob(B) – prob(A)*prob(B). However, the formula is not a mathematical relationship, merely a useful piece of arithmetic for setting priorities. Another approach is described in the next section.

P and C values may be plotted for each item for reporting purposes. The plot may also include iso-risk contours, or lines joining points of equal RF value, to provide a quick visual indication of risk priorities. Figure 5.3 shows the form of diagram that may be used. Figure 5.4 shows an example from a recent procurement project.

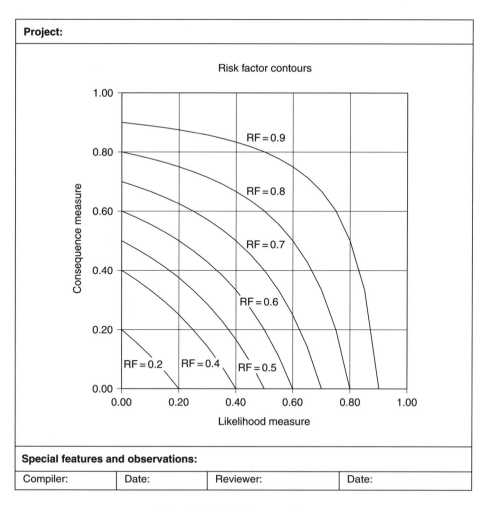

Figure 5.3—Risk contour diagram

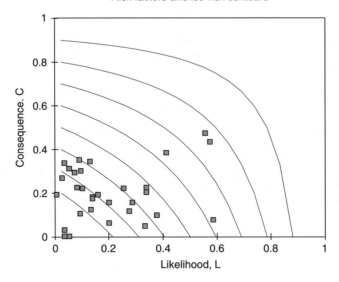

Figure 5.4—Risk factors and iso-risk contours for a technical project

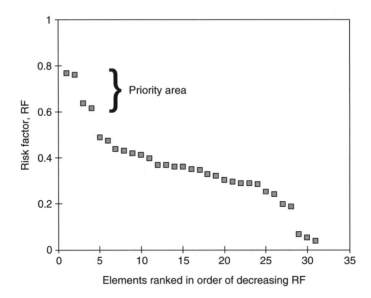

Figure 5.5—Risk profile for the project in Figure 5.4

Note: The elements have been sequenced in decreasing order of risk factors. The horizontal axis shows the rank order of the elements.

Items may be ranked in order of decreasing risk factors, to generate a 'risk profile' for the project. Figure 5.5 shows an example from the same procurement as in Figure 5.4. The risk factors, the ranking and the risk profile are used to decide which risks are acceptable and unacceptable, and to enable risk management priorities to be set.

Another way of calculating risk factors

In some circumstances, risk factors may be calculated as the product of the likelihood and consequence measures:

$$RF = P*C.$$

This form of expected value calculation is common in some forms of safety analysis. Here, P and C are not restricted to the ranges 0 to 1.

The 'product' formula has one significant disadvantage in comparison with the earlier form, as shown by the iso-risk contours in Figure 5.6: items with high consequences but low probabilities may be allocated low risk factors, and hence they may not be flagged as important. This can be a problem in practice, as there is a chance that significant risks may not be noticed. The earlier version identifies items with high likelihoods or high consequences or both, so the chance of high consequence but low likelihood items being ignored is reduced greatly.

The recommended method of calculating risk factors uses the first form:

$$RF = P + C - (P*C).$$

Semi-quantitative priorities for individual risks

Priorities for individual risks can be assessed in a similar fashion to those for project elements. However, the simpler and more direct scales discussed in the previous section are commonly used.

Potential impacts may be assessed in terms of the potential for problems to affect the criteria for the project, as identified in the initial context stage of the risk assessment.

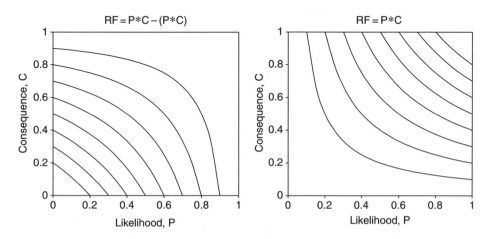

Figure 5.6—Comparison of RF calculations – iso-risk contours

Table 5.8—Typical numerical values for likelihood and impact ratings

Likelihood scale	Impact scale	Letter rating	Numerical value
Almost certain	Catastrophic	A	0.9
Likely	Very high	B	0.7
Possible	Moderate	C	0.5
Unlikely	Low	D	0.3
Rare	Insignificant	E	0.1

If appropriate, impacts might be assessed for each criterion and then combined, as was done for elements and described earlier.

Risk factors are then calculated for all risks, in a similar process to that described above. Likelihood and impact ratings are first transformed to numerical values, using scales like those in Table 5.8. The risk factor RF for a risk is calculated from the likelihood measure P and the impact measure C as:

$$RF = P + C - (P*C).$$

High, medium and low risks

Risk factors and the initial ranking in the risk profile can only be a guide to priorities for management attention, due to the constraints of the procedures used to generate them. Accordingly, a two-stage process is commonly used to set priorities.

1. Risks are sequenced in decreasing order of risk factors, calculated by the processes described above, and cut-off levels are set to provide an initial indication of priorities. The risk factors are usually based on assessments generated by the technical or commercial specialists and managers responsible for individual elements. The initial cut-off levels may be set by the manager. The choice of cut-off levels may be based on absolute criteria (for example, if safety issues are involved), pragmatic criteria related to the resources available for managing high-risk elements, or on more sophisticated trade-offs between the costs of developing detailed Risk Action Plans for major risks and the benefits of doing so.

2. Each risk in the sequenced list is examined to determine whether it has been classified correctly, and the classification is modified accordingly. In this stage, similar risks may be grouped, to be managed together. This task may be undertaken by the manager alone, but it is often preferable for other specialists and managers to be involved as well. This facilitates better communication, understanding and 'ownership' of the main risks.

Figure 5.7 illustrates the outcomes from a semi-quantitative analysis of a technical project after it had been reviewed. Risk factors were assigned to project areas, using a process similar to that described above; initial cut-off points were set, and then each area was reviewed and its priority adjusted where necessary. The figure shows the 34 project areas, sorted first by agreed priority and then by risk factor. There is considerable overlap in the risk factors between the High, Medium High, Medium Low and Low categories, justifying the value of the review process in determining the overall priority rating for each area of the project.

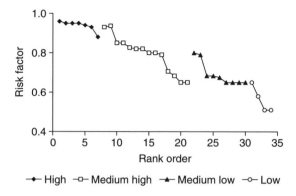

Figure 5.7—Risk factors after review

(The project manager in this case requested that the original Medium risk grouping be disaggregated into Medium High and Medium Low categories to facilitate resource allocation decisions and communication of them to the oversight committee.)

Detailed assessment scales for likelihoods

Detailed assessments may be made on a variety of likelihood measures. Table 5.1 listed measures that have been useful for projects of varying kinds, sizes and degrees of complexity. Similar measures can be developed to suit a range of specific requirements and concerns. Detailed scales for selected indicators are shown in Tables 5.3 to 5.6.

Detailed assessment scales for consequences

Detailed assessments may be made on a variety of impact measures. Table 5.2 listed measures that have been useful for projects of varying kinds, sizes and degrees of complexity. Similar measures can be developed to suit other criteria.

Detailed scales for selected indicators are shown in Table 5.7. The numerical values used in the table should be adjusted to reflect the specific characteristics of the project.

Consequences should be assessed on the basis of the impacts of risks on the project as a whole, not just on individual elements.

Environmental risk assessment example

The Australian Department of Defence has developed an environmental risk management framework that uses a semi-quantitative approach for risk analysis and priority-setting (www.defence.gov.au/environment). Consequences and likelihoods for individual risks are assessed using five-point scales, with detailed descriptions of each scale point and six

Table 5.9—Semi-quantitative scales for an environmental risk analysis

Likelihood scale	Consequence scale	Rating
Almost certain	Catastrophic	5
Likely	Very high	4
Possible	Moderate	3
Unlikely	Low	2
Rare	Insignificant	1

consequence criteria. Scale points are translated into numerical values, from 1 at the low end to 5 at the high end of each scale, as summarized in Table 5.9.

Two measures of risk level are used:

1. The primary risk level (PRL) is a conservative measure of risk, based on the most severe consequences across all the relevant criteria. It is calculated as

$$PRL = (likelihood \ rating) \times (maximum \ consequence \ rating).$$

2. The secondary risk level (SRL) is a less conservative measure of risk, which incorporates all relevant criteria, not just the most severe ones. It is calculated as

$$SRL = (likelihood \ rating) \times (average \ consequence \ rating),$$

where the average consequence is calculated across all relevant criteria for which a rating is available.

In most circumstances PRL is the preferred measure, as it is more conservative. The PRL should always be used for screening risk assessments (see Chapter 18).

Table 5.10 indicates how the risk levels may be interpreted as simple descriptors, and also shows the corresponding management actions that may follow, depending on the consideration of risk treatment activities.

Table 5.10—Risk levels and management action (example)

Risk level (PRL or SRL)	Descriptor	Indicative management action
16–25	Extreme	Immediate action required, senior management will be involved
9–15.9	High	Senior management attention needed and management responsibilities specified for further action
4–8.9	Medium	Manage by specific monitoring or response procedures, develop more detailed actions as resources allow
1–3.9	Low	Manage by routine procedures, unlikely to need specific application of resources

RISK TREATMENT

6

Chapter overview

- ### Purpose

  The purpose of risk treatment is to determine what will be done in response to the risks that have been identified, in order to reduce the overall risk exposure.

- ### Rationale

  Unless action is taken, the risk identification and assessment process has been wasted. Risk treatment converts the earlier analyses into substantive actions to reduce risks.

- ### Inputs

  The primary inputs to this step are:

  - the lists of risks and their agreed priorities from the previous step; and
  - current project plans and budgets.

- ### Method

  - Identify the options for reducing the likelihood or consequences of each Extreme, High or Medium risk.
  - Determine the potential benefits and costs of the options.
  - Select the best options for the project.
  - Develop and implement detailed Risk Action Plans.
  - Make appropriate provisions in project budgets.

- ### Outputs

  Risk Action Plan summaries are required for each risk classified as Extreme or High on the agreed risk priority scale.

> ● Documentation
>
> ● Risk treatment options worksheet like Figure 6.6.
> ● Risk Action Plan summary like Figure 6.8.

Introduction

Risk treatment consists of determining what will be done in response to the risks that have been identified, for the purpose of reducing the potential risk exposure. Any controls and plans in place before the risk management process began are augmented with Risk Action Plans to deal with risks before they arise and contingency plans with which to recover if a risk comes to pass. At the end of successful risk treatment planning, detailed ideas will have been developed and documented about the best ways of dealing with each major risk, and Risk Action Plans will have been formulated for putting the responses into effect.

In addition to these project-specific plans, risk treatment might also include alteration of the base plans of the business – for example, what should the business do if a planned manufacturing plant extension is not commissioned on time? Occasionally the best way to treat a risk might be to adopt an alternative strategy, to avoid a risk or make the organization less vulnerable to its consequences.

Trade-offs will often be required when selecting treatment options: for example, between scope, cost and schedule. The process of selecting and developing effective risk treatments involves (Figure 6.1):

- identifying the options for reducing the likelihood or consequences of each Extreme or High risk;
- determining the potential benefits and costs of each option, including the possible impact on the organization if the risk occurred, the reduced level of risk if the option were implemented, the potential benefits of the reduced level of risk, and the costs of achieving those benefits, including both direct and indirect costs and the effects of any schedule delays;
- selecting the best options for the project;
- for options that have the form of contingency plans, specifying the symptoms or trigger points at which the option might be implemented;
- identifying links to related processes or activities within or outside the project; and
- developing detailed Risk Action Plans.

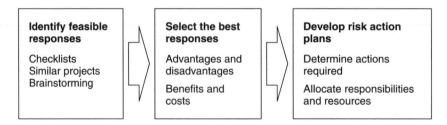

Figure 6.1—Overview of risk treatment

Risk treatment strategies

The particular Risk Action Plans developed and implemented to treat an identified risk will depend on the nature of the project and the nature of the risk. They cannot be specified in detail in guidelines like these. However, some general suggestions can be provided.

During the response identification and assessment process, it is often helpful to think about responses in terms of broad risk management strategies:

- risk prevention (including risk avoidance);
- impact mitigation;
- risk sharing;
- insurance; and
- risk retention.

In practice, these categories overlap to some extent. Nevertheless, they provide a useful framework for thinking about how to deal with risks.

These categories are in the nature of tactical responses. The organization should determine how they should be combined into its overall strategy, according to the extent to which it is prepared to accept or tolerate risk. Policy decisions such as this must be made at senior levels in the organization, not left to individual managers.

Risk prevention

Risk prevention strategies are directed to eliminating sources of risk or reducing substantially the likelihood of their occurrence.

Examples of risk prevention include:

- more detailed planning;
- the selection of alternative approaches;
- improving designs and systems engineering, or adopting enhanced design standards;
- procedural changes;
- permits to work;
- protection and safety systems;
- preventive maintenance;
- formal processes and quality assurance procedures;
- operations reviews;
- regular inspections and audits; and
- training and skills enhancement.

The specific terms of a contract also provide a means of avoiding risk. Given a reasonable feel for the risks involved, a key aspect of risk management for this purpose is risk reduction via contractual countermeasures. The aim is to avoid or neutralize significant sources of risk via contractual arrangements between the procuring organization, the ultimate client, the prime contractor or supplier, sub-contractors and insurance providers. Contract terms are likely also to involve an element of risk sharing.

Risk avoidance is a particular case of risk reduction, where undesired events are avoided completely by undertaking a different course of action.

Impact mitigation

Impact mitigation is directed to minimizing the consequences of risks. Some risks, such as those associated with economic variations or extreme weather conditions, cannot be avoided. The likelihoods of other risks arising may be reduced by risk prevention strategies, but the risks may still occur. In these cases, risk management must be directed to coping with their impacts, and ensuring that adverse consequences for the project and the project criteria are minimized.

Impact reduction strategies include:

- contingency planning;
- engineering and structural barriers;
- separation or relocation of an activity and resources;
- quality assurance;
- contract terms and conditions;
- regular audits and checks to detect compliance or information security breaches; and
- crisis management and disaster recovery plans.

Impact mitigation strategies do not preclude the use of risk prevention responses, and they are commonly used together. For example, escape and evacuation plans are essential in many areas for mitigating the consequences of major fires, but they do not avoid the need for proper prevention measures such as the use of fire retardant materials, sprinkler systems and the like.

Insurance is another important impact mitigation strategy that also has characteristics of risk sharing and transfer.

Risk sharing

Some risks can be transferred in part from the purchasing organization to another party, so the other party bears the initial consequences if the risk arises. Sharing a risk with another party usually incurs a cost for the organization.

A general principle of risk management is that risks should be the responsibility of those best able to control and manage them. Risk assessment, in identifying how risks might arise, can provide the initial guide to which party is best able to manage the risks.

Risk sharing occurs when contracts are negotiated between an organization and its suppliers or sub-contractors. Contracts are the primary means of allocating risk between the parties involved in most projects. However, sharing a risk with a contractor or supplier does not transfer it fully, and it may not really eliminate the risk – it just transforms it into a 'contractor failure' or 'contractor performance' risk. In these circumstances it is critical to ensure the contractor has a system in place for managing risk effectively, otherwise the project may end up with additional risks. In many projects, procurement contracts require sound risk management processes to be developed and implemented by the contractors, sub-contractors or suppliers of products or services, as part of prudential control and oversight procedures.

This process of allocation is called risk sharing rather than risk transfer because risks are rarely transferred completely or shed entirely. In many circumstances the contract between the buyer and the supplier is viewed as an explicit mechanism for sharing risk between them, rather than transferring risk from one to another.

The risk assessment process, in identifying how risks might arise, can provide the initial guide to which party is best able to manage risks and the most appropriate form of contract. The analysis also identifies the potential consequences, and so may aid in determining a fair price for taking the risks involved.

Insurance

Insurance is a well-known risk sharing strategy. It is normally used for physical assets and a limited range of commercial risks, particularly for the low probability but high impact residual risks that may remain after other risk treatment actions have been implemented. Sharing a risk with another party will usually incur a cost, for example an insurance premium, which provides a direct measure of the cost of sharing the risk. It should be noted that an insurance contract, like most contracts, is also a process that transforms the risk into something different: in this case, the insured party now has a credit risk that the insurer will not pay the full amount of a claim or will delay payment.

Insurance is particularly relevant to the management of 'residual' risks, where active risk prevention and mitigation measures have been implemented. The remaining variability is a prime candidate for insurance.

Some government entities do not insure their risks as a matter of policy. This policy is based on the premise that the Government has the size and consequent capacity to meet losses as and when they arise, and government contracts with suppliers should not normally involve the Government insuring assets or risks. Policies of this kind are changing as governments move towards more transparent accounting processes and user-pays principles.

Purchasing organizations frequently require their suppliers to have insurance policies in place to cover risks that properly belong to the supplier. These may be policies to cover specific physical risks, such as damage to goods in transit, or more general risks, such as professional indemnity.

Responses such as insurance, or the inclusion of liquidated damages clauses in contracts, transfer at least part of the burden of risk to another party. The payment of a claim may also be regarded as mitigating the impact of the risk, although it frequently does little to avoid the risk in the first place. However, liquidated damages clauses may provide a powerful incentive for contractors or suppliers to implement and maintain their own risk management programmes.

Many risk sharing strategies for projects or procurements require decisions to be taken at very early stages, usually in the pre-tender phases.

Risk retention

Sometimes risks cannot be avoided or transferred, or the costs of doing so would be high. In these circumstances, the organization must retain the risks. Nevertheless, risk prevention and impact mitigation measures and monitoring are usually recommended, at least in outline form.

As most businesses in the private sector know, hedging or shedding all risks is rarely possible, and in any case it often costs so much that little or no profit can be made. In these circumstances, companies may become risk takers as an integral part of conducting their business, and reap the associated rewards. In some instances, organizations may wish to consciously retain significant risks, particularly where they have the appropriate expertise to manage them.

Risk retention will become an important consideration for those government agencies with current plans or future aspirations to compete with the private sector, those that may be corporatized or privatized, or those that may be judged on commercial criteria, such as profit and return on assets.

Some organizations have statutory obligations to retain and manage risk. They will usually take particular care to select and implement risk prevention, mitigation and control strategies to ensure the residual risk they must accept is minimized.

Using likelihood and consequence information

The detailed ratings developed in the risk analysis process provide initial guidance on the risk treatment actions that may be appropriate.

The likelihood and consequence ratings are used to determine the risk priorities. They also provide a guide to the kinds of risk treatment responses that may be relevant for each risk, as shown in Figure 6.2 and Figure 6.3.

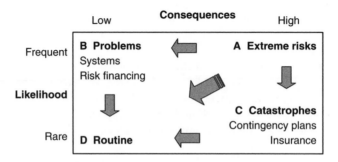

Figure 6.2—Likelihoods and consequences

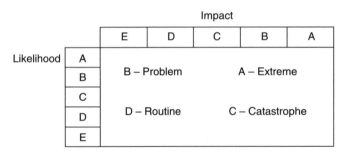

Figure 6.3—Treatment options overlay of the risk priority rating table

A. **Extreme risk area**. Detailed risk treatment action is required. This may be directed to reducing the likelihood of the risk (or avoiding it altogether), or to reducing its impacts, or both. In Figure 6.3, this has the effect of moving the residual risk to the regions labelled B, C or D.
B. **Problem area**. Risks in this area have high likelihoods, but moderate to low impacts. Treatment actions can often be directed to improving management systems and procedures. This area typically receives a lot of management attention because of the high frequency and may result in an over-allocation of resources.
C. **Catastrophe area**. Risks in this area have low likelihoods but potentially high impacts. Effective preparation and crisis management or contingency plans are often valuable options for the catastrophic residual risk. Insurance may be appropriate. Management should ensure that this area receives the appropriate resources even though the risks may seem less urgent.
D. **Routine area**. Risks in this area can often be managed by standard processes, systems and procedures, or on an ad hoc basis.

Using agreed and inherent risk information

The agreed and inherent priority ratings for each risk discussed in Chapter 4 provide a further guide to treatment actions. Table 6.1 and the detailed descriptions following outline the implications for risk treatment.

A. Risks classified as Extreme or High on both scales. These risks are likely to arise and to have potentially serious consequences, even with the controls in place. They require detailed planning and close management attention, as by implication there are few effective treatment controls that have been implemented.
B. Risks classified as Extreme or High on the inherent scale, but not on the agreed scale after taking the controls into account. These risks are potentially serious if the controls fail. Management attention should be directed to monitoring and improving the controls to ensure they remain effective.

Table 6.1—Management actions

	Agreed priority		
Inherent risk	*Extreme or High*	*Medium*	*Low*
Extreme or High	A	B	B
Medium	*	C	D
Low	*	*	E

Note: * indicates that these extremes are not possible (unless the controls that have been implemented actually make matters worse!).

C.   Risks classified as Medium on both scales. They may be likely to arise, or to have serious consequences, but not necessarily both, given the controls. These risks require planning and management attention to improve the controls.

D.   Risks classified as Medium on the inherent scale, but only Low on the agreed scale after taking controls into account. Management attention should be focused on monitoring the controls and improving them where appropriate.

E.   These risks are Low on both scales. They can usually be managed using routine procedures.

Developing and selecting feasible risk treatment responses

It is usually important to identify and list a range of responses that might be implemented if a risk event were to occur, particularly for the Extreme, High and Medium risks. The process begins with a review of the risk and how it might arise. This should be done by someone familiar with the activity, the element and the kind of risk being examined.

From the review, a list of responses to the risk should be generated. The methods for this are similar to those for risk identification: brainstorming with a selected team to generate ideas; examining the lessons learned in similar activities, or using ideas generated in similar projects; and utilizing previous organizational and other experience captured in the form of checklists. The material in the preceding sections of this chapter may provide a guide.

The list of responses may be expanded to include a brief description of what is involved in each response, the mechanisms by which it will reduce the risk and when it might be most appropriate. Initially, all feasible responses should be listed, with more extensive descriptions of the more attractive ones. It is important that the responses that are identified are appropriate and practical in the context.

For each Extreme, High or Medium risk, the most appropriate set of responses must be selected from the set of all responses to the identified risks. This usually involves trade-offs between the potential benefits of implementing a response and the actual costs of doing so (Figure 6.4). The profile in Figure 6.4 is generated by sequencing the treatment options from left to right in order of decreasing effectiveness, where the risk level is the notional risk reduction obtained from a specific option at the additional cost indicated on the horizontal axis. Options on the left-hand end of the profile have high marginal benefits in terms of the ratio of risk reduction to treatment cost and so are likely to be favoured. Those on the

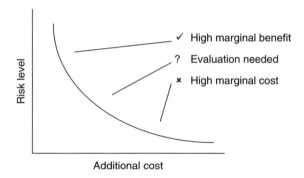

Figure 6.4—Treatment trade-offs

right-hand end have low marginal benefits compared to the treatment cost and so are likely to be less favoured if there are constraints on resources (as is usually the case). Standard forms of benefit-cost analysis may be helpful in structuring the selection process, although a generous amount of judgement is usually included, particularly in the middle region.

When assessing risk treatment strategies the following points should be borne in mind.

- The aim of the evaluation is to identify the most attractive strategies.
- While the description of the selection process is framed in terms of costs and benefits, this is simply a structure within which to organize professional judgement about the merits of alternative treatment strategies. Formal quantitative cost-benefit analyses will be very important in some circumstances, but they need not be undertaken in every case if the effort required would not be warranted.
- The screening process need not be very complex to be effective, and may rely heavily on the professional judgement of staff (who may nevertheless be required to justify their assessments). Simple forms of analysis are often adequate for many purposes: for example, scales from 5 (high effectiveness or high cost) to 1 (low effectiveness or low cost) provide a simple way of recording the initial assessment of a response and a guide to the recommendation.

As part of evaluation, risks should be examined at the level of the overall project, across the elements, to develop wider decision rules for controlling and managing risk (Figure 6.5). The aim is to identify common risks and general responses to risks that occur in more than one place or that have wide potential effects.

Responses may be specific to one risk or have wider and more general effectiveness in reducing a range of risks. They may be implemented now, or they may be contingent on particular risks arising or thresholds being attained. The evaluation and selection of worthwhile responses should take into account all the potential benefits and costs associated with each response, and for groups of responses, across the entire activity and for all the stakeholders. Points of leverage should be exploited if they will assist in maximizing the benefits of a risk treatment strategy.

General responses are capable of dealing with several specific sources of risk or with similar risks that may arise in different areas. General responses may offer economies of scale or

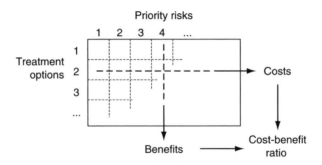

Figure 6.5—Treatment options and trade-offs

improved efficiency in dealing with risks. Responses such as better planning, improved staff training or quality assurance procedures tend to be general responses, because they contribute to the resolution of many different kinds of risks, often across an entire project.

It is important to distinguish between specific and general responses to facilitate the ordering of responses and the development of decision rules for selecting responses and when they might be applied.

Conclusions from the analysis should include recommendations about whether the response is worth exploring further, any follow-up actions required, and whether the response requires immediate action or whether it may be deferred until a risk arises or a threshold or 'trigger point' is reached.

For detailed analyses, such as might be needed for large or particularly risky projects, the potential responses for each risk may be summarized on a risk treatment options worksheet (Figure 6.6). A note may be made on that sheet of additional information needed to conduct a more extensive benefit-cost analysis should that be required (for example, in the development of a comprehensive business case for justifying a recommended course of action).

Risk and response scenarios

As part of the response identification process, risk and response scenarios may be developed. A scenario is a description of how a risk might arise, the responses that might be taken and their consequences. It is a way of describing in broad terms the processes by which risks might occur and be dealt with.

Scenarios can be useful for developing responses to unlikely or unusual events, or to events outside the usual experience. For example, they may be used to develop physical security plans for dealing with sabotage or terrorism, or to model political or community processes.

Scenarios are also useful when the consequences of different risks arising, or of a risk arising at different levels, can lead to a set of common outcomes. For example, a particular outcome described in terms of damage and consequences might eventuate as a result of a minor event having a larger than expected effect or a major event having a smaller than expected effect.

Element:	Risk:		Action Sheet: Risk Register number:	
Likelihood:	Impact:	Agreed risk level:	Inherent risk level:	

Risk description (causes, consequences, implications):

Current controls and plans:

Possible additional actions:

Response	Effectiveness	Cost

Comments and recommendations:

Sources of information and list of attachments:

Compiler:	Date:	Reviewer:	Date:

Figure 6.6—Risk treatment options worksheet

Scenarios may be developed and attached to risk and response descriptions where appropriate and useful.

Secondary risks and responses

A primary risk is a self-initiating source of risk, usually related directly to the initial list of project elements. A secondary risk arises as a consequence of a primary risk, or as a consequence of implementing a control or a treatment response. A secondary response is a response to a secondary risk. For example, in some circumstances a fire might be a primary risk, with water damage and structural collapse as associated secondary risks.

Where possible, secondary risks and responses should be embedded in the primary response, as this often simplifies the subsequent analysis. The use of scenarios provides one way of doing this.

However, it is not always possible, nor is it always desirable, to embed secondary risks and responses. This is the case particularly if the secondary risk or its associated responses may themselves have major consequences, or if they differ in significant ways from the initiating primary risks.

The same risk and response description worksheets may be used for secondary risks and responses.

A structure diagram is a useful way of summarizing the relationships, including the project items, primary risks and responses and secondary risks and responses, with their interconnections. Figure 6.7 shows an example adapted from Cooper and Chapman (1987).

Risk action plans

In any project, the development and implementation of detailed action plans for reducing risks is the key to successful project risk management in practice.

Risk Action Plans for treating identified risks will be part of project plans, coordinated and integrated wherever possible with established project management processes and procedures, and controlled and managed like any other activities in the project. This may require treatment actions to be integrated with existing procedures for project management, budgeting, capital expenditure approval, asset management, health and safety, human resources, environmental and other management as appropriate.

The manager responsible for treating a risk may belong to the project team, the sponsoring business unit, or a functional area. Generally, responsibility should be allocated according to who is best able to deal with the matter. Responsible managers should complete Risk Action Plan summaries for each risk classified as Extreme or High on the agreed risk priority scale. The structure of the summary is shown in Figure 6.8.

- **Extreme and High risks**: All Extreme and High risks must be reduced. A detailed Risk Action Plan is required, with a one-page executive Risk Action Plan summary in the form shown in Figure 6.8. Similar risks, or risks for which a common treatment is indicated, can be grouped. All the boxes in the summary are required to be completed.

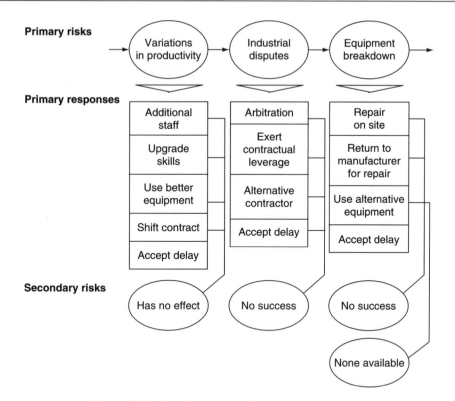

Figure 6.7—Part of a structure diagram for a large project

Note: Risks are shown in circles, responses in rectangles. Additional notes may be attached to risk circles and response boxes, indicating mechanisms, special features, probabilities or specific impacts.

The summary may be sufficient in many circumstances, but additional detail can be included if required, such as the benefit-cost analysis justifying the action. The summary can refer to existing work plans and processes. Managers should amend existing work plans appropriately.

- **Medium risks**: All Medium risks should be reviewed and, where resources are available, suitable cost-effective reduction actions should be implemented and a Risk Action Plan summary completed (Figure 6.8). The aim should be to reduce all Medium risks unless it is decided, based on an assessment of costs versus benefits, to accept the risk.
- **Low risks**: The managers responsible should take into account the identified risks, and ensure existing controls, plans and procedures are adequate to cover them. Where the risk is inherently Extreme or High, managers must also ensure that the control processes are being implemented correctly and effectively.

For all risks that have an inherent risk level of Extreme or High, a summary should also be completed, focusing on the processes for enhancing and monitoring the effectiveness of the controls.

Risk Action Plan summaries may be supplemented as necessary by more formal Risk Management Plans. These may take many forms, according to the nature of the risks and

Element:	Risk:		Risk register number:
Likelihood:	Impact:	Agreed risk level:	Inherent risk level:

Risk description (causes, consequences, implications):
Current controls and plans:
Additional actions recommended:
Responsibility:
Resources required:
Timing (key milestones, closure):
Reporting (to whom, when, in what form):
References (to other documents or plans as appropriate):

Compiled by:	Date:	Reviewed by:	Date:

Figure 6.8—Risk Action Plan summary

Table 6.2—Contents of a simple project
Risk Management Plan

1. Recommended risk management actions
   Summary
   Impact
2. Risk identification and assessment
   Element description
   Risk identification
   Risk priorities
3. Responses to risks
   Alternative courses of action
   Consequences of alternatives
   Assessment of options
4. Implementation
   Objectives
   Actions required
   Responsibilities
   Resource requirements
   Timing
   Reporting

responses and the way the organization documents its project management processes. A set of contents for a very simple Risk Management Plan is summarized in Table 6.2, and more extensive examples are provided in Chapter 9. Detailed Risk Action Plans are likely to form appendices to the Risk Management Plan for the project.

The first part of the Risk Management Plan provides an executive summary of the actions to be taken and the potential impact on the business.

Part 2 of the plan describes the project element and the risk identification process for that element. It also describes the priority assessment for the identified risks for the element, thus providing the justification and need for Risk Action Plans. This section summarizes the activities that were detailed in Chapters 3 and 4.

Part 3 describes the response selection process, the options considered, the evaluation process and the selection of the preferred responses, related to the specific set of risks.

Part 4 describes the detailed actions and implementation processes that must be undertaken to manage the risks that have been identified, expanding on the information in Figure 6.8.

Managing Medium risks

Although Extreme and High risks individually lead to the greatest potential problems, there are usually many more Medium risks than Extreme and High risks, and the effect of the Medium risks in aggregate may be significant. Accordingly, the Medium risks must be managed too. The assessment process for identifying and evaluating options for the management of Medium risks is similar to that described for Extreme and High risks. The level of detail required may be lower, but the same considerations apply.

In practice, the management and oversight processes for Medium risks tend to be more flexible and devolved than they are for Extreme and High risks. The management of Extreme and High risks usually requires formal Risk Action Plans that are presented and monitored centrally. For Medium risks, the focus for the senior manager is usually on ensuring that appropriate action is being taken, without necessarily the same degree of detailed central control and oversight.

The management processes are often simple, depending on the complexity of the project organization:

- designating the manager responsible for each risk area;
- ensuring that each manager has plans developed to a level of detail appropriate to the requirement; and
- ensuring the reporting and monitoring procedures are adequate for tracking the implementation of risk management activities.

The risk action summary in Figure 6.8 usually provides most of the detail needed for the oversight of Medium risks. Each responsible manager may have more detailed plans, but they do not always need to be examined in detail at the senior level.

In this way, risk management becomes part of the regular management processes within the project.

Implementation

Implementing the individual Risk Action Plans for Extreme, High and Medium risks is essential for the benefits to be obtained from the project risk management process. Implementation management employs standard project management techniques that are not special or specific to risk management. The requirements are straightforward:

- setting objectives;
- specifying responsibilities;
- allocating and controlling resources, including budgets;
- specifying schedules and milestones for implementing action items, and their impact on the project schedule;
- monitoring and reporting progress and achievements; and
- assisting in the resolution of problems.

MONITORING AND REVIEW

Chapter overview

- ## Purpose

  Monitoring and review:

  - link risk management to other management processes; and
  - facilitate better risk management and continuous improvement.

- ## Rationale

  Continuous monitoring and review of risks ensures new risks are detected and managed, and that action plans are implemented and progressed effectively.

- ## Inputs

  The main input to this step is the risk watch list of the major risks that have been identified for risk treatment action.

- ## Method

  - Implement a review process as part of the regular management meeting cycle.
  - Undertake major reviews at significant project phases and milestones.

- ## Outputs

  Revisions to the risk register, and a list of new action items for risk treatment.

- ## Documentation

  Update the risk register as a result of the review process.

Introduction

Monitoring and review link risk management to other project management processes. Continuous monitoring and review of risks is an important part of implementation, particularly for large projects or those in dynamic environments. It ensures new risks are detected and managed, and that action plans are implemented and progressed effectively.

The project manager should maintain a risk watch list, containing a list of the major risks that have been identified for risk treatment action. For large projects, appropriate managers at each level of management in the project will maintain their own risk watch lists for their areas of responsibility.

Regular monitoring processes

Risk management should be a regular agenda item for project management meetings. The primary tool is the risk watch list. This is used to ensure all the important risks are examined.

Initially, the risk watch list will contain all the risks classified as Extreme and High, with selected Medium risks. As risk issues are resolved or change, or as new risks arise, the risk watch list will be updated.

Under the heading 'risk management' in the meeting agenda (Figure 7.1), several items will be considered.

1. For each risk on the risk watch list, the progress and effectiveness of risk treatment actions will be reviewed, and adjustments to Risk Action Plans will be made as needed.
2. Extreme, High and Medium risks for which effective risk treatment has been completed should be reassessed and reclassified, and removed from the risk watch list if appropriate.

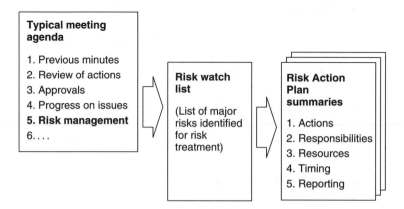

Figure 7.1—Meeting agenda for regular risk monitoring

3. Medium or Low risks that have changed in status and become important enough to be reclassified as Extreme or High will be included in the risk watch list, and responsibilities and timing for preparing detailed Risk Action Plans will be allocated.
4. Any new identified risks will be considered, and Extreme and High ones will be included in the risk watch list. For each new risk included in this way, the responsibility and timing for preparing a detailed Risk Action Plan will be allocated. Risk Action Plan summaries for all new Extreme and High risks will be included in the risk register and the project Risk Management Plan.
5. Trends and general issues in programme risks and risk management will be considered, and any necessary changes to risk management strategies will be made.

Updating the risk register

The risk register database is the main risk management tool for monitoring the risk management process within the project. It lists the ranked risks and references the associated risk action plans. Keeping the risk register up to date is the responsibility of the project manager. In practice, this task will usually be delegated to the project control function.

New risks will be identified out of planning and design review processes, further project risk assessments and other management activities. These risks will be entered into the risk register and if required risk action plans developed and referenced in the register.

Risks that have been managed, avoided or are no longer relevant can be removed from the risk register. The associated risk action plans will also be deleted from the risk register.

As resources become available, risk management options will be evaluated (in terms of costs and benefits) and appropriate risk action plans developed for the Medium risks. These will also be referenced in the risk register.

The status of specific risks and the associated risk action plans should be reviewed regularly, as noted earlier.

Major reviews of risks

The nature of risks changes as projects and implementation timeframes change. Regular reviews of risks and risk treatment will be undertaken as part of the normal project management process to revise the lists of Extreme and High risks, to generate new Risk Action Plans and to revise the risk register.

One approach to monitoring the overall status of risk in the project regularly is to use the risk survey processes described in Chapter 5. The information for this should come from the managers responsible for the individual configuration items or work packages.

The most appropriate way of doing this is likely to be in conjunction with the project's monthly project cost and schedule control system (CSCS) or equivalent reporting, quarterly system audits or equivalent formal review cycle. Incorporating semi-quantitative assessments (like those in Chapter 5) in the form of risk surveys in the CSCS 'Estimate to complete procedure' is a practicable way of doing this. The estimate to complete procedure requires managers to think about aspects of the project related to risks and uncertainty, specifically analyses of the work and resource usage to completion, based on historical performance. The risk analysis extends this thinking to more explicit considerations of what problems might occur in the future, and ways of dealing with them.

It should be noted, however, that risk surveys will rarely be needed monthly. A six-monthly reporting cycle may be sufficient for small projects; for large projects quarterly reports may be adequate, or surveys may be conducted on an 'as needed' basis.

Additional formal and more complete risk identification and assessment reviews may be needed. In general, such reviews should be undertaken at key milestones, including:

- key planning and design review activities, where there may be significant changes proposed in the project strategy, scope or processes;
- at major transition points, such as the start of tendering, contract negotiation, implementation, acceptance testing and commissioning activities, where there are significant changes in the structure and focus of the project and its associated risks;
- as part of formal project review processes;
- where there is a major change in external circumstances, including any major change in policy, organization or priorities that might impact on the project.

There are likely to be advantages in aligning major risk management reviews with other project milestone reviews. Typical milestones at which reviews may be undertaken are listed in Table 7.1.

Table 7.1—Typical milestone review stages

Review stage	Project phase
1	Scheme definition, pre-project study
2	Design proposal, plant specification
3	Detailed design
4	Construction and pre-commissioning
5	Commissioning
6	Post-commissioning

COMMUNICATION AND REPORTING

8

Chapter overview

- **Purpose**

  Project managers must report on the current status of risks and risk management as required by sponsors and company policy.

- **Rationale**

  Senior managers need to understand the risks they face, and risk reports provide a complement to other project reports in developing this understanding.

- **Inputs**

  The risk register and the supporting action plans provide the basis for most project risk reporting.

- **Method**

  Submit reports on a regular basis or as required, as part of standard project reporting.

- **Outputs**

  Reports provide a summary of risks, the status of treatment actions and an indication of trends in the incidence of risks in the project.

- **Documentation**

  - All projects are required to submit Summary Risk Reports (format like Figure 8.1, Figure 8.2).
  - Major projects may require more extensive reporting on a periodic basis or at key milestones (format like Figure 8.3).

Reasons for communication and reporting

There are many reasons for communicating and reporting the outcomes of a risk management study.

- Communication within the project team. Maintaining the consistency and 'reasonableness' of a large risk assessment in a complex project, possibly incorporating the judgements from a diverse team of experts, requires special care. Recording the assumptions that underlie each judgement and decision is important for checking purposes when the results of a risk analysis do not seem right. In practice, anomalies occur because inconsistent assumptions are made, and the documentation provides the detailed clues for resolving them.
- Communication with an owner or client. It is important that the end-users understand the risks and trade-offs that must be made in a large project, as they are usually the ones who must pay for risk. By describing the risks, their assessment and their management, the buyer ensures that all parties are fully informed, thus avoiding unpleasant surprises. This may be an important part of the negotiating process for the long-term allocation or sharing of risk between the stakeholders.
- Communication with the providers of finance and insurance support. Funding bodies, whether they are banks, bond holders, equity providers (shareholders), credit guarantors, the finance divisions of the procuring organisations, government funding agencies, or private-sector participants in a public-sector project, all require information about the risks and their allocation and management. In particular, they will often have a direct interest in the residual risks (the risks that remain after all reasonable management actions have been taken) and the 'worst-case' outcomes, after prudent risk management plans have been implemented.
- Accountability and auditability. Project managers must be accountable for their decisions. It is important that the risk assessment process is documented in such a way that it can be reviewed, to enable the structure and assumptions to be examined and the reasons for particular judgements and decisions to be identified.
- Information source for future projects. The collection of detailed information about all aspects of a project, in a structured fashion that facilitates retrieval, generates a very valuable organizational asset. It provides a database of corporate knowledge that probably only existed in the heads of the project team and its specialist advisers. In practice, many organizations have found such a database to be an unexpected bonus by-product of the risk assessment process, that can be used subsequently in other similar project analyses.
- Record for post-implementation project evaluation. All organizations should review their large projects after completion, to ensure their objectives have been met and their procedures have been adequate, and to extract the key lessons for improving performance in future projects. This becomes part of the development process towards the achievement of best practice.

Communication and reporting also makes an important contribution to planning processes.

- Risk management planning for the key stakeholders. The project Risk Management Plan described in the next chapter provides a high-level focus on risk across the entire project.

- Tactical risk action planning. The Risk Action Plans described in the previous chapter provide the basis for tactical action and implementation.
- Justification for spending money now or taking a particular course of action. Where significant risk management activity must be taken early in the life of a project, usually directed to risk prevention measures, different funding levels and spending profiles may result. The project Risk Management Plan and the detailed Risk Action Plans provide the rationale for management recommendations and actions to reduce risks.
- Communication between the project team and the contractors or suppliers. The project Risk Management Plan and Risk Action Plans should identify the problems and the solutions and convey a detailed understanding of what must be done and why. They form a valuable tactical bridge between the various parties involved in the project. In some circumstances, owners, contractors and suppliers all may be involved in the risk assessment itself, in a form of partnering process. Partnering in large projects may be an important strategy for risk reduction, but it is a topic in its own right and outside the scope of this book.
- Control of risk and risk management activities. Formal project risk management reports specify the criteria for success, the targets and measures used to assess performance, detailed accountabilities for managing risk and the allocation of budgets and resources. They provide the strategic and tactical focus for successful project risk management.

Aspects of communication as it applies to environmental risk management are also discussed in Chapter 18.

Tendering requirements

Formal reporting by project sponsors or procuring agencies may be required in some circumstances as a matter of policy. Some government agencies and private-sector organizations require their contractors and suppliers to submit project Risk Management Plans as part of their tender submissions when they bid for large projects. This provides a way of ensuring that potential suppliers have thought through the main issues of risk and its management at an early stage in their planning processes.

As an example, many government agencies regularly require Risk Management Plans as part of their tender and contract deliverables. Such tender requirements usually cover two aspects of risk and its management:

- the risks identified by the contractor, with an indication of their potential severity and the ways in which they will be managed; and
- the processes and structures the contractor will employ for the continuing monitoring and management of risk throughout the project, including the role of the purchasing authority in managing risks within its own control that are critical to successful delivery.

Table 8.1 shows extracts from the request for tender documents for a recent procurement. These two requirements, for risk identification and for management processes, are illustrated clearly.

Table 8.1—Extracts from request for tender documents

4.7.9   Risk management. The contractor shall develop and maintain a risk management programme to plan for, assess, analyse, and manage project risk in accordance with the Risk Management Plan. (ESSENTIAL)

Tenderers shall describe in their tender both perceived project risks and the processes by which risk planning, assessment, analysis, and handling procedures shall be employed throughout the execution of the Contract. When discussing perceived project risks, tenderers shall identify the possible cost, schedule, and performance impacts and classify the severity of the risks. Tenderers shall also discuss proposed courses of action to minimise, eliminate, or otherwise avoid identified risks. When discussing the planning, assessment, analysis, and risk handling procedures to be employed during the Contract, tenderers should discuss risk identification, analysis, monitoring, and controlling techniques that are proposed, the means by which the Government will be advised of the risks, and what actions may be expected of the Government to mitigate identified risks.

4.7.9.1   Risk Management Plan. The contractor shall provide and maintain a Risk Management Plan. (CDRL-MGT-07) (ESSENTIAL)

Tenderers shall include . . . a draft of their Risk Management Plan identifying risk commensurate with the level of development of the tender and proposals for managing this risk. Tenderers shall use the following definitions for risk levels when identifying risk in their draft Risk Management Plan.

Low risk	Has little potential to cause disruption of schedule, increase in cost, or degradation of performance.
Medium risk	Can potentially cause some disruption of schedule, increase in cost, or degradation of performance.
High risk	Can potentially cause serious disruptions of schedule, increase in cost, or degradation of performance.

In the example, the focus is on the three most common measures of project success: time, cost and performance. However, in this case, as in most projects, these measures are multi-dimensional and there are more than three critical factors. Table 8.2 shows some of the additional aspects of time, cost and user acceptance that may have to be considered. (Compare these with the criteria discussed in Chapter 2.)

Reports

Formal reporting may be required for large or particularly risky projects. What is large or risky depends very much on the organization and its own policies and procedures. For example, some companies undertake and report on formal risk analyses only on very large projects, while others perform them routinely on relatively small activities. Reporting requirements should be specified in the project Risk Management Plan (Chapter 9).

Where formal reporting is not deemed necessary, a summary of the main risks, risk treatment plans, responsibilities and anticipated outcomes may provide an adequate basis for reporting. This may be in the form of a summary risk report, containing a graphical representation of those risks with Extreme or High ratings, taking controls into account

Table 8.2—Extended concepts of time, cost and user acceptance for a project

Basic measure	Factors that may be considered
Time	Time for practical completion and delivery of the procured items, often defined as the time to successful completion of trials and acceptance tests.
	Time to the start of operational implementation, including the time required for manning and training to operational skills levels.
	Operational in-service life of delivered systems.
Cost	Capital cost.
	Other sponsor expenditure during the procurement process on management, personnel and sponsor-supplied facilities and equipment.
	Through-life cost, including the cost of operating the delivered systems and their associated spares.
User acceptance	Performance against specific operational criteria.
	Integrated logistics support aspects, including reliability, availability and maintainability.

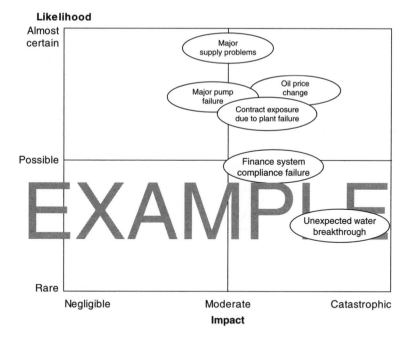

Figure 8.1—Example of a risk reporting graphic

(Figure 8.1), together with a summary of the risks and the treatment actions that are being implemented (Figure 8.2). In many cases at least part of the information is available from the risk register database.

For major projects, more extensive reporting may be required on a periodic basis or at key milestones. Figure 8.3 provides an example of an extended reporting format.

Project summary risk report	Period:	Submission date:

Summary of Extreme or High risks			
Risk number	Risk description	Risk treatment and control summary	Responsibility

Commentary on significant changes during the period:

Commentary on the status of the risk management system in the project:

Project Manager: Date:	Reviewer: Date:

Attachments: Risk Action Plan summaries for Extreme and High risks

Figure 8.2—Project summary risk report

Major project periodic risk report	Period:	Submission date:

Commentary on Extreme or High risks to the project and their management:

Summary risk profile:

Agreed priority	Impact			The number of risks in each inherent risk rating	
Likelihood ⇩	High (A or B)	Medium (C)	Low (D or E)	Extreme	
High (A or B)				High	
Medium (C)				Medium	
Low (D or E)				Low	

Summary of Extreme or High risks:

Figure 8.3—(Continued opposite)

Risk number	Risk description	Risk treatment and control summary	Responsibility

Commentary on significant changes during the last period:

Commentary on the status of the Risk Management system in the project:

Project Manager:	Reviewer:
Date:	Date:

Figure 8.3—Major project periodic risk report

PROJECT PROCESSES AND PLANS

Chapter overview

- ### Purpose

  The project Risk Management Plan specifies how risk management will be conducted in the project, and integrates it with other project management activities and processes.

- ### Rationale

  Risk management should be part of 'business as usual' for everyone in the project. The project Risk Management Plan specifies how this is to be achieved for the project team.

- ### Inputs

  The project Risk Management Plan is based on the organizational guidelines, adapted as necessary for the project, and integrated with other project plans and documents.

- ### Method

  Develop the project Risk Management Plan at an early stage in the project, and keep it updated as the project progresses throughout its life.

- ### Outputs

  Major projects require a project Risk Management Plan, but this is not usually required for smaller or less risky projects.

- ### Documentation

  Project Risk Management Plan (contents in Table 9.5).

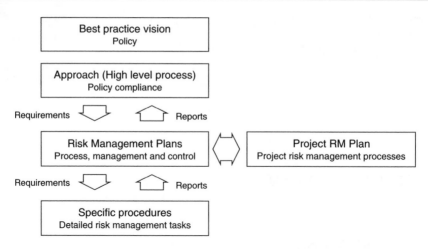

Figure 9.1—Structure of organizational risk management processes and procedures

Project and organizational risk management

The structure of the risk management processes in an organization is usually multi-levelled. At the highest level there is a best practice vision and policy. This provides the direction for the organization. A high-level risk management approach outlines the method that guides the implementation of risk management in all activities, within the policy guidelines. In each project, specific risk management plans outline how each project will implement the risk management approach. The specific risk management procedures describe in detail how the plans are to be implemented. The structure is outlined in Figure 9.1.

Risk management procedures

Most large organizations that manage projects as part of their regular business activities have processes that are well documented in a set of project management procedures, planning guidelines or similar manuals. These may contain provision for a project Risk Management Plan and describe the requirements in more or less detail. Where no such plan exists, new risk management procedures may have to be developed, since many large contracts now require them. In any case, it is good practice to manage risk explicitly, even for medium and small projects, and good procedures provide an efficient way of doing this.

To achieve their best impact, project risk management procedures should satisfy the following criteria:

- Procedures should be compatible with existing project procedures and fit within the company's established operating framework;
- They should be broadly compliant with the requirements of Government and other procurement and regulatory authorities for major contracts, so they achieve their external purposes;

- They should be written as general procedures that can be adapted to specific projects where necessary, to provide greatest efficiency and flexibility;
- Any periodic risk reporting required by the procedures should become part of the regular project reporting cycle, so that managers are not burdened with excessive additional administration.

Typical risk requirements for large projects

This section outlines the general requirements for risk analysis for large projects, particularly those involving significant technical development. It uses examples from specific defence projects as the basis for describing the common requirements. The details of the projects are not important, since the requirements reflect those included for many large procurement activities. Risk management is often referenced in the request for tender documents and in various mandatory contract data items, as noted in Chapter 8.

Most large procurement projects carry an obligation for the contractors to implement risk management (Table 9.1). At the project level, this is often seen as primarily a coordinating and integrating function, but this obviously depends on the size and complexity of the project.

The implementation of risk management in a project must be supported by appropriate plans. These specify how the contractor will undertake risk analysis, recognize high-risk areas and reduce risks in the project. Risk management plans may be required in the Project Management Plan, in the system engineering management plan, or in a separate project Risk Management Plan (Table 9.2). The contents of a typical Risk Management Plan are outlined in the next section.

Table 9.1—Typical general risk management requirements

Project Risk Management

General Requirements

a. The contractor will identify sources of risk, including any issue that may impede or impair the attainment of contract requirements for technical performance, operational performance, support, quality, or cost and schedule performance.

b. Risk management at the project management level of the project organization will coordinate the risk management activities implemented at functional levels to address sources of risk particular to each function.

Table 9.2—Typical Risk Management Plan requirements

Project management plan

Part X dealing with systems and procedures shall include details of the contractor's systems and procedures to satisfy the requirements for the following:

a. Project risk management . . .

Most projects require monthly reports on status and progress to a contract supervisory authority. This may be an internal body such as a project review board, or linked to the project sponsor, owner or users. Risk reporting is usually required as part of overall reporting (Table 9.3).

There are likely to be other requirements concerned with specific aspects of risks and hazards in high-technology projects. These are frequently contained in other detailed technical plans. Depending on the project characteristics, they might be included in reliability and maintainability plans, failure modes, effects and criticality analysis (FMECA) plans, design safety plans, facilities plans or test and evaluation plans (Table 9.4). Most large engineering contracts require detailed safety and environmental Risk Management Plans (Chapters 17 and 18).

Table 9.3—Typical reporting requirements

Monthly status report

The monthly status report will include . . . a project risk report . . .

The project risk report will contain summary details of risks from all sources, and will include the following information for every major source of risk identified:

- description of the risk, its nature and its source;
- assessment of the risk, its impact, the probability of failure, the consequences of failure, and if previously reported, any changes in these parameters since the previous report;
- responsibility for risk treatment; and
- an abstract of the risk treatment plan, which will summarize the salient details of recommended actions, principal decision points and criteria for closure, and will provide a reference to the detailed risk treatment plan for the source of risk in question.

Table 9.4—Typical related requirements

Reliability and maintainability plan	*FMECA plan*
The Reliability and Maintainability Plan will be based on appropriate standards. It will include information on the following topics: • The contractor's procedures for reliability and maintainability (R&M) risk identification, assessment, analysis and treatment; • The contractor's procedures for integrating R&M risk management into the technical risk management programme . . .	The FMECA plan will include the following information: • A description of the contractor's established systems and processes for performing FMECA; • Sample worksheet formats used; • The rules and assumptions that the contractor has established for FMECA specific to this project, including the definition of a failure in terms of performance parameters and allowable limits; • The lowest level of system decomposition at which FMECA will be performed; • The interrelationship between FMECA, R&M analyses and technical risk management; • The manager responsible for FMECA and the organizational unit that will perform the analyses.

Project Risk Management Plan

The Risk Management Plan for a project summarizes the results of the risk management process described in the previous chapters. In particular, it describes the detailed risk treatment plans to be implemented to reduce and control risks, and it provides for continuing monitoring of the implementation.

A project Risk Management Plan is usually required for all major or risky projects. For smaller or less risky projects, the elements of a Risk Management Plan may be incorporated in the project execution strategy or equivalent. In practice, many of the requirements for reporting on risks and the implementation of risk treatment plans will be combined with regular management reporting.

A project Risk Management Plan takes a high-level view of risk. It is neither appropriate nor practical to include in it a mass of detail about particular functional areas of the project nor specific items in the WBS, particularly if they may change as the project and its risk profile develops. It is more useful to confine the detail to individual risk treatment plans to be implemented and maintained in the functional areas, and to specify the control and reporting procedures necessary for senior managers to maintain oversight of them. The Risk Management Plan may contain summaries of the treatment plans.

Typical contents of a detailed project Risk Management Plan are outlined in Table 9.5. (Compare this with the contents of a simple Risk Management Plan described in Chapter 6, Table 6.2.)

The Risk Management Plan may include references to incident management and risk management training.

- Incident management describes the processes for managing incidents and responding to problems, such as site accidents, fires or security breaches. This section is likely to be brief and refer to the organization's existing procedures and other relevant plans in the operating areas, including security manuals, safety manuals and hazard procedures.
- Risk management training is an important element of continuing risk management. This section specifies the responsibility for training, its content and objectives, and the individuals for whom training should be provided.

Links to project management

There are several management processes linked to projects that require integration with project risk management (Table 9.6). These may be discussed in the organization's general procedures or the project Risk Management Plan.

Monitoring and plan review

For all projects, the nature of the risks will change as the project moves through different phases. Risk management should begin at the strategic planning stage of a proposed

Table 9.5—Contents of a detailed project Risk Management Plan

Plan section	Purpose
Background and objectives	Defines the scope of the project and the Risk Management Plan, and states the objectives.
Project risk management responsibilities and functions	Specifies the structure, roles and functions relating to risk management of members of the project management team, and the way they link with organizational risk management functions.
	Risk management relationships between the sponsor, contractors, sub-contractors, financiers, insurers and regulators may also be described here.
Project risk management process	Specifies the risk management processes to be followed in the project. Usually this will be done simply by reference to organizational guidelines, but this section will also describe any project-specific modifications to the standard process.
	This section may also describe the processes for managing incidents and allocate responsibilities for training.
Managing risk in the project	
• Monitoring and review	Specifies the processes for regular monitoring and review, including timing and responsibility.
• Reporting	Specifies the processes for regular and exception reporting, including timing, format and responsibility.
• Project risk register	Specifies the structure and location of the project risk register, and responsibility for its maintenance.
• Major reviews	Specifies the timing for and nature of major reviews of project risks.
Risk register	Contains the current list of project risks, with priority ratings. This will be a dynamic part of the Risk Management Plan, and may be incorporated as an appendix or by reference to a risk register database.
Risk treatment	Contains summaries of the risk treatment plans for major risks. This will be a dynamic part of the Risk Management Plan, and may be incorporated as an appendix or by reference to a project schedule or other status document.
Links to project processes	Specifies how risk management integrates with other project management tasks and processes.
Appendices	Lists and summarizes key documents relating to risk management and control, including standards, specifications and handbooks, project documents, plans and publications, the company's project management procedures, and other general references.
	Names and contact details for managers with project risk management and incident management responsibilities may be listed.

project or programme, and continue through its life. The project and the risks should be reviewed periodically to ensure the Risk Management Plan is still relevant. As the project proceeds and the focus changes from strategic planning to more operational issues, different forms of risk analysis and risk management will be needed.

The Risk Management Plan should not be a static document. It should reflect the current analysis and thinking about risk in the project, and it will change as the procurement progresses and the risks change or become more urgent.

Table 9.6—Project and risk management integration for sponsors

Process	Risk management activities
Engineering design	During the engineering design process a range of hazard and risk studies should be performed.
	At the concept and preliminary design stages concept and preliminary hazard analyses should be performed and, using a simplified risk assessment process, a statement of the risks should be prepared that includes an initial risk register.
	Detailed engineering potentially involves a range of hazard studies such as Hazops, fire safety, construction safety and appropriate updates of them during the construction period.
Project brief, contract form and tender documentation	The project brief should include the major risks from the user's perspective, and any special conditions required to minimize the risks.
	For major projects the brief should include the requirement for a risk assessment and a project Risk Management Plan.
	The risks associated with the form of contract must be understood. If a change to the standard form of contract is to be made then the risks associated with the change should be fully understood and authorized by a senior contract person with the appropriate knowledge of the issues.
Tender appraisal and acceptance	In the tender appraisal process the risks associated with each short-listed option should be noted. A prompt list should be developed that will assist individuals to identify the risks.
	The list should include typical issues such as: supplier failure, experience, level of supervision, cost and price uncertainty, schedule, resources, dependence on suppliers and quality.
	Bidders should be required to provide risk management plans with bid submissions.
Capital expenditure	Risk assessment is required for capital expenditure authorization. The depth of the assessment depends on the value and risks associated with the project.
Scope changes and variations	This area must be addressed and the risks understood at the beginning of a contract. Significant changes may require hazard studies, simple risk assessments or both.

Specific monitoring of risks and the implementation of Risk Action Plans is an important part of the process. For example, in long procurements the identification and priority setting processes form the basis for regular surveys of risks and responses, leading to revised lists of Extreme, High, Medium and Low risks and new Risk Action Plans. The responsibility for conducting surveys, and their frequency, should be specified in the Risk Management Plan.

As Extreme and High risks are managed or avoided, the associated Risk Action Plans are superseded and so can be deleted from the Risk Management Plan. Risk Action Plans can be developed for the higher-priority Medium risks as management resources become available for more detailed analysis or as the timing becomes more critical.

The Risk Management Plan, like all key plans for any large project, should provide up-to-date guidance for the project manager and the project team on the current state and future plans for risk management activity.

Summary

Modern project management processes impose stringent management and reporting requirements on prospective contractors. Previously the emphasis was primarily on cost and schedule control and the maintenance of product quality, but risk management has become a recent focus of attention. Most companies see the new requirements for comprehensive risk management procedures not as an additional burden, but rather as another step towards best management practice.

SIMPLIFYING THE PROCESS

10

Chapter overview

- ### Purpose

  This chapter shows how the risk management process can be simplified when a full assessment is not warranted.

- ### Rationale

  Not every project requires a full risk management study. The rigour required for risk management in a large or risky project will be much greater than that for a small or routine service activity. The approach can be tailored to suit the perceived risk.

- ### Inputs

  Inputs are provided by the activity manager, individuals from inside and outside the project, and appropriate functional specialists.

- ### Method

  A simple risk review follows a similar procedure to the risk review workshop, but there may be no formal workshop, or one with limited scope.

- ### Outputs

  One output of the process is a statement of the risks and their priorities. Risk summary sheets and the proposed treatment actions form the main outcomes for management.

- ### Documentation

  Risks are documented in a simplified risk register, possibly in the form of a risk summary sheet (Figure 10.2), and summary lists of treatment actions.

Overview

The full risk management process is not always needed, although each stage in the process should be addressed. Various simplifications are possible, according to the characteristics of the project, the anticipated level of risk, the time and resources available and the perceived need. The appropriateness of using a simplified approach is usually determined during initial context analysis (Chapter 2).

Table 10.1 shows an example of an organizational policy that describes the characteristics of projects for the purpose of specifying the kinds of risk assessment that are needed. The values were set by the organization according to the management team's view of the risks they were willing to bear and the delegated authority limits set by the board. Broad characteristics like these can be used as a guide to the initial level of risk.

These characteristics are indicators only. It would be usual to choose the best fit, but to take a conservative approach and select the higher risk level if there were any doubt.

The detail of the risk management process should be tailored to the need. Table 10.2 and Figure 10.1 show the way in which the process can be simplified for Type 1 (Low risk) activities. Type 2 (Medium risk) activities follow the pattern described in the earlier sections; so do Type 3 (High risk) activities, but they may also need a distinct Project Risk Management Plan and a nominated risk coordinator may be appointed.

Table 10.1—Project risk characteristics

	Type 1	*Type 2*	*Type 3*
Perceived level of risk	*Low to Medium*	*Medium to High*	*High*
Contract value	<$150,000	<$5 million	Over $5 million
Time frame	<3 months	<12 months	Over 12 months
Scope	Simple to moderate	Moderate to complex	Complex
Potential impact on project quality or production	Little or no quality or production impact	Potential for some quality or production impact	Potential for significant impact on quality or production
Potential health, safety and environmental (HSE) impact	Little or no HSE impact	Potential for minor HSE impact	Potential for significant HSE impact
Potential for commercial impact	Little or no commercial impact	Potential for minor commercial impact	Potential for significant commercial impact
Number of parties	Few	Several	Many
Commercial structure	Standard terms of engagement, or existing agreement	Standard terms, but augmented by special conditions	Unique contract conditions

Table 10.2—Simplified risk management processes

	Type 1	*Type 2*	*Type 3*
Context	Project manager to identify stakeholders and objectives		
	Use the project risk management criteria Confirm suitability of risk summary sheet (Figure 10.2)	Project manager to add to the criteria (if necessary) to address the particular project objectives and decide on key elements. Review with key staff and senior manager (e.g. project director, business unit manager)	
Risk identification and assessment	Project manager to conduct a simple risk review.	Project manager to conduct a risk review workshop	
		Risks to be recorded in a spreadsheet or database that will become the risk register	
	Risks to be entered into a project risk register		
Treatment	Project manager to document risk treatment actions (summary of actions in risk register) and incorporate them in normal work plans		
		plus: Risk Action Plans for all Extreme and High risks	
		Outline approach for Medium risks	
Monitor and review	Project manager to create a risk watch list, and review risk in regular management control meetings		
		plus: monitoring and review of Risk Action Plans for Extreme and High risks	
			plus: project Risk Management Plan
Documentation	Project summary and context description, risk register and risk watch list spreadsheets		
		plus: Risk Action Plans for Extreme and High risks	
			plus: project Risk Management Plan
Responsibility	Project manager to ensure actions are carried out and documents prepared Project manager's manager to review and authorize documents All Extreme and High risks in the risk register will be reported as part of the normal risk management process		
			plus: a risk coordinator may be nominated to ensure that the process continues

Simple risk reviews

A simple risk review may follow a similar procedure to the risk review workshop, but there may be no formal workshop. The project manager or another nominated person completes a risk summary sheet (Figure 10.2). The project manager should also request lists of risks

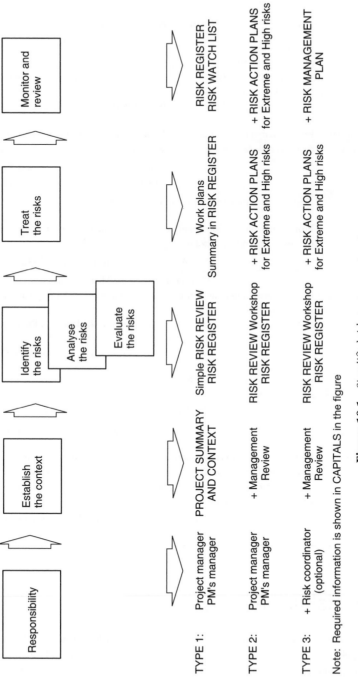

Figure 10.1—Simplified risk management processes

and assessments from appropriate individuals, both inside and outside the project, and consult specialists from appropriate disciplines.

The specific risk summary sheet shown in Figure 10.2 contains a default list of key elements. Each organization should review and tailor these key elements to suit its own needs and the requirements of the project (see Chapter 2).

All the key elements in the sheet should be considered and others added and addressed as required. The identified risks are recorded in the sheet along with the current controls and the consequence and likelihood ratings. These ratings are drawn from the general risk assessment process, including the criteria for assessing the consequences.

The initial ratings should be reviewed and agreed ratings selected. As with the full assessment process, this will assist in setting priorities for the risks and in allocating resources. Risk treatment actions should be recorded for all the Extreme and High risks and for those Medium risks where the benefits outweigh the costs.

The output of the process is a statement of the risks and their priorities. The risk summary sheet, which forms the risk register in this simplified process, along with the proposed treatment actions, provide the main outcomes for management.

The following important points should be considered when undertaking and interpreting the outcomes from a simple risk review:

- A simple risk review is not as effective as a workshop for identifying risks, as the idea-generating benefits of the brainstorming approach are more difficult to obtain.
- Care must be taken to ensure the likelihood and consequence assessments are consistent, particularly if they are provided by different people.
- The team agreement and 'ownership' benefits of the workshop may have to be obtained by other means.

A simple risk review should only be used for Type 1 (Low risk) activities.

Case study: tender for an SPM overhaul

This case study concerns a tender evaluation in which a very simple consideration of risks was a primary determinant of the preferred tenderer for the overhaul of a single point mooring (SPM). In particular, it demonstrates that a quick risk review can provide useful information without a large effort, and this can add significant value to a business decision.

An SPM is a device used in loading crude oil onto tankers. There are many SPM designs, varying in size and complexity according to the oil volume requirements for tanker loading, the depth of the water and the weather conditions. This particular SPM was relatively simple. It consisted of:

- a floating steel structure, moored to the sea bed;
- under-buoy hose connections to on-shore oil storage tanks;
- connections to floating flexible hoses for tanker loading;
- pumps, valves, measuring devices and control systems on and inside the SPM structure.

Key elements and issues (Prompt list)	No.	Risks	Controls	C	L	Initial priority	Agreed priority	Actions and responsibility
Regulatory regime								
Business objectives								
Commercial								
Political and community								
Contractual and legal								
Safety								
Industrial relations and human resources								
Capital requirements								
Resources								
Timing and schedule								

Figure 10.2—(Continued opposite)

Technical and performance					
Customers					
Suppliers					
Infrastructure					
Assets					
Monitoring and management systems					
Finance and administration					
Others					
…					

Figure 10.2—Example risk summary sheet for a simplified risk assessment process

Table 10.3—Summary of tenders

Feature	Tender A	Tender B
Quoted price, inclusive of owner's costs	Less than US$ 500,000	Less than US$ 500,000
Planned schedule duration	35 days	45 days
Mobilization (advance warning)	30 days	60 days
Experience	Worked with the client before on SPM overhauls, over a period of about 12 years	Never worked with the client before, but had undertaken similar tasks for other clients
Lifting process	Dry dock	Cranes

The overhaul was a routine activity conducted after a specified number of years of operation. It required the SPM to be towed to a harbour and either placed in a dry dock or lifted onto the dockside by crane for refurbishment.

There were three respondents to the request for tenders. Of these, one was discarded as technically non-compliant, as its cranes did not have enough lifting capability for the task. The other two were both technically compliant, and the costs associated with each were almost identical, with Tender B marginally cheaper. (The cost difference, after including differential owner's costs, was less than 0.5% of the total price.) The main features of each tenderer's response are summarized in Table 10.3.

The question was asked: which tender should be selected, and could a quick risk review assist in the process? This question was linked to the company's commercial procurement processes – after non-compliant tenders have been eliminated, the cheapest remaining tender should be chosen, unless a special case could be made to the company's tender committee. This process does not take any account of the risk associated with an otherwise compliant tender, and the manager responsible for the smooth operation and maintenance of the SPM was concerned that the risks associated with the cheaper tender far outweighed its minor cost advantage.

A quick risk review was undertaken. It involved a risk analyst and an experienced marine manager. It took less than an hour to complete.

The benefits of selecting Tender A rather than Tender B are summarized in Table 10.4.

Overall, the cost difference was negligible and owner's costs were already included in the budget. The benefits of using the established provider of services were substantial when risk was included in the commercial evaluation. Tender A was recommended, and the recommendation was accepted by the tender committee.

Case study: planning for an industrial water pipeline

Background, scope and objectives

A mine site in the mountains required additional water. This was to be generated by desalination of seawater near the coast; it would then be pumped to the mine. The water was suitable for industrial purposes, but not for domestic consumption nor agricultural use.

Table 10.4—Benefits of selecting Tender A (summary)

Benefit	Implications
Duration of work shorter by 10 days	With the stand-by buoy and its restricted flow rates, loading is expected to take about 29 hours. Demurrage is payable if loading extends beyond 30 hours. Delays are unlikely with careful management of loading operations. Nevertheless, if there were a delay it would be costly for the owner. The extended use of the stand-by buoy increases this risk.
Faster mobilization	This provides more flexibility and allows better planning, with less risk to the loading schedule.
More experienced personnel	More experienced personnel will do a better job. This is particularly important when refurbishing some of the control equipment in the SPM, which requires careful handling.
	More experienced personnel are likely to generate fewer contract variations, and the speed (and price) of rectification of latent defects is likely to be better.
Long history with the client	This is likely to provide better project and commercial outcomes, due to the good working relationships between the companies.
Dry dock instead of crane	Tenderer A will use a dry dock for the overhaul, while Tenderer B will use a crane. The dry dock will impose less structural stress on the buoy, providing better life extension.

The landform and the presence of a nearby village restricted the possible pipeline route. The 28-inch (711 mm) pipeline had to cross the back of a hill behind the village. Along this section the water was at a very high pressure, with a high static head and large inventory due to the length of the pipeline run to the end of the first section.

A major failure of the pipeline above the village could result in a disaster, with water and mud running through the village, potentially killing people and destroying homes. Pipeline failure could arise from natural causes such as earthquake, from accidental damage by an excavator or other digging equipment, or from intentional tapping into the line to gain access to the water.

The risk assessment considered only the section of pipeline that ran past the village. The objectives of the assessment were to:

• understand the risk of pipeline damage, its likely causes and consequences;
• assess the level of risk; and
• develop risk treatment actions appropriate to the level of risk.

The assessment was conducted by four people over a period of three hours.

Risk assessment approach

Prior to starting the assessment, it had been suggested that a detailed quantitative risk analysis would be needed. This would have been time-consuming and costly, and it was noted that quantitative estimates of the likelihood of pipeline failure could be only guesses. It was concluded that a quantitative assessment would be difficult and based on data that could not be suitably supported, and so a simpler approach was adopted.

The assessment team examined the risk of pipeline failure and developed plausible failure scenarios. The consequences and likelihood of each scenario were analysed to provide qualitative estimates of the levels of risk. Based on these estimates, treatment actions were developed and evaluated. The risks were reassessed with the proposed treatments in place and confirmed as tolerable.

Context and risk analysis scales

After considering the stakeholders and their needs, a set of criteria was developed (Table 10.5).

The analysis of scenario risk used a process similar to that discussed in Chapter 4. The consequence scale (Table 10.6) was linked to the criteria, and a simple likelihood rating was adopted (Table 10.7). The matrix shown in Figure 10.3 was used to derive risk priorities.

Table 10.5—Criteria

Criterion	Notes
Safety and environment	Safe and environmentally acceptable implementation and safe and environmentally acceptable resultant facility
Public image and reputation	Government, shareholder and community support
Performance	Performance, reliability and availability as required
Costs and timing	Capital, operating and maintenance costs within budget Implementation to schedule

Table 10.6—Consequence scale for the water pipeline

Rating		Potential impact on the criteria
A	Catastrophic	Most criteria may not be achieved, several severely affected, includes multiple fatalities
B	Major	Most criteria threatened, one severely affected, includes a single fatality
C	Moderate	Some criteria affected, considerable effort to rectify, includes severe injury
D	Minor	Remedied, with some effort the criteria can be achieved, includes injuries requiring treatment
E	Insignificant	Very small impact, rectified by normal processes, includes very minor injuries

Table 10.7—Likelihood rating for the water pipeline

Rating		Interpretation
A	Almost certain	Very high probability of occurrence, could occur several times during a year
B	Likely	High probability, may arise once in a one to two year period
C	Possible	Possible, reasonable probability that it may arise during a five to ten year period
D	Unlikely	Plausible, but could occur during the next ten to twenty years
E	Rare	Very low likelihood, but not impossible, unlikely during the next ten years

Consequences

Likelihood	Severe A	Major B	Moderate C	Minor D	Insignificant E
A Almost certain	Extreme	Extreme	High	Medium	Medium
B Likely	Extreme	High	Medium	Medium	Medium
C Possible	High	High	Medium	Medium	Low
D Unlikely	High	Medium	Medium	Low	Negligible
E Rare	Medium	Medium	Medium	Low	Negligible

Figure 10.3—Priority matrix for the water pipeline

Scenarios and risk assessment

Four scenarios were developed (Table 10.8). They were discussed individually and relevant factors influencing the consequences or likelihood of the associated risk were noted (Table 10.9).

The consequences and likelihoods of the scenarios were analysed and combined to derive the levels of risk shown in Table 10.10.

Table 10.8—Pipeline failure scenarios

Scenario	Description
1. Natural disaster	A landslip or earthquake that breaks the pipeline across its full diameter. The water would generate a mudslide that impacts on the village, kills many people, destroys many homes and receives national and possibly international press coverage.
2. Accidental digging into the pipeline	A large leak due to mechanical impact. The water would generate a mudslide that impacts on the village, kills many people, destroys many homes and receives national and possibly international press coverage.
3. Purposeful attempt to tap into the pipeline to obtain water	The effect would be a hole in the pipeline (estimated as a 25–50 mm hole near the top of the pipe) and the likely death of the person tapping into the pipe. The leak would have to continue for an hour or more to cause any flooding damage, but it would be very obvious (a fountain). There would be no other fatalities.
4. Pipeline failure due to poor installation and testing	A failure when the pipeline is fully pressurized with water, with a break in the worst case up to the full diameter of the pipe. This would cause a flood and mudslide into the village with the potential for multiple fatalities.

Table 10.9—Contributing factors to pipeline failure

Scenario	Contributing factors
1. Natural disaster	Earthquakes have occurred in the region, but none have involved faulting and shear forces capable of breaking a pipeline.
	A major earthquake of this magnitude would cause a great deal of damage of which the pipeline rupture would be a relatively minor part.
	The frequency of this was estimated as less than once per 1,000 years, a very rare event.
2. Accidental damage	The only excavators in the village belong to contractors, most of whom have a working relationship with the company and are therefore highly likely to know of the line.
	There will be a maintenance access road beside the line. It will be used for regular inspections.
	There will be signage along the route indicating the pipeline location.
	The villagers do and will know of the existence of the line.
	The local authority has a strict permitting system for the kind of work that might dig into the line. The process would involve consideration of the pipeline.
	A second pipeline maybe installed in the future, and this would most likely run in the same easement. It is conceivable that the installation contractor for the new line could accidentally dig into the operating water line.
3. Wilful damage	It is most unlikely that an attempt would be made to tap the pipeline in the open above the village. It is more likely to occur in a concealed location, such as in the valley and therefore with a lower risk of a significant impact on the village.
4. Poor installation	Poor pipeline installation and testing procedures without precautions would contribute to this.

Table 10.10—Pipeline scenario risk assessment

Scenario	Consequences	Likelihood	Level of risk
1. Natural disaster	Catastrophic (multiple fatalities and large scale damage)	Rare	Medium
2. Accidental damage	Catastrophic (multiple fatalities and large scale damage)	Unlikely	High
3. Wilful damage	Major (single fatality and significant damage)	Possible	High
4. Poor installation	Catastrophic (multiple fatalities and large scale damage)	Unlikely	High

Risk Treatment Options

Possible risk treatment options were generated for the High risks, commencing with Scenario 2 (Table 10.11). Scenarios 3 and 4 were addressed and additional options generated and short-listed (Table 10.12). The Medium risk, Scenario 1, was then reviewed. Risk

Table 10.11—Scenario 2 options

No	Prompt	Feasible option	Evaluation
1	Prevention	Horizontally drill from the plant to the valley beyond the village. (This eliminates much of the risk.)	Price and review
2	Prevention	Pressure test the line before burying. (This also reduces Scenario 4.)	Adopt
3	Prevention	Use line testing procedures that are thorough and enforced. (This also reduces Scenario 4.)	Adopt
4	Prevention	Maintain signage and other items agreed to protect the line from being accidentally damaged by digging.	Adopt
5	Prevention	Regular inspections – at least twice per week.	Adopt
6	Prevention	Give the villagers water. (Pipeline water is unsuitable for use; the company may have to generate potable water separately; this would introduce a new liability and risk.)	Discard
7	Protection	Install an outer sleeve.	Discard
8	Protection	Dig into rock and backfill with concrete.	Discard
9	Protection	Design extra thickness in the pipe wall such that the machines most likely to dig into the line are most unlikely to be able to penetrate it.	Adopt
10	Protection	Install a concrete slab over the line.	Adopt
11	Protection	Install warning tape in the trench between the slab and the surface.	Adopt
12	Protection	Dig to a depth of at least 2 m (the normal depth is 1 m).	Adopt
13	Mitigation	Construct a major water drain downhill of the line to prevent the water and mud from getting to the village.	Discard
14	Mitigation	Install a check valve (able to be pigged) downstream of the village.	Adopt
15	Mitigation	Install a second flow measurement device on the inlet to the tank at the end of the first pipeline section. On detection of a major leak shut down the pumps at the desalination plant.	Adopt
16	Mitigation	Install an alarm line above the concrete slab that if broken either raises an alarm at the desalination plant or automatically shuts down the pumps.	Review

treatment options were prompted in the areas of prevention, protection and mitigation to aid in generating a comprehensive list.

Scenario 1 will benefit from the extra pipeline wall thickness and the mitigation strategies recommended for Scenario 2. The horizontally drilled pipeline option could remove the pipeline from the area and eliminate the risk entirely.

Residual risk

The recommended actions for all four risks were considered effective in reducing the risks to tolerable levels. Table 10.13 shows the risk levels after taking all the actions marked Adopt, and after taking all those marked Review as well. Figure 10.4 shows the intended effects of the options on the design and installation of the pipeline.

Table 10.12—Additional options from other scenarios

No	Scenario	Feasible option	Evaluation
17	Scenario 2	Control the access to the inspection road and the pipeline route above the village, for example, with a fence and locked gates.	Adopt
18	Scenario 2	Enhance the access road to make it a more accessible route for inspection.	Adopt
19	Scenario 2	Inspect the valley area as part of the regular inspection.	Adopt
20	Scenario 2	Include signage along the pipeline route with a suitable warning sign denoting the dangerous pressure and the fact that the water is industrial quality and unsuitable for agricultural or domestic use.	Adopt
21	Scenario 2	Ensure that all the village is informed about the hazards associated with the water.	Adopt
22	Scenario 2	Review the flow meters at both ends (option 15) of the first section of the line and determine if it is feasible to detect 50 mm, 25 mm and even smaller leaks.	Price and review
23	Scenario 4	Specify a high quality of installation, inspection and testing prior to water being admitted into the line.	Adopt
24	Scenario 4	Develop monitoring and line failure contingency plans when the line is first filled and pressurized.	Adopt
25	Scenario 1	Sleeve the pipe such that a leak can be captured and directed from the ends of the sleeve away from the village. There are some concerns about corrosion, inspection and effectiveness.	Discard

Table 10.13—Effect of actions on risk rankings for the pipeline failure scenarios

Scenario	Initial risk level	Residual risk after Adopt actions	Residual risk after Adopt and Review actions
1 Natural disaster	Medium	Medium	Low (a drilled line would not affect the village)
2 Accidental damage	High	Low	Low
3 Wilful damage	High	Medium	Low
4 Poor installation	High	Low	Low

Conclusions

This case illustrates the level of detail that can be generated by a focused team in a short period, using an approach that covers all the main steps of the risk management process but in an abbreviated form. The assessment was simple to understand and the results were

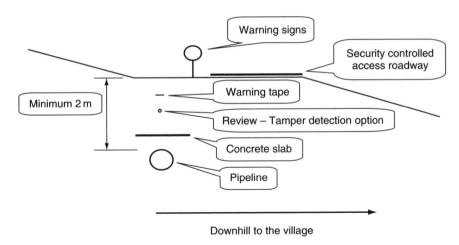

Figure 10.4—Recommended options

acceptable to the organization. There was no need for quantitative analysis, as the outcomes from the qualitative approach were quite sufficient for making the necessary decisions about the pipeline, its design and its route. Option 1, using horizontal drilling through the hill to avoid the risk altogether, had not been considered previously, and more detailed analysis of this option was planned.

Summary

Simple approaches can generate excellent results when used appropriately. It is important not to short-cut the risk management process by eliminating any of the steps, but the steps themselves can be trimmed and tailored according to the need.

MANAGING OPPORTUNITIES

11

Chapter overview

- ### Purpose

  Risk management is concerned with changes or deviations from what is planned or expected. This chapter shows how the positive deviations, the opportunities, can be identified and exploited in just the same way as the risks or negative outcomes can be identified and treated.

- ### Rationale

  If they are identified and exploited early enough, opportunities can provide significant benefits for a project. The benefits can be identified and realized using a straightforward extension of the standard risk management process.

- ### Method

  The general risk management process described in the earlier chapters applies equally well to opportunities, requiring only minor adjustments.

- ### Outputs

  The process produces an opportunity register, analogous to the risk register outlined in Chapter 4, and a set of action plans that parallel those described in Chapter 6.

- ### Documentation

  The documentation for opportunities is identical to that for project risks.

Project risks and opportunities

Risk is defined as exposure to the consequences of uncertainty. In a project context, it is the chance of something happening that will have an impact upon objectives. It includes the possibility of loss or gain, or variation from a desired or planned outcome, as a consequence of the uncertainty associated with adopting a particular course of action.

Much project risk management focuses on the negative consequences of uncertainty, and the early chapters of this book reflect that emphasis. However, the opportunities embodied in positive consequences may be important and can provide additional benefits and improved project outcomes. For example, changes in external conditions often provide opportunities as well as problems, and it is important to be able to recognize the opportunities and be able to respond swiftly enough to capture them and, through careful management, realize the associated benefits.

Some individuals and organizations have become so used to thinking of risk management solely in terms of the negative outcomes of uncertainty that they recoil from using the same process to address opportunities. Some believe that all project plans start life with so much built-in optimism that the only significant uncertainty is risk. Others might accept the value of addressing opportunities but insist on using a separate process to do so.

Each case must be taken on its merits but it is certainly worth considering whether a plan does embody opportunities. If it is worth considering opportunities, integrating them into the general risk management activity is a proven way to achieve a cost-effective process and better project outcomes.

The definition of risk is broader than 'hazards'. The risk management process can embrace this broader definition, within the same basic approach as is used to manage the undesirable consequences of uncertainty.

As a project matures, highly focused processes, such as value management or value engineering, often have the effect of identifying and exploiting opportunities. In the early stages of projects, when strategic issues are vitally important, the scope for capitalizing on opportunities through an explicit process may be considerable. At this early stage, the process described here for risk management is an effective means of dealing with opportunity management.

Establishing the context

When considering opportunities, the context stage of the risk management process is similar to that for risks, and in many cases it is identical to that described in Chapter 2. The criteria are the same, but the focus is on improvement of outcomes rather than minimizing detrimental effects.

The key elements used to structure the process may need to be adjusted to suit opportunity management on some projects. Because thinking about opportunities often requires a different thought process from thinking about risks, the key elements may need to be structured to encourage a productive frame of mind for identifying and evaluating opportunities. In particular, in early project stages the key elements for opportunities may need to emphasize important strategic aspects of the project to a greater extent than for risks.

Identification of opportunities

The processes for identifying opportunities are similar to those used for identifying risks, described in Chapter 3. In much of our own work, we favour a structured brainstorming approach, but 'opportunity workshops' need to be conducted carefully and often differently from workshops that focus only on risks.

Members of project teams are usually less familiar with 'opportunity thinking' than 'risk thinking', and process facilitation must be adjusted to take account of the different mental perspective and approach that is needed if workshops are to be effective and generate good outcomes. In particular, the strategic focus noted in the previous section often needs to be emphasized when addressing opportunities. Pre-seeding of risk and opportunity registers can be a useful aid, providing examples of the kinds of topics that should be raised.

On some occasions, the process of identifying project risks and associated treatment actions will also result in the identification of opportunities. For instance, the successful resolution of a particular risk may open up significant opportunities for the project. Workshop and brainstorming sessions should be flexible enough to allow for this.

Analysis of opportunities

When risk management is directed to the negative consequences of risks, the consequence scales reflect the losses or undesirable outcomes that might arise. The risk management approach can be used to identify and prioritize opportunities (or 'positive' risks) with little change to the analysis, but the consequence scales must be adjusted.

The simplest approach, when opportunities are being considered by themselves (without negative impacts), is to use a consequence scale similar to that for risk analysis, but with only positive outcomes; an example is shown in Table 11.1. As with any scales of this kind, the measures used should reflect the objectives, needs and nature of the organization and the characteristics of the project, as identified during the context phase (Chapter 2).

Table 11.2 shows a further example of scales for opportunities and risks. In this example, the words are substantially the same for the positive and negative impacts. This is not necessary in all cases, particularly if the scales are disaggregated with different measures for each criterion of interest (like some of the extended consequence rating tables in Chapter 4). It may be possible to use 'mirror image' scales for criteria measures in monetary

Table 11.1—Example of detailed description for positive consequences

Level	Descriptor	Description
A	Outstanding	Significantly enhanced reputation, huge financial gain
B	Major	Enhanced reputation, major financial gain
C	Moderate	Some enhancement to reputation, high financial gain
D	Minor	Minor improvement to image, some financial gain
E	Insignificant	Small benefit, low financial gain

Table 11.2—Impact rating scales for risks and opportunities

Rating	Potential impact, in terms of the criteria for the project	
	Risks	Opportunities
A	Catastrophic: Most criteria may not be achieved	Outstanding: Most criteria may be enhanced substantially
B	Major: Most criteria threatened, or one not achieved	Major: Most criteria may be improved, or one enhanced substantially
C	Moderate: Some criteria affected	Moderate: Some criteria improved
D	Minor: Easily remedied	Minor: Some benefit
E	Negligible: Very small impact	Negligible: Very small benefit

units, but even then the value to the project of a particular financial gain may not be equivalent to the pain associated with the same level of financial loss – in most cases the negative utility of breaching budget allocation with a million-dollar loss is greater in absolute terms than the utility of a million-dollar gain. Safety criteria can be difficult too, although it may be possible to measure safety benefits in terms of reduced costs for workers' compensation insurance and similar surrogates.

When considering opportunities, the likelihood scale need not change, as this reflects the chance that a beneficial outcome will arise. In fact, to use different likelihood scales for opportunities and risks may generate confusion and reduce the effectiveness of the exercise.

A qualitative opportunity analysis matrix can be used to combine the likelihood and consequence ratings to determine the level of opportunity. For example, Figure 11.1 shows a matrix for setting opportunity and risk priorities. This is almost the same as the priority-setting matrices shown for risks in Chapter 4; all that has changed is the legend.

When risks and opportunities are being considered together, a 'two-directional' scale of consequences may be useful, with −A representing a catastrophic risk and + A representing an outstanding opportunity. The analysis matrix may be adjusted, as shown in Figure 11.2.

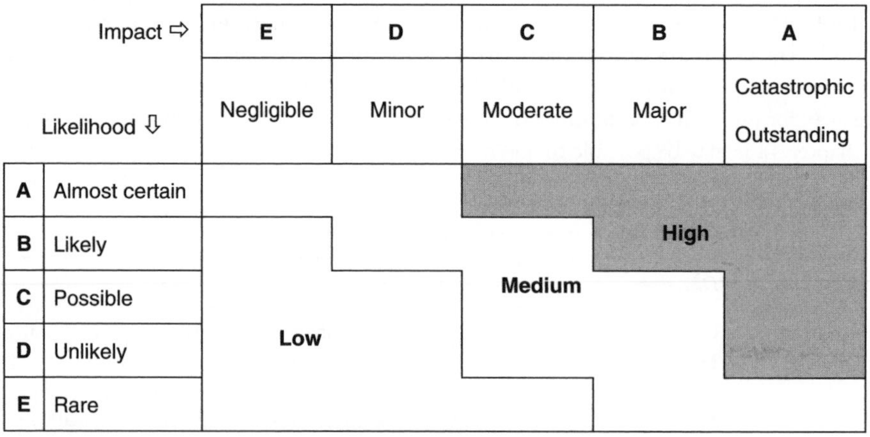

Figure 11.1—Initial risk and opportunity priorities

	Negative consequences				Likelihood		Positive consequences			
Catastrophic	Major	Moderate	Minor	Insignificant		Insignificant	Minor	Moderate	Major	Outstanding
−A	−B	−C	−D	−E		+E	+D	+C	+B	+A
−E	−E	−H	−H	−M	**A** **Almost certain**	M	H	H	E	E
−E	−H	−H	−M	−M	**B** **Likely**	M	M	H	H	E
−E	−H	−H	−M	−L	**C** **Possible**	L	M	H	H	E
−H	−M	−M	−L	−L	**D** **Unlikely**	L	L	M	M	H
−H	−M	−M	−L	−L	**E** **Rare**	L	L	M	M	H

Figure 11.2—Combined opportunity and risk analysis matrix

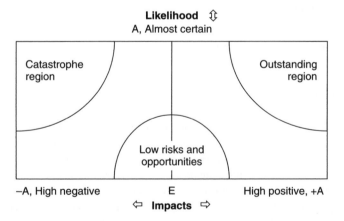

Figure 11.3—Risks and opportunities

In this expanded form the priority matrix need not be symmetric between risk and opportunities.

Individual risks and opportunities can be plotted on the same graph to show their relative priorities. Figure 11.3 shows an example in which the horizontal consequence scale ranges from −A (catastrophic negative outcome) to +A (outstanding beneficial outcome), and the likelihoods are shown on a vertical probability scale from E (rare) to A (almost certain).

Treatment

The priorities that are generated for opportunities in the analysis and evaluation process can be interpreted in much the same way as risk priorities, with the focus of action being on capturing and exploiting the opportunities rather than avoiding or mitigating the problems.

- **Extreme opportunity**: detailed planning is warranted at senior levels to prepare for and capture the opportunity.
- **High opportunity**: senior executive management attention is appropriate and management responsibility should be specified.
- **Medium opportunity**: manage by specific monitoring or response procedures.
- **Low opportunity**: manage by routine procedures that are unlikely to need the specific application of resources.

Treatment options for risks having positive outcomes (opportunities) are similar in concept to those for treating risks with negative outcomes, although the interpretation and implications are clearly different. Options include:

- actively seeking the opportunity by deciding to proceed with or continue the activity likely to create it (where this is practicable);
- changing the likelihood of the opportunity, to increase the chance of beneficial outcomes;
- changing the consequences, to increase the potential gains;
- sharing the opportunity with others who can assist in any of the other strategies; and
- retaining the residual opportunity.

After opportunities have been changed or shared, there may be residual opportunities that are retained with no further immediate action specified. This may be described as 'leaving it to chance'.

As opportunities offer potential gains, it may be possible to interest another party in sharing the effort to capture a specific opportunity. They might provide additional capabilities or resources that increase the likelihood of the opportunity arising or the extent of the gains if it does. Mechanisms may include the use of incentive contracts and organizational structures such as partnerships, joint ventures, royalties and farm-in arrangements. Sharing the positive outcomes usually involves sharing some of the costs involved in acquiring them.

Sharing arrangements often introduce new risks, in that the other party may not deliver the desired capabilities or resources effectively and the organization and management of the work may become more complex. Public private partnerships and alliance contracting can be seen as opportunity sharing and transfer as much as being risk sharing and transfer mechanisms.

The selection of options for treating opportunities is part of the allocation of resources across an entire project, including any new risks and opportunities that may be introduced by exploiting an opportunity. As discussed in Chapter 6, the combined effects of all treatment actions should be considered, for both opportunities and risks, in order to select that package or portfolio of actions that maximizes the overall net benefits to the project.

Examples of project opportunities

This section shows case examples of opportunities and priority ratings identified in project workshops we have conducted. In practice these were part of much larger risk and opportunity registers and, in most cases, there were far more risks than opportunities. Indeed, in a typical combined risk and opportunity workshop for a project we would not normally expect more than a quarter of the items to be opportunities, although we have obtained higher proportions in some strategic projects. This may also depend, to some extent, on whether the specific objective was to identify risks, or risks plus opportunities.

Table 11.3 shows the High opportunities identified in a public-sector project to establish a motor vehicle emissions-testing regime to improve air quality. As is often the case with projects having public policy implications, many of the High risks were related to the perceptions (or misperceptions) of the stakeholders, and many of them had to be dealt with in the project's communication and consultation processes. All three of the High opportunities depended on communication and consultation to some extent for their benefits to be realized. In this case, the identification and assessment process included an analysis of the urgency with which actions should be taken.

Table 11.4 shows the High opportunities identified when developing the business case for a computer-aided despatch system for emergency service vehicles. All arose in the key element 'Service capability'. The likelihood here was the chance of realizing the benefit within the available budget, either during the contract negotiation process or as part of project implementation. As in the previous case, an indication of the appropriate timing for action was recorded during the analysis.

As part of the analysis for a multi-nation services delivery project, the potential management structures under which the consortium companies might operate to provide a high-quality service to the customer were reviewed. The review was undertaken from the perspective of the benefits and risks to the participating companies and from the perspective of the customer (or our best guess about that perspective at the time). The potential management structures that were considered are outlined in Table 11.5.

Twenty specific features were noted, discussed and rated as either risks or opportunities under each of the structures and for both major stakeholders. Table 11.6 shows a summary of the analysis. In the table, the columns headed P show the ratings from Company P's perspective, and those headed C show ratings from the customer's. It should be noted that the simple counts of ratings in Table 11.6 do not necessarily provide a complete guide to

Table 11.3—High opportunities with communication and consultation treatments

Element	Opportunities		C	L	Urgency
5 Business rules	5.20	Clear test standards and processes increase the perceived fairness and consistency of the system	B	B	Prior to tender
13 Agency activities	13.07	Publish air quality improvements and outcomes	B	A	Prior to tender
14 Repairers	14.08	Repair industry gets more work, and supports the programme actively	B	B	Prior to tender

Table 11.4—Outstanding opportunities identified when developing a business case

Opportunities	Comments	C	L	Urgency
1.01 Increased effectiveness and higher standards of service, with significant community benefits	Improved response times, more appropriate responses, better definition of service in terms of outputs	B	A	Immediate, urgent
1.02 Improved work practices leading to more efficient and more effective service provision	Opportunity to understand the business better, leading to improvements in efficiency, development of better performance measurements than are available now	B	B	After contract award
1.03 Improved capability to enter data in the field	Field data entry via mobile data terminals, leading to more complete and accurate data capture, once-only entry	C	A	After contract award
1.04 Improved access to data in the field leading to safer operations and more appropriate responses	Examples: chemical spills, hospital databases, firearms registers	B	A	Prior to selection

Table 11.5—Potential management structures

Structure	Notes
Prime	Company P is the prime contractor, with companies Q, R and S as sub-contractors
Independent Alliance	For example: • Company P offers services for all countries except Korea; • Company Q offers services in Korea, with companies R and S as nominated sub-contractors; • Companies P and Q form a high-level alliance to ensure service delivery synergies are achieved through compatibility of systems and common data analysis processes
Incorporated JV	Special-purpose incorporated company structure
Unincorporated JV	Special-purpose partnership or JV contract arrangement

the overall opportunities and risks associated with each management structure, as some features were far more important than others; the individual opportunities and risks were used in determining the structure that would be most beneficial for the consortium while remaining acceptable to the customer.

The outcomes from analyses like this may lead to adoption of specific forms of contract or contract terms for the inter-company arrangement, with cost and risk sharing mechanisms that have been tailored to the identified opportunities. More information on risk allocation within contracts is provided in Chapter 14.

Table 11.6—Summary of items in each category

Rating	Prime		Independent Alliance		Incorporated JV		Unincorporated JV	
	P	C	P	C	P	C	P	C
3 Major opportunity	9	9	1	0	6	7	1	1
2 Medium opportunity	6	4	6	2	10	9	4	5
1 Minor opportunity	1	1	1	2	1	1	6	5
−3 Major risk	0	3	2	5	0	1	0	0
−2 Medium risk	1	0	1	8	0	0	1	1
−1 Minor risk	0	0	4	0	1	0	1	1
0 Not relevant	3	3	5	3	2	2	7	7

Table 11.7 shows a selection of the Extreme and High opportunities for a business unit with responsibilities for conducting small and medium projects within its organization and for managing the provision by other companies of large projects. There are a number of points of interest in this example.

- Consequence ratings were on the scale −A to −E for risks and A to E for opportunities.
- The criterion that was most affected by each opportunity was noted.
- The assessment of agreed priorities was extended to consider the inherent levels of opportunity. The inherent priority was interpreted as the potential opportunity that might be obtained if current plans and processes were implemented. In some cases the inherent priority was less than the agreed priority, indicating current plans and processes might not work or be difficult to implement effectively.
- Item 17.16 is worded as a fact that could be interpreted as major problem or risk. However, the members of the business unit preferred to think about it as an opportunity, in the sense that changing the pay and reward structure would generate far better business and project outcomes. Several other opportunities were described and evaluated from this standpoint.
- Item 27.03 was originally rated as a risk, with a negative consequence of −B, as shown in the table. However, when all the risks and opportunities were reviewed it was decided that there was a High opportunity for the company if the procurement process and the traditional contract structure could be changed to provide a more appropriate (and more equitable) distribution of risk.

Summary

The general risk management process described in the earlier chapters of this book applies equally well to opportunities, with only minor adjustments. By identifying opportunities as well as risks, and taking appropriate action to exploit them, additional benefits and improved project outcomes can be obtained.

Table 11.7—Extreme and High opportunities for a project management business unit

Element	Opportunities		Comments, controls	Criterion	C	L	Agreed priority	Inherent priority
17 People and culture	17.16	Inequities in pay rates and conditions within the company cause organizational, managerial and morale problems.	Performance appraisals and rewards are not always appropriate for developing and retaining the best people and hence for achieving the outcomes.	Employees	A	A	Extreme	Extreme
18 Structure, systems and process	18.11	Increasing the frequency of audits (external and internal) would provide an opportunity to improve performance by identifying areas where we can do better and move towards best practice.	There have been several external reviews of aspects of our business and facilities that have generated good ideas for improvements.	Business and facility integrity	B	C	High	High
20 Performance and reward	20.01	Meaningful key performance indicators (KPIs) are hard to define.	KPIs do not always include customer performance impacts.	Business and facility integrity	B	B	High	High
27 Procurement	27.03	We attempt to place too much risk with the contractor, thus increasing the prices we pay.		Financial impacts	–B	C	High	Low
27 Procurement	27.08	Pre-qualification and short-listing are not done well. This wastes time and resources.	The pre-qualification system is not implemented effectively. Vendors often withdraw after pre-qualification, ask for extensions or submit responses that do not meet the specifications.	Project performance	B	C	High	High

The quantitative analysis processes described in Chapters 19 to 23 perform a similar function, by considering distributions of consequences in terms of ranges of outcomes that often extend on both sides of an expected or likely outcome. Opportunities are often incorporated into a quantitative risk analysis without any distinction being made between positive and negative consequences of uncertainty, as the range of outcomes of an uncertain quantity may easily extend from negative to positive values and pass through zero in between.

The same principle can easily be adopted in the cost-effective qualitative analysis and management process described here. The process is discussed in terms of risks to avoid complicating the language but it is equally relevant to opportunities or positive risks. These two sides of uncertainty can be dealt with together in an efficient and integrated process.

It is logical for project managers to consider both risks and opportunities. To manage only risks is effectively to ignore one half of a project manager's responsibility.

Further reading

Some of our early thoughts on opportunities and their assessment were included in a Standards Australia Handbook HB 142-1999, *A Basic Introduction to Managing Risk*. Hillson (2004) has written extensively about opportunity management in projects.

OTHER APPROACHES TO PROJECT RISK MANAGEMENT

12

Chapter overview

> ### ● Purpose
>
> This chapter compares four widely used approaches to project risk management: the Australian and New Zealand Standard AS/NZS 4360, *Risk Management*, on which this book concentrates; Chapter 11 of the US Project Management Institute's *Project Management Body of Knowledge*; the UK Association for Project Management *Project Risk Analysis and Management (PRAM) Guide*; and the UK Office of Government Commerce *Management of Risk* (M_o_R) guideline.
>
> ### ● Rationale
>
> These approaches have much in common but they also differ in some areas. It is important to understand the similarities and differences in objectives, style and terminology, to enable the material described in this book to be applied most effectively.

Risk management guidelines and standards

Project risk management is a particular application of risk management. The same principles apply to project risk management as to any other application. However, projects face some specific issues relating to the way they are organized and managed and there are opportunities to develop general risk management principles into more detailed guidance.

There are two professional organizations that issue guidelines on project risk management, the US-based Project Management Institute (PMI) and the UK-based Association for Project Management (APM). There are three sources of guidance on project risk management a project manager might turn to:

- the Australian and New Zealand Standard AS/NZS 4360, *Risk Management*;
- the PMI publishes a general guide to project management called the *Project Management Body of Knowledge* (PMBOK), Chapter 11 of which deals with risk management;
- the APM's *Project Risk Analysis and Management (PRAM) Guide*; and,
- the UK Office of Government Commerce (OGC) *Management of Risk* (M_o_R) guideline.

Each of these has a lot to offer but there are significant differences in their objectives, styles and approaches.

AS/NZS 4360

The Australian and New Zealand Standard was first published in 1995 and updated in 1999 and 2004. It is a generic risk management standard that is readily applied to project risk management and is the basis for the processes described in this book. It is not confined to projects, and it is just as relevant to safety, financial or security risk management as to project risk management. It works well at all levels from individual activities to an entire business; in particular, it can be used as the basis of an integrated programme or business risk management process spanning a portfolio of projects.

The Standard describes an overall approach to risk management, not just risk analysis or risk assessment. It deals with the links between the risk management process and both strategic direction – the context – and day-to-day actions and treatments. However, because it is a generic approach, the Standard itself says nothing about project-specific issues and, as the preceding chapters have illustrated, it has to be developed in some detail to operate as a project risk management method.

The main features of the Standard are illustrated in Figure 12.1.

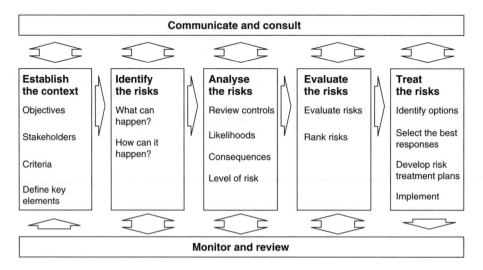

Figure 12.1—The AS/NZS 4360 risk management process

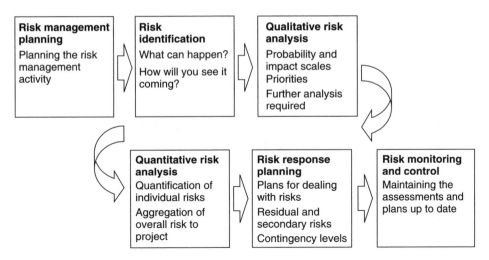

Figure 12.2—The PMBOK project risk management process

PMBOK, Chapter 11

Chapter 11 of the PMI's PMBOK is written specifically for project risk management. It is structured in a framework of inputs, processes and outputs. It deals with management responsibility for the process and links to the wider project management process contained in the rest of the PMBOK.

The details of risk management itself are not as clear as the approach described in AS/NZS 4360. Chapter 11 of PMBOK ranges across qualitative and quantitative risk analysis methods but does not link these together directly. The approach owes a lot to large technologically complex project operations and this shows in the material. Figure 12.2 illustrates the process.

PRAM Guide

The *PRAM Guide* is a stand-alone project risk management guide. It deliberately separates the risk management process from detailed techniques or methods that might be used to implement various stages in the process.

It is written within a project management structure and deals with the process and responsibilities for managing the process. It provides examples of techniques for individual process steps. The team who produced this guide included practitioners, consultants and academics. The core material is well structured and easy to follow.

Figure 12.3 illustrates the key stages and data flows in the PRAM Guide process.

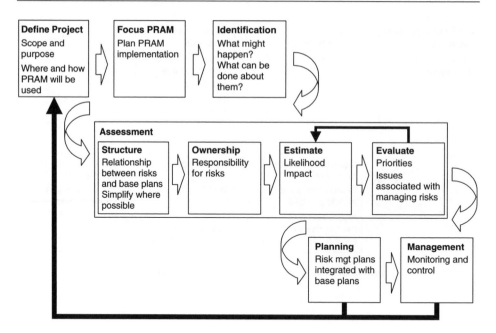

Figure 12.3—The PRAM Guide risk management process

M_o_R guideline

The *Management of Risk* guideline, known as M_o_R, is written for public sector organizations. It deals with all risks to an organization's success and includes guidance on the risk management process, management structure, roles and responsibilities as well as checklists to assist various stages of the process. It discusses the application of risk management from the strategic level, including corporate governance, through to programmes, projects and operations.

There is a strong emphasis in the M_o_R guideline on the organizational framework and management structure within which risk management takes place, echoing the priorities set in the PRINCE2 guidelines for project management. The guideline touches on cultural and other issues relating to the successful implementation of effective risk management within an organization.

In the same way that the *PRAM Guide* separates the process from specific tools and techniques, the M_o_R guideline separates the general risk management process from details of its implementation in strategic, programme, project and operational contexts, and from specific tools and methods that might be employed to execute a part of the process.

The process flow described in M_o_R is illustrated in Figure 12.4.

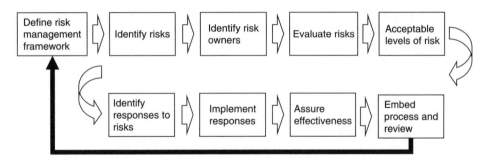

Figure 12.4—The M_o_R Guideline risk management process

Comparison of processes

These alternative sources of risk management guidance do not conflict with one another and there is value in each of them. Some features of each one that might affect how they are used are set out below.

AS/NZS 4360

1. This process evaluates risks individually, except where common factors are identified that link risks or offer opportunities for strategic initiatives that address several risks at once.
2. It is often applied with qualitative evaluation scales, as discussed in earlier chapters, although quantitative likelihood and consequence measures can be used.
3. It lends itself to a process based on a risk register.
4. It can be highly structured:

- it suits a facilitated process with cost-effective use of participants' time; and
- it is easy to support with data management tools.

5. It is readily scalable to suit the size and complexity of a project:

- simple round table discussions are suitable for small jobs;
- formal workshops can be used for medium-sized projects;
- a series of linked and integrated workshops and analysis may be needed for large programmes.

PMBOK, Chapter 11 and PRAM Guide

1. These are primarily management process structures.
2. Some analysis techniques are described and references are made to others.

3. They encompass the use of qualitative scales, decision trees, influence diagramming, sensitivity analysis and Monte Carlo simulation.
4. Risk evaluation is addressed both in terms of individual risks issues and the aggregate risk in a project as a whole.
5. They are explicitly set in a project management context.

M_o_R guideline

- This guide is, in principle, as generally applicable as AS/NZS 4360 but it is targeted at and described in terms of public sector organizations.
- Some analysis techniques are described and there is extensive reference to related OGC publications.
- Its coverage of analysis methods is as broad as that of the *PRAM Guide* and they are dealt with separately from the risk management process, as in the *PRAM Guide*.
- The methods recommended for use at the project level include some that deal with individual risks and others that can be used to understand the aggregate risk to a project as a whole.
- The overall context of the guide is the organization within which risk management is being applied and the achievement of that organization's objectives.

The stages in the processes outlined here can be related to one another roughly as shown in Figure 12.5. This illustrates the fact that they all cover essentially the same ground, as might be expected. M_o_R and AS/NZS 4360 are less task-oriented than the other two approaches, being more concerned with high-level process requirements. M_o_R in particular focuses on the organizational context and roles and responsibilities of stakeholders across the entire process so that its alignment with the steps in the other approaches is less clear cut than the alignment between those three.

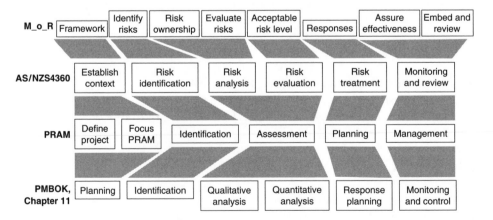

Figure 12.5—Process comparison

In this book, we have used AS/NZS 4360 as a foundation of our description of risk management activities. It is well proven, it covers everything you need to consider and it has substantial and growing support in both the public and the private sector in many countries around the world.

Sources of information

The Standard is available from Standards Australia at www.standards.com.au A description of its application to projects is available at www.broadleaf.com.au/services/proj_rm.htm

The PMBOK, including Chapter 11, is available from the PMI at www.pmi.org/publictn/pmboktoc.htm

A summary of the *PRAM Guide* is available from www.eurolog.co.uk/apmrisksig/publications/minipram.pdf and the full document can be obtained through the APM at www.apm.org.uk/pub/public.htm

Information about the M_o_R guide, including sources of documentation, can be found on the OGC website at www.ogc.gov.uk

Part II
Extending the basic process

CASE STUDY: TENDER EVALUATION 13

Chapter overview

● Purpose

The processes described in this chapter assist in identifying potentially high-risk aspects of a tender submission. They provide an important input to tender evaluation, particularly for high-risk and high-technology projects.

● Rationale

The risks associated with specific tender responses are identified at an early stage, so they can be addressed explicitly in the tender evaluation. The high-risk areas on which the greatest attention and effort should be focused in the evaluation of tender responses are identified.

● Inputs

Initial information used in Phase 1 of the assessment process is based on project documents and the request for tender itself. Information for Phase 2 is derived from individual tenderer's responses.

● Method

In Phase 1, develop an appropriate system or element structure for examining the tender; use a semi-quantitative approach to assess the likelihood of risks arising in each element, and their consequences, and derive a baseline priority for each element and the project.

In Phase 2, modify the evaluation according to the detailed approach each tenderer intends to adopt, and that tenderer's capabilities.

- **Outputs**

  - A list of elements prioritized by 'riskiness' for each tenderer, with consequence and likelihood ratings, and agreed priorities for the elements.
  - Deviations for each tenderer from the baseline assumptions.

- **Documentation**

  Detailed descriptions of the assumptions underlying the initial evaluation and the evaluations for each tenderer, to justify the assessments and the process followed.

Introduction

This chapter describes how an initial risk assessment process can be undertaken for tender evaluation. The focus is on thinking about how the project might be performed by the competing tenderers, and the implications for tender evaluation and selection procedures. It spans the pre-bid activities of the owner's project team, where it assists in developing an understanding of potential risks and how they might arise, and their post-bid activities, where it contributes to more rigorous tender evaluation.

The description here is based closely on an evaluation conducted for a major high-technology project for which request for tender documents had been issued. The process has been applied successfully in several other major procurements for high-technology equipment and systems, and it has wide applicability in other forms of tender assessment, as part of the bidding stage of the procurement process.

The objectives of the risk assessment in tender evaluation are:

- to provide an initial indication of where the major risks might arise in the project, prior to receipt or detailed examination of tender responses, based on a set of credible assumptions about how the project might be conducted;
- to develop a risk baseline against which individual tender responses can be compared;
- to assist the project team to focus on potential risk areas in their evaluations of offers and in their evaluation visits to tenderers' sites;
- to provide a risk profile for each tender offer submitted, developed on a consistent and justifiable basis; and
- to provide a documented audit trail of the project team's assumptions about potential risk areas and their reasons for adjusting their assessments in the light of individual tender responses or site evaluation visits.

The process makes use of a number of the risk management tools and techniques described in earlier chapters. In particular, it shows how the semi-quantitative priority-setting approaches and indicators of likelihoods and consequences described in Chapter 5 can be extended in their application to tender evaluation.

Basic structure of the assessment and evaluation process

Figure 13.1 shows the two phases of the risk assessment and tender evaluation process for the procurement. Phase 1 is concerned with establishing a baseline against which tenders can be assessed, prior to bids being received. Phase 2 compares each submitted tender offer with the baseline, to develop a comparative risk assessment for each one. The process does not attempt to derive an 'absolute' measure of risk. The focus is on providing a comparison between the tender responses and proposed methods for fulfilling the contract, as one part of the wider tender evaluation process.

The structured and documented risk assessments produced in Phase 1 and the subsequent adjustments in Phase 2 provide consistency and auditability throughout the evaluation. These assessments, generated by qualified specialists from the project team, form the input to a simple risk model. The structured approach to risk assessment and quantification assists greatly in the comparison of risks between individual tenderers in the source selection process.

Phase 1: establishing the risk baseline

Phase 1 is concerned with establishing and documenting a risk baseline against which individual tender responses can be compared.

The structure of Phase 1 is illustrated in Figure 13.2. The first three parts involve a detailed assessment of the project from a risk perspective by the project team, using the

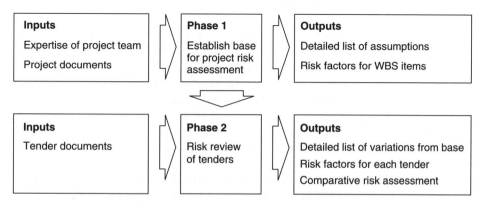

Figure 13.1—Overall structure of the process

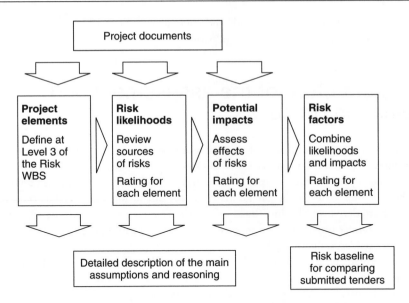

Figure 13.2—Outline of the steps in establishing the project risk baseline

project documents and their own specialist knowledge. The final part uses the assessments to calculate risk factors and baseline variances.

The assessment process

The initial assessments of risk WBS items are usually undertaken by the project team in an interactive working session. The process involves several stages:

1. The project structure is reviewed with the project manager and key staff, and an agreed risk WBS is generated. This may be based on the contract WBS contained in the request for tender documents, or the WBS may be modified for risk assessment purposes as discussed in Chapter 2.
2. A training session is conducted for the project team. The objectives of the training are to introduce the key concepts of risk and risk management and to exercise the project team in the processes to be used in the assessment workshops.
3. If there is no adequate WBS Dictionary, the members of the project team produce an outline description of what is included in each risk WBS item.
4. An assessment workshop is conducted, involving all the members of the team concerned with the project. The first part of the workshop reviews the objectives of the risk assessment study, the way it is proposed to relate this to the overall assessment, and the tasks to be completed during the session.
5. The team reviews each risk WBS item in turn. The definition is read aloud and any clarification needed is provided by the team member most familiar with the item. Key assumptions are discussed and documented for the item, and then for each likelihood

and impact indicator. Risk likelihood and impact factors are assessed, as described below.

Each WBS element is examined in detail by the project team. The project team's assumptions about the way in which the WBS element would be performed are discussed in a structured workshop attended by the key members of the team. Details are recorded on a summary sheet. Figures 13.3 to 13.5 show examples of the work sheets used in

WBS number:	**Element:**			**Page 1 of**
WBS dictionary:				
Project team assumptions:				
			Assumptions continuation pages: Yes/No	
		Assessment summary		
Likelihood measures			**Impact measures**	
Hardware maturity			Performance	
Hardware complexity			Cost	
Software maturity			Schedule	
Software complexity				
Dependence				
Integration and interfacing			**Risk factor**	
Management processes				
Compiler:	Date:		Reviewer:	Date

Figure 13.3—Summary sheet for recording workshop assessments

WBS number:	Element:		Page of
Project team assumptions			**Rating**
Likelihood, hardware maturity			
Likelihood, hardware complexity			
Likelihood, software maturity			
Likelihood, software complexity			
Likelihood, dependence			
Compiler:	Date:	Reviewer:	Date:

Figure 13.4—Detailed assumptions and ratings, sheet 1

WBS number:	Element:		Page of
Project team assumptions			**Rating**
Likelihood, integration and interfacing			
Likelihood, management processes			
Impact, performance			
Impact, cost			
Impact, schedule			
Compiler:	Date:	Reviewer:	Date:

Figure 13.5—Detailed assumptions and ratings, sheet 2

a recent assessment. The workshop uses brainstorming processes similar to those described in Chapter 3.

After the working session, the assessments are combined in a spreadsheet and converted to numeric ratings. The scales used are those discussed in Chapter 5. Risk factors are calculated, as described below.

Risk likelihoods

Risk likelihoods are assessed for each project element (Figure 13.6), using processes similar to those described in Chapter 5. Indicators of the likelihood of problems are usually used; for example:

- hardware maturity;
- hardware complexity;
- software maturity;
- software complexity;
- dependency;
- integration and interfacing;
- management processes.

Each indicator is expressed as a six-point descriptive scale, ranging from Low to Very High.

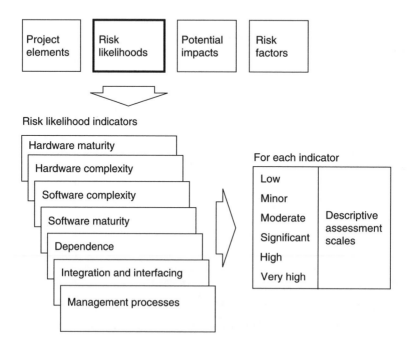

Figure 13.6—Likelihood assessment

As described in Chapter 5, US Department of Defense studies have found the first five of these factors to be good indicators of the likelihood of problems in high-technology projects. In other words, problems are more likely to occur in project elements that involve new or complex hardware or software, or that are highly dependent on other systems or contractors. Recent procurements with which we have been involved have included the final two additional factors to reflect specific aspects of concern to other client organizations. Other indicators can also be used, as discussed in Chapter 5.

In the assessment workshop, each item is assessed against each relevant factor, and any specific assumptions are noted on the detailed assessment sheets (Figure 13.4, Figure 13.5). The resulting assessments are recorded on the summary sheet (Figure 13.3). Not all factors are relevant for all items. For example, hardware maturity and complexity are not applicable to non-technical risk WBS items such as project management.

Potential impacts

The potential impacts of risks on the whole project are assessed for each project element (Figure 13.7). Three measures of impact are commonly used:

- reduced user acceptability, often measured in terms of performance reduction;
- cost increase; and
- schedule delay.

Behavioural considerations such as integrity, fair dealing, ethical behaviour and competence may also be included as a fourth measure in the impact assessment process.

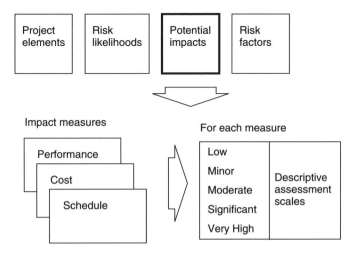

Figure 13.7—Assessment of potential impacts

Descriptive assessment scales are used, similar in concept to those used for the risk likelihood indicators, as described in Chapters 4 and 5. They rate the potential impacts of risks on the whole project, not just on the element being examined.

In the assessment workshop, each item is assessed against each impact measure. Key assumptions about each impact measure for the item, if risks arise, are recorded on the detailed assessment sheets (Figure 13.4, Figure 13.5), and the resulting assessment is recorded on the summary sheet (Figure 13.3).

Risk factors

The descriptive assessments of risk likelihoods and potential impacts are converted to numerical values and used to derive risk factors for each element (Figure 13.8). The method of calculation is that described in Chapter 5.

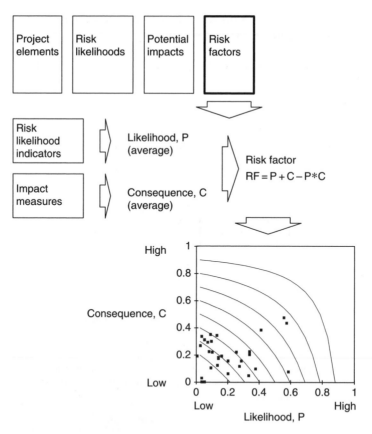

Figure 13.8—Risk factor derivation

For each element, the relevant risk likelihood values are averaged to generate a single likelihood measure P, in the range from 0 to 1. For those elements for which not all indicators are relevant, the average is over the number of relevant values.

Similarly, the impact measures are averaged for each element to generate a single impact or consequence measure C, also in the range 0 to 1.

A risk factor or combined risk measure is calculated for each element:

$$RF = P + C - (P * C).$$

The risk factor RF varies from 0 (low) to 1 (high). It reflects the likelihood of a risk arising and the severity of its impact. The risk factor will be high if a risk is likely to occur, if its impacts are large, or both.

Phase 1 outcomes

The risk factors from a recent procurement are depicted graphically in Figure 13.9 and Figure 13.10. Figure 13.9 shows the scatter of likelihood and impact measures. Figure 13.9 also shows iso-risk contours – lines of equal risk factor – to indicate the main partition of risks into High, Medium and Low risk areas.

Figure 13.10 shows the risk profile for the procurement, in which WBS elements are ranked in decreasing order of their risk factors. The risk profile provides a different view of the High, Medium and Low risks for setting risk management priorities.

A review of the risk profile for the procurement determines the cut-off point between High and Medium risks. In this example, it lies at about RF=0.65, and the cut-off between Medium and Low lies at about RF=0.40.

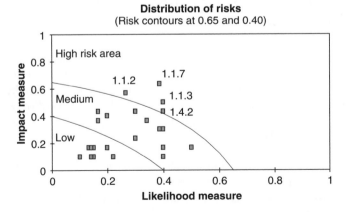

Figure 13.9—Risk likelihood and impact measures

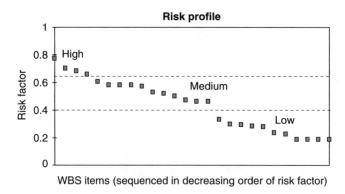

Figure 13.10—Project risk profile

Phase 2: review of tenders

The tender review process builds on the risk baseline established in Phase 1 and the documented assumptions associated with it. Its objective is to provide comparative guidance to the tender evaluation team on the potential effects of risk on the project, given each tenderer's approach. Absolute measures of risk are of secondary importance.

The key to an accurate evaluation is the generation of consistent and verifiable risk assessments by those functional project groups most qualified to make the judgements. Worksheets similar to those used in the risk assessment in Phase 1 make the process a measured and repeatable task and provide an audit trail of the assumptions.

Figure 13.11 shows the structure for Phase 2. The steps are described in detail below, set out as procedures to be followed for each tender.

Project elements, risk likelihoods and potential impacts

The assessment in Phase 1 makes a number of assumptions about the individual project elements. These are documented in the working papers of the Phase 1 assessment session.

The first step of the tender evaluation is to compare the approach taken by the tenderer with the assumptions made in the initial assessment, for each item in the WBS. Any differences in approach that could affect the likelihood or impact of risks should be noted. These might include, for example:

- Is the requirement commercial-off-the-shelf? Does it require major development or does it involve a mixture of new and developed components or sub-systems?
- Has the tenderer demonstrated an adequate understanding of the requirement?
- Has anything been omitted from the proposal?
- Does the tenderer have a proven track record in this field?
- Is the contractor a good project manager, with suitable management systems?

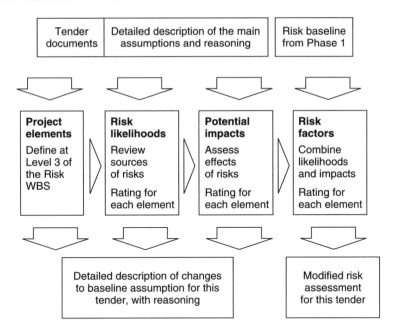

Figure 13.11—Structure of Phase 2 for each tender

- Are the production, delivery and installation schedules optimistic or realistic?
- Are there other uncertainties surrounding this element of the proposal?

Individual risk likelihood indicators should be examined for each element. Any differences between the tenderer's proposed approach and the baseline assumptions should be documented, and any differences in the risk likelihood rating for the element should be noted. Factors that might alter the way an indicator is assessed might include different methods of working, the use of sub-contractors and the tenderer's level of skill and experience with work of a similar kind.

Risk impact measures should be examined for each element, and any proposed revisions to the initial baseline assessment should be documented. Factors that might alter the way impacts are assessed include less risky approaches to the work required to deliver the element, methods and procedures for early detection of problems and well-developed risk management plans.

The revised risk likelihood and impact measures should be converted to numeric scales and risk factors recalculated. The process is identical to that followed in Phase 1.

Any significant variances from the baseline assessment should be examined in detail to ensure the reasons are understood and documented.

Conclusions

The approach described in this chapter has been used successfully in the evaluation of tender submissions for a number of large high-technology procurements. On the basis of our experience, the benefits for the procuring organization can be significant.

- The project team develops a reasoned, quantified view of the nature of the risks throughout the procurement, based on credible and documented assumptions. A defensible baseline is developed.
- The assessment is conducted before tender responses have been received, so it is largely independent of any specific technical approach and is seen to be independent of specific tenderer approaches and responses.
- Potential risks and threats are identified for the tender evaluation team at an early stage, to provide a guide for detailed examination and inquiry.
- The detailed documentation assists the team and others in the approval chain to gain an understanding of the main risk assumptions and mechanisms. In particular, it underpins the formulation of strategies for contract management and project implementation that take risk into account, the selection of a preferred tenderer from a risk management perspective and the development and negotiation of detailed contract conditions relating to risk management.
- The entire process is documented, and thus it can be reviewed and audited.

CONTRACTS AND RISK ALLOCATION 14

Introduction

- ## Purpose

Risks can be allocated or transferred to parties to a contract through specific wording in the contract or through behaviour. The contract is a risk allocation or transfer tool as is the way in which individuals manage it.

- ## Rationale

In any contractual relationship, the responsibility for managing specific risks should fall to the individuals or organizations best placed to manage them.

- ## Input

The risk register and outputs of the risk assessment activities form the basis of inputs to the contract and contract negotiations.

- ## Method

Select contract types and draft contract clauses to minimize the assessed risks by allocating them to the parties who can best manage them.

- ## Outputs

A contract, with correctly allocated risks, documents how risks will be managed by each party to the contract.

- ## Documentation

Risk register, Risk Action Plans, risk allocation table and contract documentation.

Allocation of risks in a contract

Contracts are agreements between parties for the conduct of specific actions or functions, in return for consideration. Contracts of all sizes and for all purposes are intended to transfer risks, allocating them to an individual or an organization to be managed for the duration of the arrangement.

This can be demonstrated when looking upon a simple construction contract for a domestic residence. The owner determines that it is too risky to build or extend a house himself, so he contracts a builder to do it. Through the contract, the owner transfers the technical and project risks associated with building the house to a party, the builder, who is presumably better placed to manage those risks. The owner must source the funds for the construction, and the builder takes an element of credit risk associated with the owner's payments for the work.

This is a basic example of risk allocation via contract. It can be a very complex process at times, but the principles remain the same – allocate risk to the party best placed to manage it, through specific wording in the contract document.

An unreasonable or imbalanced allocation of risks under a contract can occur as a result of the inexperience of the negotiating parties or one party's strong negotiation position. This imbalance may introduce new risks to the project, particularly where the parties do not fully comprehend the nature of the risks or do not possess the necessary capabilities to manage or control them.

By understanding the nature of risks and how they can be allocated appropriately through the contract, project managers can select the most suitable contract form, and then develop and execute the contract to manage risk effectively.

It is worth noting that the transfer of risk, or allocation to another party, can be accomplished either explicitly through drafted and agreed contract wording, or implicitly if the entity responsible for the risk is expected to have a level of capability or professional skills in that area. Implicit transfer of risks is, of itself, a more risky approach as this relies upon unwritten or implied conditions.

Contract types and price basis

Over time, the business world has developed contracts from simple handshake agreements between two parties to powerful, complex documents involving many parties. The fundamental basis of these documents remains the same – the allocation of risk. Today we are able to choose from a large number of contract types that have been developed by experience to allocate and manage a variety of kinds of risks under a variety of circumstances.

When considering a particular type of contract, we can assume that where a contract allocates a great deal of risk to one party, the other party is normally not exposed to the same level in that area.

An example of this is a cost-plus contract, where a contractor is to provide a service in return for the cost of providing the service plus an agreed margin of profit. In this case, the risk of cost overruns has been allocated to the customer in total, leaving the contractor financially risk-free apart from the credit risk of the client not paying as promised. At the

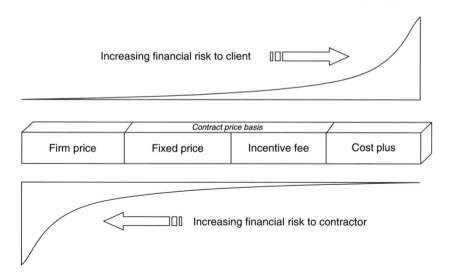

Figure 14.1—Contract types and financial risk allocation

other end of the spectrum, firm-price contracts release the client from risks associated with cost overruns, with this risk allocated to the contractor who must perform the services for a set price, with profit at stake if unanticipated cost increases occur.

There are many price bases for contracts. Figure 14.1 illustrates how financial risk is allocated to either the client or the contractor in the four major forms of contract that are addressed here.

- firm price;
- fixed price;
- incentive fee; and
- cost plus.

Each form of contract addresses the issue of financial risk differently, and allocates risk to the parties in different ways. The following sections look at these four contract forms in more detail. In the latter parts of this chapter, we address the different types of services provided under contract, and how risks to service delivery can be allocated.

Firm-price contracts

Contracts with a firm-price basis allocate all financial risk to the contractor or service provider. In this type of contract, the parties agree to a contract price that remains unchanged for an agreed scope of work or services, no matter what the actual cost to the contractor of providing the work or services. The contractor accepts the risk of cost overruns but may also make additional profit if costs are lower than expected.

Firm-price contracts are common and best used for low-risk, non-developmental, off-the-shelf requirements of a short duration, usually less than two years. Frequently, the customer will want this kind of contract, even though the risks involved in the services to be provided may not suit the contract type, as the customer generally derives the greater benefit.

Fixed-price contracts

Contracts with a fixed-price basis allocate most financial risk to the contractor, but allow some relief in the area of economic fluctuations. In this type of contract, the parties agree to a contract price that remains fixed and does not vary for an agreed scope of work or services, except to allow for changes in exchange rates or inflation. The contractor accepts the risk of cost overruns and also may achieve additional profit through cost savings, but will gain relief from cost increases that are caused by inflation or exchange rate variations. The customer is responsible for the risk that exchange rates may vary or that inflation will cause the contractor's labour, equipment and material costs to rise. In this case the customer makes good any changes to the contract price caused by these economic variations.

Fixed-price contracts are common and best used for low-risk, non-developmental, off-the-shelf requirements of a longer duration, usually more than two years, where the effects of economic changes over a longer period can have a significant impact on the actual contract costs. Frequently, the customer will want this kind of contract, even though the risks involved in the services to be provided may not suit the contract type, as the customer generally derives the greater benefit.

Incentive fee contracts

Contracts with an incentive fee share financial risks between the contractor and client more evenly. In this type of contract, the parties agree to a target contract price that remains fixed for an agreed scope of work or services. The contractor and customer agree to accept a share of the risk of cost overruns and also agree to accept a share in the benefits of any cost savings. In some cases, an incentive fee contract will also set a maximum or ceiling price to the customer, above which the contractor will take on all financial risk, as per a fixed- or firm-price contract.

The exact figures set for the target and ceiling price, and the sharing ratio between the client and contractor will be influenced by the allocation of risk within the contract itself, who is best placed to manage the risks and the outcome of negotiations. For example, if the incentive fee contract allocates the great majority of risks to the contractor, it may be appropriate for the target and ceiling prices to be set quite high or for the sharing ratio for profit and loss to favour the contractor as a form of consideration for taking on that risk. The reverse might be the case if the contract allocates risks substantially to the customer. An example of risk-sharing in an incentive contract is discussed in Chapter 22.

Incentive contracts are best used for moderate- to high-risk developmental requirements where the scope of work is difficult to specify precisely and hence the costs are not easy to estimate accurately. Frequently, the contractor will want this kind of contract, even though the risks involved in the services to be provided may not suit the contract type, as the contractor generally derives the greater benefit.

Cost-plus contracts

Contracts with a cost-plus basis allocate all financial risk to the customer. In this type of contract, the parties agree to a scope of work for which the contractor will be paid all costs incurred in providing the goods or services, plus a profit agreed as either a fixed price or a percentage of the actual costs incurred. The customer accepts the financial risk of contractor cost overruns as well as the agreed profit margin. Unless other contract provisions are included, there is little incentive for the contractor to minimize costs incurred, irrespective of the risks encountered in providing the goods or services.

Cost-plus contracts are rare and best used for high-risk developmental requirements. Often, the contractor will want this kind of contract, even though the risks involved in the services to be provided may not suit the contract type, as the contractor generally derives the greater benefit.

Risks through the procurement life cycle

The very presence of risks in the business environment has a strong influence over the need to develop formal contract documents. The total absence of risk in business and projects, highly unlikely as it is, would result in simple or virtually non-existent contract terms. If there are no risks to allocate, the need for a contract would diminish markedly.

In the real world, however, contracts are required to formally assign risks to the contractual parties and to describe in detail how these risks are to be managed. The identification and assessment of risks and how they are to be allocated should start at the earliest stages of contract formulation and drafting and continue through to contract closure.

Project managers should be aware that risks through the procurement cycle are likely to include risks inherent in the acquisition process itself, such as probity and good management in the tendering and evaluation processes, as well as risks associated with the delivery mechanisms and the project deliverables. An example in which 'project performance' and 'contract process' criteria were used to assess the consequences of risks is provided in Chapter 24.

Drafting contracts

Contracts are generally drafted in one of two ways:

- from first principles, where parties to the contract draft terms and conditions as they see fit; or
- from a draft template that provides initial guidance and structure to the contract.

Both approaches to contract drafting have their merits and one is not normally favoured over the other. What is important is that the contract drafting process recognizes and reflects the risks in the scope of work. The most appropriate allocation for the risks should be considered in the draft contract and the necessary protection mechanisms, or risk mitigation strategies, be provided for the parties. With this protection successfully drafted, the contract document may form the basis upon which an agreement may be reached.

When developing a contract from first principles, the drafter should take into account the risks that may arise and their impacts on the parties to the contract. Contract clauses should be developed to mitigate the risks, placing responsibility for managing them on the contract party best placed to do so. Broad categories of project risks that may be addressed in a contract include:

- ownership and title;
- design, construction and acceptance;
- contract-price basis and payment; and
- liability and indemnity.

The drafter may use existing risk registers, lists of risks or other sources of risk information to assist in creating a contract structure and drafting specific clauses. The contract should cover all the identified risks and allocate responsibility for their management explicitly. Project managers sometimes use a risk allocation table to itemize the risks and indicate the preferred allocation of them to the parties to the contract. An example is provided in Chapter 16.

Contracts developed from a template should follow the same principles as if they were drafted from scratch, although they offer a different set of considerations for the drafter. The template will already contain a set of clauses that have been developed and refined to mitigate common risks in this kind of contract. The drafter will need to review the contract template to ensure that:

- existing clauses adequately address the risks to the scope of work;
- existing clauses allocate the management of the risks to the appropriate party in this particular instance; and
- any other risks are effectively covered by the inclusion of additional clauses or modification of existing ones.

Existing project risk information, in the form of risk registers, risk lists or lessons learnt, provides a valuable source of information for the contract drafter. The drafter should ensure that, wherever possible, the risks and their allocation are effectively addressed through terms and conditions in the contract. Such allocation decisions should be made based on the capabilities of each party, their willingness to accept responsibility for managing the risks, and the position the drafter's organization wishes to take on entering contract negotiations.

Some project risks are not appropriately addressed through contract clauses; for example, the availability of contract management staff to manage the contract post-signature. These must be addressed through other project management strategies within the parent organization.

Links to tender documents and tender evaluation

In many cases, a draft contract is provided as part of the request for tender (RFT) package to assist tenderers to develop their proposals. The draft contract provides tenderers with guidance on the ultimate agreement between the parties and the client's attitude to risk and its allocation. The indicative allocation of responsibility for managing risks through the draft contract will have important ramifications for tenderers in how they structure and cost their responses, and in deciding whether they will submit a response to the RFT at all.

The draft contract should assist tenderers to gain an understanding of the risks identified by the customer and this should, in turn, help in developing detailed strategies for delivering the scope of work required. The allocation of risks, as described in the draft contract, also assists tenderers in developing negotiation plans and their own risk management responsibilities and strategies.

Plans for the evaluation of tenders should explicitly describe the way in which risk and risk management is to be dealt with. No formal tender evaluation process should be without this.

Evaluation of tenderers' risk management capabilities

Tender responses should be evaluated to establish the risk management capabilities of each tenderer. It is no longer adequate for tenderers simply to state that they have the capacity and capability to manage risks. Astute customers assure themselves that the companies they select to deliver projects and services have formalized, integrated risk management processes that systematically identify and treat risks before they become significant problems. Tenderers need to indicate that they:

- have risk management processes that are consistent with an appropriate standard;
- have project management systems that are integrated with the risk management process; and
- can link well with the customer's approach to risk management.

Tenderers should be required to identify and assess risks to the scope of work. They should also be asked to demonstrate the mitigation strategies that they have developed to manage the risks within their overall strategy for managing the project delivery. Tenderers will need to indicate that they:

- have identified the risks to delivering the scope of work or services;
- have developed effective mitigation strategies to manage the risks and costed them in the tender price; and
- are willing to work with the customer in proactive management of all risks throughout the life of the contract.

Examples of RFT clauses that require tenderers to have integrated risk management processes and plans were provided in Chapters 8 and 9.

Contract negotiation

As discussed previously, contracts are an agreement for the allocation of risks between two or more parties. Contract documents commonly group like kinds of risks into sections or clauses and deal with them, instructing one or other of the parties to manage the risk in a particular way; for example:

- the contractor shall deliver the preliminary design documents to the client within 90 days of contract signature . . .
- the client shall provide to the contractor all material required for designated task 5.2 under the contract by 25 June . . .

Contract negotiation is the process by which the parties agree who is best placed to manage which risks, and the cost of doing so.

Prior to negotiations, each party should develop a detailed register of risks under the proposed contract and a strategy for negotiating each of them. An assessment of the severity of each risk indicates how significant it is and provides an insight into how critical it is to negotiate the risk successfully.

For instance, a risk within the draft contract that is assessed as being critical to one party, to the extent that to fail to negotiate it successfully would cause the contract to be unacceptable, would be deemed a critical negotiation point. In such a case, the contract would not be executed if this risk was not resolved satisfactorily.

Contract negotiations frequently are conducted in a sequence from the front page to the back page of the contract document. This is a poor way of structuring negotiations, as there is no focus on resolving high-risk areas and the contract is simply negotiated on a clause-by-clause basis. A more effective way is to develop an agenda for negotiating that is based on the risks each party must successfully resolve. Instead of starting negotiations on page 1, the parties should agree to start with those areas of the contract considered to be the greatest risks for each of them.

Early focus on the high-risk aspects of the contract concentrates the parties' attention on those matters that ultimately determine whether the contract will be agreed and executed, or rejected as unachievable. Clauses relating to lower-level risks can be dealt with later, or set aside if the risk assessment indicates there is little or no impact if the clause is not negotiated to the complete satisfaction of either party.

Contract management

It has been said that a well-drafted and negotiated contract can fail through poor management and, conversely, a poorly constructed or flawed contract can be successful through good management. Nevertheless, the objective should be to negotiate a good contract and then make it even more successful through good management throughout its life.

It takes more than a good contract to achieve a successful project outcome. Contracts can have their problems – most of them do – and it is the responsibility of managers from both parties to actively manage their resolution. This means, amongst many other things, managers must proactively identify and mitigate risks that have the potential to cause the contract to fail to meet its objectives.

Managers may accomplish this through regular monitoring and review of risks. Monitoring is the process of observing the status of risks and how they are being managed. This takes place frequently and is not a time-consuming activity, often being done in weekly or monthly meetings as a part of normal business. Contract management forums should monitor risks as part of normal business, and risk management should be incorporated into meeting agendas. For example, risk management should be a regular agenda item for project management meetings, as discussed in Chapter 7.

A review is the process by which managers formally take stock of the identified risks and their status. Reviews are often conducted using a formal workshop process, with the participation of project executives and key stakeholders. They are usually conducted only once or twice a year, in conjunction with other management activities.

Risks that emerge in the early stages of developing a contract, perhaps in the drafting or negotiation stages, may have an impact on a specific area of the project, such as in the design solution of a component. The nature of the risk will change over the life of the project as treatment plans are developed and implemented. Effective monitoring of risks is required to ensure they do not ultimately have adverse effects on key project criteria, such as system performance or safety, and that they don't have long and expensive lives.

Contract closure

Ultimately, all contracts come to a close, as projects are completed either successfully or unsuccessfully. Ideally, risks would have been identified, managed and mitigated to their completion at or before contract closure. On occasions, however, risks can remain open at contract closure, and this requires decisions about how they may best be managed and what actions should be taken.

For example, risks may not be resolved fully at contract completion if the full potential of the asset, facility, system or equipment purchased has not been demonstrated during acceptance and testing. In such a case, there is a risk that the asset or system may not live up to its promised levels of performance. This may not be evident until some time after the contract is completed and the asset or system is already operational. A strategy for managing this risk, outside the construct of the contract, will need to be developed by the project manager.

In other cases, the risks remaining at the end of the contract are a direct result of one or both of the parties not fully completing their contract obligations. This often happens in large and complex contracts, usually despite the best intentions of the parties. In closing the contract, adjustments are often made in terms of the price, the equipment delivered or other measures, to make allowance for the remaining risks.

But there is still work to do, however, even if the contract is closed. Many risks still exist and may need to be passed on to another party. In large organizations, especially public sector agencies, it is commonplace for one organization to undertake the procurement action and then to pass the deliverables on to the end customer, the users. In situations where risks remain at contract closure, their details should be communicated to the end-users so they can continue to be monitored and managed. Some end-user organizations may require funding to be provided from the procurement agency to allow for treatment of the remaining risks. What matters most, though, is that appropriate information on the nature and severity of any remaining risks is communicated to the end-user or client.

Asset delivery and service projects

The discussion in this chapter applies to contracts for the provision of both physical assets and facilities as well as capabilities and services. As with construction projects, contracts developed to deliver services should allocate the risk of effective delivery to organizations that have, or should have, better capabilities for managing the associated risks. For example, an industry specialist that already has extensive national networks, logistics support chains and a skilled workforce may be willing and able to provide services more efficiently than a customer organization can do in-house, hence with a lower service delivery risk. If the contract is formulated well and risks are allocated properly, the customer is free of the risks involved in providing the services internally.

The price basis of a service contract depends on the duration and nature of the services to be provided. As risks in the provision of well-defined services are often reasonably low, incentive fee or cost-plus service contracts are not typical, although fixed-price contracts may be geared to service volumes where there is an identifiable and measurable driver for the variable price component of the delivery and the customer is willing to take the volume risk. Examples of this latter form include IT or communications contracts where there is an agreed fixed price per transaction, facility management contracts with prices linked to occupancy rates, or asset maintenance contracts with prices linked to traffic levels.

Most problems that arise from service contracts occur where risks have not been identified clearly in the first place, or not dealt with effectively in the contract. In these cases, risks are likely to return to the customer, who may believe mistakenly that the risk has been passed to the contractor via the agreement. For example, problems are likely if a large organization has outsourced the support of its IT infrastructure to a contractor, but has not correctly identified the processes and responsibilities for managing technology changes in the equipment in the contract. In this case, it is inevitable that the organization will be left with the responsibility for paying for and managing necessary technology upgrades.

Many service contracts involve outsourcing, as in the IT example above. Outsourcing is discussed in detail in Chapter 15. Another particular form arises where the purchasing organization requires a specified capability and the provider must source the necessary assets, equipment and people for its delivery. Where government is the purchaser, public–private partnerships or private financing arrangements may be appropriate. These forms of arrangement are discussed in detail in Chapter 16.

MARKET TESTING AND OUTSOURCING

15

Chapter Overview

- ### Purpose

  This chapter discusses the application of risk management in market testing and outsourcing activities.

- ### Rationale

  Outsourcing of the provision of goods and services is an important function for many organizations. Because outsourcing often involves long-term contractual or partnering arrangements and risks that may be new or unfamiliar to the organization, sound risk management can lead to better relationships and help to avoid costly mistakes.

- ### Method

  The overall risk management process is the same as that described in earlier chapters. Some aspects of its implementation change to suit the specific application.

Introduction

Outsourcing is a contractual arrangement where an external provider takes responsibility for performing some or all of an organization's functions. It may involve a partial or complete transfer of staff or resources to the external provider.

Market testing is the process by which an organization compares its internal service delivery capability and cost against a competitive market. This is a necessary prelude to any informed decision about whether or not the organization should outsource functions to an external provider.

All organizations outsource in one form or another. Many organizations buy in the materials required for their manufacturing processes, while some contract out the marketing and distribution of their products. Other organizations divest themselves of an entire integrated activity by creating a subsidiary organization and selling it. (Governments achieve similar outcomes through the creation and privatization of government business enterprises.)

In both the public and private sectors, the outsourcing of support services and non-core activities is becoming increasingly common. Examples of functions that may be outsourced include:

- information technology support and help desk functions;
- property, facilities and asset management, including maintenance, fleet management cleaning, security and gardening;
- provision of clothing, catering, laundry and 'hotel' services;
- marketing; and
- warehousing and distribution.

The advantages of outsourcing may include:

- access to specific technical expertise or innovative technologies for the provision of particular goods and services that may not be sustainable internally;
- improvements in efficiency and reduced costs through economies of scale;
- more flexible industrial conditions or organizational culture;
- improved focus on critical or core functions of the business.

Outsourcing

The outsourced provision of goods and service in an organizational framework can be considered in terms of three functions (Figure 15.1):

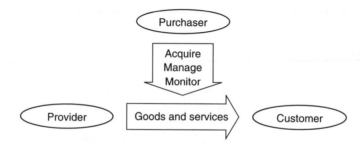

Figure 15.1—The three core functions of goods and service delivery

- the internal or external customers who require goods or services;
- the outsourced provider of the goods or services; and
- a purchaser who must acquire those goods and services and ensure they continue to meet the customers' needs to an appropriate standard.

To achieve organizational efficiencies many organizations have segregated and formalized these three functions. Many of the risks associated with outsourcing are associated with these three functions and their interrelationships.

Adverse impacts of outsourcing may be associated with the purchaser, the provider or the customer or their interactions.

- For the customer, outsourcing usually involves more formal and complex arrangements for the supply of goods and services and their payment.
- For the purchasing function, this may require the organization to develop new skills and expertise for establishing, managing and monitoring the contractual relationship between the provider and the customer.
- For management, outsourcing may mean a loss of technical expertise from the organization, with no guarantee it will be available if required in the medium to long term.

Outsourcing may cause major changes to the nature and competence of organizations, particularly if the outsourced activity is a critical link in the organization's value chain. Once implemented, outsourcing may be difficult and expensive to reverse, due to the loss of in-house skills coupled with the difficulty in re-acquiring such skills.

Outsourcing does not necessarily transfer the governance, accountability or risks associated with the outsourced function. The manager responsible for the outcomes of that function generally retains accountability for performance and the management of the risks associated with it. In addition, new risks emerge with outsourcing that in turn require management attention.

The outsourcing process

Outsourcing can be thought of in three distinct phases, each of which can be regarded as a project and in each of which risk management can be applied (Figure 15.2, Table 15.1):

- strategic analysis is undertaken in order to decide whether to outsource and, if so, what functions or services to outsource;
- transition planning develops the plans needed to outsource and then to move between in-house and outsourced activities; and
- implementation refers to the implementation of those plans and strategies.

A thorough risk review of each phase and the establishment of detailed transition and implementation plans should be undertaken prior to the execution of any contractual arrangements. This should ensure the organization will take a more proactive approach to any identified risks encountered in the implementation of an outsourcing initiative. Table 15.2 identifies a number of issues and strategies to be addressed in the process and included in

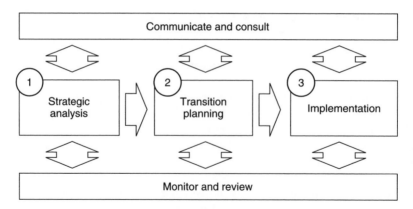

Figure 15.2—The three phases of outsourcing

Table 15.1—Risk management at each phase of outsourcing

Phase	Context	Risk focus	Treatment outcomes
Strategic analysis	Strategic and organizational context: vision, objectives, goals, value chain, competitive strengths, capabilities	Strategic risks	Strategic decisions: what to outsource, if anything; costs and benefits analysis of internal improvement initiatives
Transition planning	Policies, strategic issues, organizational structure and culture, patterns of work and behaviour, capabilities	Transition risks	Review of strategic outsourcing decisions Transition plans Outline tendering strategy
Implementation	Draft contract, potential contractors, required service standards	Tendering, contract and delivery risks	Revised contract terms, implementation plans

plans. The comprehensiveness of these plans should be commensurate with the complexity and magnitude of the outsourcing initiative.

Risk management processes

The project risk management process described in earlier chapters does not change in significant ways when it is applied to market testing and outsourcing activities. As always, establishing the context provides the basis and structure for a sound risk management process that is focused on achieving the desired objectives.

The key elements depend on the phase of the outsourcing activity as well as its characteristics. The left-hand columns in Table 15.3 and Table 15.4 show examples of key elements from market tests of technical capabilities and facilities services. The tables also show a selection of the risks that were identified. Further risks that are more specific to outsourcing are discussed in the next section.

Table 15.2—Topics to be considered in the transition planning phase

Area	Topics to be included in plans
Procurement strategy	Open, restricted or closed tenders
	Contract period and extension options
	Structure of tender evaluation team
	Contractual relationship
	Contract performance criteria to match stakeholder expectations
	Contractual terms and conditions to deal with identified risks
People and HR management	Roles and responsibilities
	Communication and consultation with staff and representatives
	Staff support
	Retention of corporate knowledge
	Management of excess staff
	Recruitment of skilled contract managers
	HSE
	Redundancy packages
Finances and resources	Budget allocation
	Project team resources
	Timeframes
Transition and implementation	Transition strategy: phased or clean-break
	Security of business information
	Communication plans
	Marketing
	Stakeholder support
	Change management

Monitoring and review take particular importance in an outsourcing environment, both for risk management and for contractual purposes. Once the decision has been taken to outsource an activity, monitoring the quality of the services provided and the costs and risks associated with their delivery provides an important means of identifying and consolidating benefits. Monitoring of contractor performance and service quality against specified key performance indicators determines whether stakeholder and organizational expectations are being met. If delivery quality and risk management are linked appropriately to payments, and with contractual terms that allow for sharing of efficiency benefits, there are incentives for all parties to improve performance.

Specific risks associated with outsourcing

Loss of corporate knowledge and skills

When an outsourcing initiative is implemented, staff undertaking the activities involved are likely to be redeployed elsewhere within the organization, transferred to the new service

Table 15.3—Examples of process risks from a technical market testing activity

Element	Risk examples
Contractor performance and capability	Inability of contractor to achieve required performance levels
	A sub-contractor fails to perform to the required standard
	Contractor does not have the necessary technical competence
	Poor specification of the capability to be delivered and the levels of service required; unclear or unrealistic performance criteria
	Lack of suitably qualified personnel, short-term and long-term
	Inability of contractor to react to unexpected increases in demand (surge requirements)
	The contractor fails to achieve required accreditation (e.g. quality accreditation)
	The contractor's other commercial work is given a greater priority than contract work
	Lack of a common understanding between stakeholders on how the service is to be delivered
	Inadequate planning for business interruption
Organization capability	The competence of contract management staff is inadequate
	Inappropriate organizational structure and numbers for contract management
	Inability to retain competence and core skills within the organization
Contract	Mismatch in expectations between the parties (despite the contract terms)
	Contractor bids on a 'win-lose' basis then plays catch-up with contract variations
	Inappropriate contract documentation for the kind of service to be provided
	Unclear or incompatible levels of authority for control, approvals and contract changes
	Insufficient incentive for innovation
	Conflicts of interest
	Loss of other commercial work affects the viability of the contract
	Contractor goes out of business
	Failure to flow down contract requirements to sub-contractors
	Poor visibility of sub-contractors
HSE	Liability for HSE resides with the landlord, who does not have control of activities
	Equipment not up to standard, causing safety problems
Information	Poor data integrity, inconsistent or incomplete data, inaccurate usage forecasts and failure rates, inaccurate inventory and spares holding records
	Configuration and standard of existing assets not as anticipated
	Inappropriate transfer of information to unauthorized parties or sub-contractors
	IT failure results in loss of accounting information
	Lack of contractor capability to manage numerous databases in different configurations
Transition	Poor specification of transition requirements
	The contractor overestimates recruitment from the existing workforce
	Industrial relations problems with the existing workforce (resentment, work to rule, disruption, slow to provide information)
	Extended transition time to the new contractor

Table 15.4—Examples of specific risks from a facility services market testing activity

Element	Risk examples
General risks	HSE problems due to incorrect application or handling of hazardous chemicals
	Damage to the environment due to incorrect choice, application or spillage of chemicals
	Accident when using hazardous equipment or working at heights (such as gutter clearing)
	Incorrect storage of dangerous goods
	Injury when moving heavy items or equipment
	Failure to perform some work due to non-availability of equipment
	Insufficient trained personnel
	Insufficient resources for major events
Grounds maintenance	Damage to structures, roads, fences
	Cutting or digging damages utilities supplies
	Extended period of bad weather (wet weather and droughts) results in failure to perform all duties
Cleaning	Electric shocks from faulty equipment
	Accidents caused by slippery floors
	Ineffective cleaning results in health risk or infections
	Damage to health due to contact with contaminated materials
	HSE problems due to use of chemicals in confined spaces
Security	Access of unauthorized personnel leading to damage or theft of physical assets or information
	Insufficient qualified staff to deal with major incidents
Transport	Insufficient drivers or vehicles to meet surge requirement
	Incorrectly licensed drivers, e.g. for carriage of hazardous goods
	Accident while transporting hazardous goods
	Accident while transporting passengers or non-hazardous goods
	Limited vehicle recovery capability, especially for heavy vehicles
	Poor management of fuel stocks resulting in insufficient fuel
	Supply of inappropriate vehicles for the assigned tasks
	HSE incidents in workshop
	Insufficient capability and resources to service firefighting vehicles and other critical vehicles and equipment, e.g. fuel bowsers
Fuel services	Fire during refuelling or de-fuelling operation
	Spillage during refuelling or de-fuelling operations
	Fuel tanker overturns
	Incident due to incorrect operation of refuelling or de-fuelling
	Incorrect truck or pump operation
	Poor fuel quality control
	Overfilling of stock tanks and trucks
	Fuel fire in the fuel farm escalating through the farm
	Fuel farm major spillage in bunds
	Fuel farm major spillage outside bunds around lower installations, results in release into the environment
	Fuel delivery equipment failure

(Continued over leaf)

Table 15.4—(Continued)

Element	Risk examples
Firefighting and rescue	Failure to respond to fire in time resulting in greatly increased damages
	Failure to respond to rescue in time resulting in additional loss of life
	Failure to correctly maintain first aid equipment
	Failure of fire alarm and detection system
	Inadequate hazardous materials (Hazmat) register leads to inappropriate response
	Over-stockpiling of hazardous materials
	Spillage incident larger than can be handled by the on-site Hazmat unit
	Inability to release firefighters for continuation training
Waste removal	Personnel infected by contact with hazardous and contaminated waste
	Incorrect disposal of hazardous and contaminated waste
	Insufficient portable toilets organized for an event
	Contamination of recyclables
Pest and vermin control	Personnel stung, bitten or infected when removing live or dead pests
	Contamination of food preparation areas resulting in minor poisoning or spoilt food
Laundry and dry cleaning	Loss or damage of items
	Infection from contaminated items
Hospitality and canteen	Inability to get correct or planned stock from suppliers
	Unexpected demand resulting in inability to feed all personnel
	Breakdown of food storage equipment or facilities resulting in loss of stock and failure to supply agreed menus
	Contamination of food
	Theft of bar cash or stock
	Serving of alcohol to intoxicated or underage personnel
	Poor quality or inappropriate food
	Cross-contamination from cleaning to food preparation
Remote locations	Inability to provide adequate supervision for personnel at remote locations
	HSE incident or accident at a remote location
	Vehicle breakdown or accident at remote location
	Inability to deliver fuel to remote areas

provider or made redundant. In practice, potential contractors are likely actively to pursue recruitment of these experienced and skilled staff, but this often occurs at the expense of the organization. In particular, the consequential impacts on the organization may include:

- inefficient or ineffective contractor management;
- inability fully to articulate requirements and be a 'smart customer';
- over-dependence on the contractor for innovation;
- inability to reverse the outsourcing decision except by paying a high premium to re-acquire the skills;
- Inability effectively to evaluate competing bids at the next round of tendering.

Loss of control over intellectual property

While intellectual property rights may not seem to be an obvious source of risk in relation to outsourcing, the use and development of intellectual property is an inevitable consequence of outsourcing. For example, records created by a contractor in the course of providing services to an organization are subject to copyright, and ownership must be agreed at the outset. An organization entering into outsourcing arrangements may face a broad range of intellectual property risks that may include:

- Failure to protect confidential information, thus enabling a contractor to use or disclose confidential information to which it has access.
- Copyright infringement or other intellectual property infringement if a contractor is allowed to copy and use third-party copyrighted material or other protected intellectual property without having obtained a licence or permission to do so from the third-party owner.
- Loss of opportunity to own and exploit intellectual property developed by the contractor in the course of undertaking outsourced activities for the organization. Furthermore, the organization may not be able to stop the contractor from using the same intellectual property for another client.
- Inability to use intellectual property developed by the contractor under the outsourcing arrangement without paying a fee, particularly on the completion of the contract.

The primary means of managing these risks is through the outsourcing agreement. Before developing the outsourcing agreement, an intellectual property audit may be needed to identify all intellectual property that may be affected by the arrangement, and which confidential information will need to be disclosed to the contractor.

Occupational health, safety and environment (HSE)

Responsibility for the safety of employees and contractors usually rests with the person in control of the workplace. This means that outsourcing does not relieve the organization of its legal obligations to identify, assess, control and monitor HSE risks associated with the work to be outsourced, unless the work is carried out on the contractor's site. HSE risks (in terms of accountability) can rarely be transferred by contract.

There may also be implications for the health and safety of the organization's own employees from the way in which outsourced work is performed: for example, poor quality cleaning or poor quality equipment maintenance may lead to injury or illness. The HSE performance of tenderers should be a criterion considered when awarding a contract.

A further HSE risk relates to employees' lack of familiarity with safety procedures that have now become the prime responsibility of a contractor. For example, critical safety procedures may change to comply with a contractor's normal practice; this may mean that internal staff need to be familiar with, and comply with, several different procedures depending on the contractor. This is a particular issue where the organization has a competition policy of not awarding multiple contracts to a single supplier.

Phantom benefits

Improved resource utilization is often cited as an organizational benefit of outsourcing, but sometimes these and other planned benefits are not realized in practice. Within an organization, the monitoring of resource utilization may reveal a shift in deployment. That is, resources utilized previously to perform the activity have been diverted to other tasks within the organization, with no consequential resource savings being achieved. In the meantime, the organization has taken on the additional costs of managing and administering the outsourced activity.

Case study: outsourcing of asset management

This case illustrates some of the functions that must be performed in managing a portfolio of geographically dispersed assets for a government agency (Figure 15.3). It was developed as part of an assessment of the skills the agency would need to acquire before it embarked on a market testing or outsourcing exercise. The nature of the specific assets is not really important: similar analyses would apply to assets such as schools, hospitals, employment offices or fire stations. The link to central Government is primarily associated with funding matters.

Table 15.5 shows the functions that were identified as necessary within the agency if each level of asset management were to be outsourced to an external contractor. The interfaces were also considered, but they are not shown in the table. A list of functions like this – including their interactions – might be a useful basis for a set of key elements for structuring a risk identification and assessment exercise.

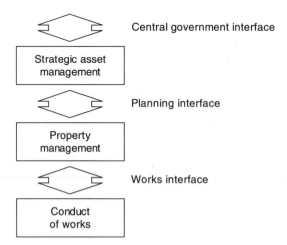

Figure 15.3—Asset management structures and roles

Table 15.5—Required functions at each level of management

Management level	Necessary functions	
Strategic asset management: functions performed centrally by the agency	Provision of strategic planning and advice Contracting the property managers Setting and monitoring performance targets Asset acquisition and disposal Data collation and analysis	
Property management: functions for individual facilities or groups of facilities in a region	Physical management	Maintenance Minor works Technical advice Data collection
	Financial management	Payments and account management Budgets and forecasts
	Asset management	Asset and utilization review and advice HSE requirements
	Project management	Feasibility, design, documentation, tendering, contract administration
Conduct of works: construction and asset service delivery functions associated with specific tasks	Maintenance	Replacement and repair of assets Painting, electrical, floor coverings, fences, graffiti, grounds
	Minor works	Upgrading of assets Installation of ramps, refurbishments, extensions, HSE compliance

In this case, though, the functions were used to initiate a review of existing agency capabilities to identify skills gaps that would need to be filled before any further detailed work could be undertaken, and the risk assessment was deferred. In effect, the agency recognized some of the organizational skills risks noted above, under 'Loss of corporate knowledge and skills' and determined they would need to be resolved before significant progress could be made in any other areas. Figure 15.4 shows the revised implementation path.

As part of the more general planning for market testing, options for outsourcing functions at each of the three levels of asset management were examined. Not all combinations were considered practicable, as Table 15.6 illustrates – specifically, it was not thought feasible for the agency to attempt to undertake low-level works if property management were to be outsourced. This reduced the number of feasible pathways from the current in-house provision of all services by the agency to an arrangement where asset management functions were totally devolved to contractors (Figure 15.5). Intuitively, the pathway across the top in which low-level tasks were considered for outsourcing before higher-level ones (AAA > AAC > ACC > CCC, shown in heavy lines) was assessed as offering the lowest risk. This 'toe-in-the-water' approach would also be compatible with the development of the agency's asset management skills.

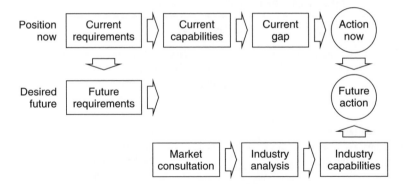

Figure 15.4—Revised implementation path

Table 15.6—Options for service provision

Management level	Service provider							
Strategic asset management	Agency				Contractor			
Property management	Agency		Contractor		Agency		Contractor	
Conduct of works	A	C	A	C	A	C	A	C
Feasible?	✓	✓	✗	✓	✓	✓	✗	✓

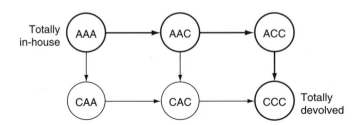

Key: A – Agency provision; C – Contractor provision

Figure 15.5—Pathways from in-house (AAA) to fully devolved (CCC) provision of services

Acknowledgements and further reading

Dennis Goodwin made significant contributions to this chapter. Additional useful material is contained in Goodwin *et al.* (2000).

PUBLIC–PRIVATE PARTNERSHIPS AND PRIVATE FINANCING

16

Chapter overview

- ### Purpose

  This chapter shows how risk management processes can be used to identify and allocate the risks in the non-standard procurement structures typically associated with private finance initiatives and public–private partnerships for acquiring capability for the public sector.

- ### Rationale

  A sound understanding of risks and where they lie is essential for equitable risk allocation and pricing decisions.

- ### Method

  The method is similar to that used for project risk management, extended to include project financing aspects. Additional quantification is often needed.

Private financing for public-sector capability acquisition

Private financing (PF) is the term used when the private sector invests in the equipment and employs the workforce to provide a service to the public sector, including capability and facilities, rather than the public sector acquiring the necessary assets itself through a traditional procurement process. The public sector engages the private sector for the provision of services, or for the use and control of an asset that is owned and supported by the private sector. The arrangement is also known as a public–private partnership (PPP).

The main characteristics of a PF or PPP arrangement are:

- one or more private parties, fully accountable to Government for delivery of the specified services;
- clear and accountable risk allocation, with associated prices;
- clearly specified outputs, with measurable key performance indicators (KPIs);
- payments only on delivery of the specified services;
- relatively long-term commitments; and
- ongoing value for money throughout the contract.

The principle is that private-sector processes and efficiencies are traded-off against a higher cost of capital, generating a net benefit for Government (Figure 16.1). There may also be budgetary benefits for Government as the cash flow requirements are spread through time, although this is rarely a primary motivation.

There are a number of ways in which public-sector services can be provided with the assistance of the private sector. They merge into one another as we move from left to right in Figure 16.2, and the private sector takes more risk as we move from left to right. PPP lies between the extremes of full government provision and full private-sector provision.

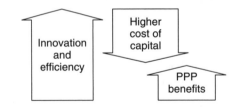

Figure 16.1—PPP benefits

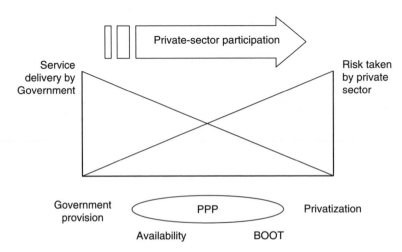

Figure 16.2—Approaches to providing public-sector services

In an 'availability' model, the private sector provides an asset that is available for public sector use to an agreed standard and level of availability. A number of school and hospital projects are like this, where the private sector builds and maintains an asset and the Government provides the expertise and equipment to deliver the service to the public.

In a build-own-operate-transfer (BOOT) model (or one of its variants), the private sector provides all the assets and the services, with the assets reverting to the Government after the expiry of a concession period. Examples include toll roads, prisons, ports and airports. In some areas, schools and training facilities have been provided on this basis, with the private sector delivering the basic education services as well as building and maintaining the assets.

Privatization transfers the assets and the service delivery to the private sector, and Government sources all services from industry. Examples include vehicle fleets and power generators.

Under a PF or PPP arrangement, a three-way relationship is normally established between the public sector, the supplier of a capability and a guarantor, commonly a financial consortium (Figure 16.3). The strength and nature of the financial and commercial arrangements between the parties depends on the specific nature of the structure involved. For example, where the finance is provided by the supplier under a BOOT model, facets of the arrangement peculiar to the private-finance provider would transfer to the supplier, and the direct link between the finance provider and the public sector might be limited to takeout undertakings, demand guarantees or commitments on the minimum use of the asset or services.

On the face of it, arrangements like this look risky, with many stakeholders. However, many of the individual parts are well known, and their risks can be managed. It is the integration issues that are often complex.

PF procurement generally follows the same process and the same contracting principles as traditional procurement. However, it does contain a number of unique steps, primarily concerned with ensuring competitiveness and value for money of the procurement outcome under the non-traditional arrangements (Figure 16.4). A key feature of PF procurement analysis is the development of a project cost benchmark (PCB). The PCB is a base cost estimate for the delivery of the capability by traditional direct purchase processes, used to

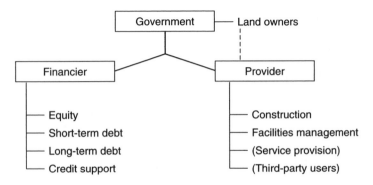

Figure 16.3—Relationships between the parties

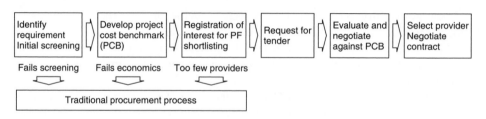

Figure 16.4—PF procurement process

assess the economics of the procurement and the comparative value-for-money of specific PF tender options.

Integration of risk management and private financing

Risk management should be integrated with PF procurement so senior managers can make informed decisions at critical points in the process. An integrated process facilitates:

- an effective exploration of PF procurement options for the capability requirement that takes into consideration opportunities and risks associated with each option;
- the establishment of criteria for evaluating tender responses;
- the development of strategies for preliminary allocation and resolution of risks during contract negotiations;
- the identification of key terms and conditions to be included in draft contracts;
- the kind of contract to be employed;
- a prioritization for the effective allocation of resources; and
- the identification of control measures for identified risks to be included in statements of work, performance specifications and contracts.

The risk management process applies across all phases of the acquired capability's life cycle, irrespective of whether the capability has been acquired through a PF initiative or through traditional procurement. It is a process that assists managers at all levels of PF acquisition and capability management.

Establishing the context

The objectives and criteria are developed by reviewing key requirement documents such as the requirement concept, major capability submissions, cost and schedule assumptions, scope definitions, engineering studies and designs, economic analyses, and any other relevant documentation about the requirement and its purpose. The process is identical to that described in Chapter 2.

Quantitative risk analysis for private financing activities

Quantitative risk analysis aggregates and quantifies risk and uncertainty in terms of distributions of PF characteristics such as time and money, often using mathematical modelling and simulation modelling techniques. It increases the accuracy with which risks are valued in a number of PF processes. These include:

- improving the accuracy of project cost estimates;
- establishing contingency levels;
- improving the accuracy of cash flow estimates;
- ranking competing PF tender responses with different levels and areas of risk;
- providing a more accurate comparison between competing PF tender responses and the project cost benchmark; and
- determining the financial impact of retained and transferable risks.

Quantitative risk modelling is a means of:

- describing the detailed mechanisms at work in a set of risks;
- evaluating the uncertainty in the requirement and the overall risk that this places on stakeholders;
- establishing targets, commitments and contingencies consistent with the level of uncertainty and the risk the public sector is willing to accept;
- exploring the relationship between detailed instances of uncertainty and an overall level of risk, to facilitate risk management resource allocation; and
- quantifying, with some level of accuracy, the effects that risk might have on cost, schedule or other measurable outcomes.

Quantitative risk modelling provides a framework within which to integrate the consequences of individual risks into an overall assessment to support decision-making and management control. In the case of large and complex PF requirements, quantitative modelling may also play a part in the evaluation of individual risks.

Quantitative risk modelling comes into its own when there is a need for a view of the overall risk associated with a PF requirement. This may arise when:

- establishing contingency levels;
- improving the accuracy of cash flow estimates;
- selling a proposal on the basis of confidence in the forecast outcome;
- ranking competing PF tender responses with different levels and areas of risk;
- providing a more accurate comparison between competing PF tender responses and the project cost benchmark;
- determining the financial impact of retained and transferable risks;
- establishing and negotiating delivery schedules, performance targets and contingency levels, or accepting commitments;
- choosing between alternative technologies or approaches with different risk profiles;

- planning risk treatments that will reduce overall uncertainty;
- prioritizing sources of uncertainty and establishing the extent to which different stakeholders can control the overall uncertainty in the PF requirement; and
- undertaking life cycle costing analysis and dealing with the variable nature of supplier-provided information.

Quantitative risk analysis modelling and processes of the kind noted here are addressed in detail in Chapters 19 to 23.

Risk allocation and pricing

Risk allocation and pricing determines the appropriate party to manage each identified risk and the pricing consequence of allocating the risk to that party. The general principles are:

- each risk should be allocated to the party best able to manage it at least cost;
- not all risk need be transferred: inappropriate risk transfer incurs penalties and may create new risks;
- worthwhile risk transfer requires flexibility in the contract: the party allocated the risk must be able to choose how to handle it;
- the partnership structure should take account of responsibility for managing risks.

To take advantage of the opportunities created through PF, public sector procurement organizations must change the ways in which they seek to accept and allocate risks. Public sector managers must focus on:

- articulating the policy objectives they wish to achieve through PF;
- identifying the service they are seeking from the PF contractor and specifying the outcomes and outputs of that service;
- identifying the core capability that is required to be delivered by the equipment, system or facility being financed; and
- structuring the most suitable payment mechanism for the provision of the PF contractor's service or output specification in accordance with the public sector's objectives for the initiative.

A fundamental principle underpinning the success of PF is the opportunity created for greater innovation and more effective utilization of funding appropriations. This often includes leaving the risk of ownership and operation of the asset with the PF contractor. Risk of ownership and operation includes the design, procurement management, defect rectification, fitness for purpose, maintenance and disposal of the asset, and is consistent with the principle that the party best able to control the risks should be responsible for their management.

Optimal risk allocation seeks to minimize both the costs of providing a public-sector capability and the risks to the PF initiative itself by allocating risks to the party best able to manage those risks. Allocating the risk in this way requires the responsible parties to use their specialist skills and capacity to implement appropriate risk strategies to ensure that the contract requirements are fully met.

While the PF contractor retains the risks associated with asset ownership, the responsibility for provision of the capability remains with the public sector. In addition, through the allocation of asset ownership risks to the PF contractor, the nature of risks associated with the successful outcome of the asset's intended use will change and new risks will emerge. These new risks in turn will need to be assessed, allocated, treated where appropriate and managed.

There are particular PF risks, such as those associated with sovereignty rights, capability, military operations and security, where the allocation of responsibility must be negotiated between the public sector and the service provider. In the provision of facilities, other examples include risks associated with ground contamination, statutory approvals, land acquisition, indigenous and native title issues, heritage aspects and environmental matters such as the presence of endangered flora or fauna. Well-developed performance specifications and clear responsibilities should reduce the impacts of these risks and facilitate their management, should they occur.

In some circumstances the public sector may seek to shed risks inappropriately to a supplier because it has a stronger negotiating position. This has several consequences.

- It results in a sub-optimal allocation of risks for which either the public sector or the contractor will have to develop management strategies through the life of the contract.
- Costs to the public sector may be higher, as the contractor makes additional allowance for risk.
- New risks may be created, resulting in unexpected increased costs to one of the parties in the longer term.

The public sector will always have responsibility for the management of some aspects of the capability requirement and its risks. From an accountability perspective, the public sector will ultimately bear the consequences of contractor performance failure.

Care must be taken in deciding which control measures should be imposed upon the design and performance of the equipment or services provided by a PF contractor as this may undermine innovation opportunities or transfer back to the public sector some of the risks associated with asset ownership.

For example, should the public sector insist on the right of approval to the design, modify proposed designs, or otherwise interfere in the design and delivery process under a PF arrangement, the impact may limit the PF contractor's scope for innovation and transfer some of the design risks back to the public sector. Insistence on approving levels of spares to be held, or limiting the annual expenditure on spares would transfer the risk of availability of equipment back to the public sector. Similarly, should the public sector retain the right to control the customers who use training facilities, the risk to the financial viability of the facility and hence the success of the PF initiative overall could transfer to the public sector.

The project cost benchmark

The project cost benchmark (PCB) is a quantitative indicator of the cost of delivering the project by the public sector. This provides a benchmark for comparing procurement options and tenders. The basis should be service delivery by the public sector, operating in the same way it usually does, with responsibility and asset ownership being retained and a mixture of public- and private-sector entities carrying out operational tasks. Service levels and material risks must be specified and costed.

Characteristics of the benchmark project are:

- project delivery by the Government, in the same way as it usually operates;
- same service levels as the private sector;
- all material risks are valued and included;
- competitive-neutrality adjustments are included for in-house bids;
- total capital and through-life costs are expressed as a net present cost (NPC).

The competitive-neutrality adjustment is needed if there are government in-house bids. The adjustment typically involves full costing of overheads and the inclusion of an appropriate commercial cost of capital, to ensure an in-house option is not given an unfair advantage.

Figure 16.5 shows the components of the PCB, all estimated as net present values:

- transferable risk, ideally to be taken by the contractor;
- retained risk, to be retained by the sponsor; and
- base cost, reliant on a good initial estimate.

The estimates are revised as the procurement proceeds, to assess:

- first, is PPP procurement better than direct purchase?
- later, does a specific PPP offer good value for money?

The evaluation of a specific PPP offer involves several steps:

- identifying general and tenderer-specific risks;
- reviewing the risk allocation;
- generating distributions of net present costs;
- adjusting for risk transfer assumptions different from the benchmark project;
- adjusting for competitive neutrality (if needed);
- comparing the adjusted bid price with the PCB (Figure 16.6).

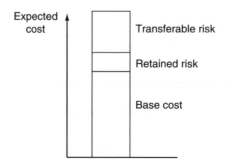

Figure 16.5—Components of the project cost benchmark

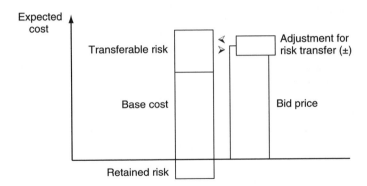

Figure 16.6—Comparing a bid with the PCB

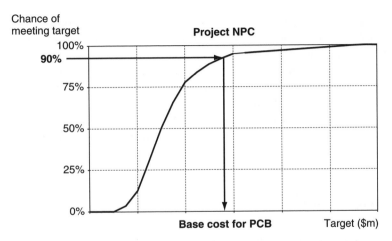

Figure 16.7—Setting the risk allowance

The base cost for the PCB includes an allowance for risk (Figure 16.7). The graph shows the way in which the chance of achieving the target (on the vertical axis) increases as the cost target (on the horizontal axis) increases. A policy decision is required to set the percentile at which risk is priced. In this example, the percentile has been set initially at 90%. This is relatively conservative – it implies only a 10% chance of failing to achieve the cost target. Note that this distribution has a long tail to the right; setting targets and budgets becomes an interesting exercise in balancing risk and reward in these circumstances, and additional attention must be paid to risk management and project management.

We have participated in one PPP where the 95-percentile was used, and in another where the 50-percentile was preferred. (Using the 50-percentile seems overly optimistic, while the 95-percentile might be a bit too conservative. It depends on the agency's appetite for risk.) The same confidence level should be used for evaluating the cost estimates for bidders and the PCB.

Payment structuring

Under a PF initiative, the contractor is required to deliver a service to prescribed standards to meet specified capability requirements, and contractual payments are structured around the delivery of those services. The public sector should not be obliged to make any payments under a PF arrangement until the services are provided satisfactorily. Through the payment structure, the public sector implicitly transfers the risks of service delivery and the associated infrastructure provision to the PF contractor. The public sector in turn avoids all the risks associated with the process that produces the services and concentrates on its performance outcomes.

In effect, capital expenditure on a risk-laden asset is replaced by recurrent expenditure on a service for which the PF contractor bears the bulk of the risks. If this can be achieved at a full life cycle cost to the public sector that is less than the cost of acquiring and supporting the asset itself, while allowing for risks and competitive-neutrality considerations, the outcome may represent value for money.

There may be benefits to the contractor in refinancing the PF arrangement at some stage. Generally, the public sector does not share in any upside benefits of contractor refinancing, on the assumption that the opportunity to refinance following completion – when the risk profile lessens because commissioning risk is no longer relevant – has been factored into the tendered price. However, where the PF contractor receives a windfall gain from a refinancing as a result of lower interest margins or benchmark interest rates, the public sector may seek to share in those benefits. Where such an arrangement is sought, appropriate mechanisms must be provided in the terms and conditions of contract.

Extraneous risks

The likelihoods of occurrence of some risks such as natural events (fire, flood, cyclone, earthquake) are largely outside the control of the contracting parties. If the public sector were to insist that these risks be managed by the contractor, a high premium might be incurred. In such cases, the public sector might decide to either share the costs with the PF contractor or take on completely the overheads involved in mitigating the impact of a risk occurrence or the costs associated with risk recovery activities. Such arrangements must be expressly provided for in the terms and conditions of contract.

Risks such as changes to tax or employment laws, movements in exchange rates and inflation, which are beyond the control of either party but have a reasonable likelihood of occurring, must also be dealt with through express conditions within the contract. The long-term nature of PF arrangements should not preclude PF contractors from adjusting their prices from time to time to reflect changes in general price levels on pre-agreed formulae. Other economic changes may be best dealt with through an equilibrium adjustment clause in the contract providing for changes to the base contract price or escalation formulae.

Risk premiums

In theory, the public sector could transfer most risks associated with the provision of a capability to the private sector if the price it pays to transfer them is sufficiently high to create interest in industry and the contractor is prepared to manage them. Industry may be keen to assume risks for which the public sector would pay a high price relative to their likelihood and impact.

The question for the public sector is whether the risk premium to transfer a risk provides value for money, or whether by accepting the risk itself it would achieve a more cost-effective outcome across the life cycle of the capability. The project cost benchmark establishes mechanisms for pricing risks to ensure that the public sector is not charged an excessive risk premium. It is designed to assist in optimizing value for money in risk allocation and, in particular, determining when the public sector should retain a risk.

Comparative risk allocation table

Table 16.1 demonstrates a typical allocation of risks under a traditional procurement, compared to that under a PF initiative. As a part of the initial screening carried out to see if PF is appropriate for the provision of a capability, during RFT preparation and documentation, and in the detailed preparation for contract negotiations, the public sector should prepare a risk allocation table similar to Table 16.1, but without the traditional risk allocation column, as a guide to formal negotiations. The risk allocation table should represent a reasonable starting position for negotiations, not an ambit claim.

Communication and reporting

Risk communication includes any two-way communication between stakeholders about the existence, nature, form, severity or acceptability of risks. Failure to develop an effective PF risk communication strategy may result in:

- misunderstandings about the nature and scope of the requirement by the contractor;
- underestimation of the complexity of the requirement by public-sector stakeholders; and
- underestimation of the complexity of public-sector culture by the contractor and consequently underestimation of the need for and scope of the integration of its business processes into those of the public sector.

Reporting provides a mechanism for public-sector managers to ensure the contractor has thought through the main issues of risk and its management at an early stage of planning. The contractor should have provided a Risk Management Plan as part of the tender response, covering:

Table 16.1—Traditional and PF risk allocation

No.	Risk	Description	Risk allocation	
			Traditional	*PF*
1	**Location**			
	Site selection	The selected site is not suitable for the capability	Public sector	Public sector
	Site conditions	The conditions on the site make construction difficult	Contractor	Contractor
	Approvals	Approvals are delayed, or onerous conditions are imposed	Public sector/contractor	Public sector/contractor
	Native title	The site is subject to claims by indigenous owners, leading to disputes, delays and compensation payments	Public sector	Public sector
	Cultural heritage	The site is subject to heritage or preservation conditions that impose additional design and construction costs	Public sector/contractor	Public sector/contractor
2	**Design**			
	Design parameters	The equipment, system or facility fails to meet design standards	Public sector	Contractor
	Design fit for purpose	The design fails to meet the performance specifications	Public sector/contractor	Contractor
	Design inter-operability	The equipment, system or facility is incompatible and fails to operate with other equipment or systems	Public sector	Contractor
	Design system integration	System and sub-system designs do not facilitate complete integration	Contractor	Contractor
	Design interface	The provided systems are unable to interface with public sector systems	Public sector/contractor	Public sector/contractor
	Design acceptance	Public sector stakeholders will not accept the design	Public sector/contractor	Contractor
3	**Construction or acquisition**			
	Technology and technical issues	Suitability and reliability of components, sub-systems and infrastructure to meet production standards and performance requirements. Complexity of design, integration and interface complexities	Public sector/contractor	Contractor
	Variations	Risks that arise as a consequence of variations to the scope, design or capability of the asset	Public sector	Contractor

(Continued opposite)

Delivery schedule and costs	Risks associated with maintaining the delivery schedules, costs of components, materials and labour	Public sector/ contractor	Contractor
Bank guarantees and performance bonds	Risk associated with obtaining the necessary guarantees or bonds for the amounts specified, and the risk that underperformance may result in these being called upon	Contractor	Contractor
Insurance cover	Risks associated with maintaining insurance cover and the volatility of insurance premiums	Public sector	Contractor
Security measures	Commercial and security risks (personnel and systems) and system security against hacking and virus attacks	Public sector/ contractor	Public sector/contractor
Environmental matters	Environmental risks, such as the presence of existing rare fauna or flora	Contractor	Contractor
Community acceptance	The community does not accept the activity in its vicinity	Public sector	Contractor/ public sector
Asset acceptance	The asset fails delivery acceptance trials	Contractor	Public sector
Force majeure	Obligations under the contract are suspended because the contract becomes frustrated	Public sector/ contractor	Public sector/contractor
Custody of information including duty to provide and to withhold access	Risks associated with acquiring proprietary information, including failure to obtain export licences for equipment or systems	Public sector/ contractor	Contractor
4 Finance			
Asset financing	Risks associated with acquiring the necessary finance to fund the acquisition of the asset	Public sector	Contractor/financier
Interest rates	Volatility of interest rates over the period of the contract	Contractor	Contractor/financier
Exchange rate fluctuations	Volatility of exchange rates over the period of the contract, for those elements of the asset purchased overseas	Public sector	Contractor

(Continued over leaf)

Table 16.1—(Continued)

No.	Risk	Description	Risk allocation	
			Traditional	*PF*
	Price escalation	Volatility of inflation over the period of the contract and the impact it will have on prices associated with the acquisition, maintenance of the asset and the provision of services	Public sector	Contractor (acquisition); Public sector (asset ownership and provision of services)
	Tax and industrial law changes	Risk of changes to the tax laws and the impact it may have on labour and material costs, overhead rates etc. during procurement or through life services	Public sector	Public sector / contractor/investor
5	**Quality assurance**			
	Quality assurance	The equipment, system or facility acquired does not meet specified quality standards	Contractor	Contractor
6	**Ownership and provision of services**			
	Performance	The asset does not meet performance specifications and consequently fails to satisfy public sector performance objectives	Public sector	Contractor/financier/ public sector
	Technology and technical issues	The technology acquired is unreliable, technically complex or expensive to maintain, or its market volatility results in early obsolescence	Public sector	Contractor/financier
	Demand	The utilization demand for the asset is different from that estimated by the public sector	Public sector	Public sector
	Third-party revenue	The third-party revenue stream is different from that expected	Not applicable	Contractor/financier
	Accidental damage or loss	Accident or loss due to negligence, misadventure or natural events	Public sector	Contractor
	Repairs and maintenance	Poor estimation of mean time between failures, mean time between repairs, failure rates, or costs of labour and materials	Public sector	Contractor
	Availability	The asset is not available at the times and places required to meet public sector operational needs	Public sector	Contractor/financier
	Human resource availability	Staff turnover, availability of suitably skilled and experienced staff	Public sector	Contractor

(Continued opposite)

Industrial disputes	Volatility of the labour force providing the service	Contractor/ public sector	Contractor
Occupational health and safety (HSE)	Failure to maintain HSE standards	Public sector	Contractor
Insurance	Failure to maintain appropriate insurance cover over the period of the contract	Public sector	Contractor
Business continuity	The capacity to continue providing the required service in the event of a major or extreme risk occurrence	Public sector	Contractor/financier
Regulatory	Failure to meet statutory requirements	Public sector	Contractor/ public sector
Facility or infrastructure viability	The asset is under-utilized or the estimated return on investment is such that the venture is not commercially viable	Not applicable	Contractor/financier
7 Disposal			
Residual value	The anticipated return on sale of the asset is less than anticipated	Public sector	Contractor/financier
Disposal	The asset cannot be sold, and other risks associated with disposal of the asset such as removal of unwanted waste material or equipment	Public sector	Contractor

- the risks identified by the contractor, with an indication of their potential severity and the ways in which they will be managed; and
- the processes and structures the contractor intends to use for risk management throughout the provision of services, including the role of the public sector.

Throughout the period of the contract, the contractor should be required to report on those risks at regular intervals. Similarly, PF management organizations within the public sector should report on the current status of risks and risk management to senior public-sector management.

Examples of private financing risks and treatments

Table 16.2 provides examples of risks that may be encountered in a PF initiative. The list is not exhaustive, and other risks not on this list are likely to arise from time to time. Table 16.2 also indicates some of the risk treatment options that may be available to control the risks or reduce the exposure.

Please note that the treatments shown are examples only. They may not suit the context of your particular project, and they may not be feasible given your project's specific circumstances. Use Table 16.2 as a guide, and with care.

Table 16.2—Examples of PF risks and treatments

Category	Examples of risks	Examples of treatment options
Assurance of supply	• The service provider goes out of business or encounters difficulties in supplying the service through the required life of the capability. • Material or spares become hard to source or become obsolete. • Contract terms for provision of services become unworkable or unenforceable due to changes in the external environment.	• Choose a financially robust supplier with a good business record. Require performance and financial guarantees to be included in the contract. • Incorporate tighter controls within the contract for ongoing life-of-type support. • Choose widely used commercial items. • Ensure contracts are adaptable, flexible and provide for equitable adjustment and contract changes.
Commercial	• Support for acquisition is not guaranteed over long periods. • Financial or maintenance systems are not compatible between suppliers, users and the public sector. • Government does not understand the new PF environment in which the public sector and industry must interact, and it is not able to facilitate the necessary relationships. • The way organizations function and business is conducted changes over the prolonged period of a PF arrangement. • The residual value of assets at the end of the PF contract is uncertain. • The asset acquired may cease to be the most effective solution to the requirement during the life of the PF arrangement. • The costs and benefits of price changes are not reflected appropriately in the contractual arrangement. • Contractors cannot guarantee the availability of critical personnel. • The use of offshore contractors causes practical administration problems.	• Incorporate tight controls within the contract for ongoing support. • Identify systems and equipment with which compatibility is required and require tenderers to demonstrate how they will comply with public-sector compatibility requirements. • Undertake independent audits on a regular basis to ensure that business relationships remain at arms length. • Ensure the public sector retains employees with appropriate project and contract management skills. • Negotiate allocation of ownership risks, including depreciation, with the contractor. • Structure the contractual agreement to ensure contractor services keep pace with technological development. • Include provision for equitable adjustment in the contract and ensure project staff possess appropriate financial management skills. • Require contractors to maintain critical skill sets and link to contractor performance guarantees.

(Continued over leaf)

Table 16.2—(Continued)

Category	Examples of risks	Examples of treatment options
Contractual	• There may be restrictions on the deployment of contractor personnel in operational areas. • Economic volatility requires adjustments to equilibrium PF arrangements. • Technology changes alter the way we do business. • Short-term considerations may override long-term PF arrangements. • Predicted demand volumes may not be as high as envisaged. • There are latent defects within existing infrastructure. • *Force majeure* may prevent the PF contractor from performing the contract. • Appropriate performance measures are not available, data has not been collected or is not collectable, or the base for comparison is not available for effective performance benchmarking.	• Develop contract clauses dealing with deployment of contractors to areas of operations. • Build flexibility into contract arrangements. • Include in the contract public sector 'step-in' and remedial rights in case of a default or *force majeure* situation. • Initiate early collection of performance data for the current process to allow realistic performance targets to be set and monitored.
Financial	• The public sector may have to invest in developing contractor knowledge of the business, and may have to contribute to the contractor's investment in such development. • Entering into long-term PF arrangements may lock in a significant proportion of public sector funding, thereby limiting flexibility to respond to new priorities. • Contractors require investment to develop a rapid-response capability. • Long-term exposure to foreign currency fluctuations • Stability of pricing over long contractual periods • The contractor may not remain financially stable over the life of contract.	• Provide industry briefings and contractor awareness programmes. • Ensure long-term public-sector budgeting includes project long-term bids. • Require tenderers to demonstrate their ability to meet short-term surge requirements. • Transfer foreign currency fluctuation risk to a central treasury agency or a financier who has responsibility for management of such risks. • Tie prices to robust and relevant indices, and provide equitable adjustment clauses within contracts. • Include in the contract a requirement to report on key business indicators to highlight financial duress and allow the public

(Continued opposite)

Category	Risk	Mitigation
	Initial risk-sharing arrangements, income streams, performance incentives and penalties may not be suitable over the life of a long contract.	sector to initiate a 'step-in' or remedial right under the contract.
	Insurance premiums for contractor equipment and personnel may be more expensive than for the public sector.	Ensure only essential insurance is purchased. Where the risk of loss is so high as to render insurance prohibitive, the public sector may have to assume the risk, even if it is not considered tolerable for the project.
	The contractor may fail to set aside from the regular contract payments sufficient funds for major capital equipment replacement or refurbishment.	Require the contractor to establish an independent 'sinking fund' for major capital items and equipment purchases.
Industrial	Different industrial agreements between the contractor and the public sector may create tension over prolonged periods.	Ensure project management staff skill sets are maintained to ensure competent management of both public sector and contract staff.
Operational	The contractor's resources may be limited and unable to support changing business needs.	Require tenderers to demonstrate capacity to meet surge requirements.
	Medical fitness of contractor staff may not be sufficient for deployment in hostile or remote area activities.	Include the development of contractor support preparedness in planning.
	Deployment of civilians in hostile or remote areas may cause unique problems (support obligations, political debate, new employment terms)	Avoid the risk by not allowing civilian contractors into hostile or remote areas.
	Contractor may not want to participate in a particular business for fear of gaining a bad reputation.	Where it is possible that contractor personnel may need to participate in deployed operations, include the potential requirement in draft contract material and tender evaluation criteria.

(Continued over leaf)

Table 16.2—(Continued)

Category	Examples of risks	Examples of treatment options
Security	• The use of PF contractors in some public-sector businesses may raise specific security issues. • The contractor's security integrity may not meet operational management information systems requirements.	• Ensure contractor and contractor personnel are appropriately security-cleared and possess appropriate facilities security clearances. • Conduct security audits of contractor management information systems (MISs), and require contractors to adhere to public sector MIS security requirements.
Supportability	• The contractor may not be able to vary supply either upwards or downwards, for example to meet operational contingencies or surge requirements, at an acceptable cost. • The contractor may not be able to provide support over geographically dispersed locations. • Conditions of employment of contractor staff may not ensure that the contractor is able to provide intense or sustained support when needed. • Contractor communication equipment may not be inter-operable with public-sector users. • Civilian contractors may rely on public-sector transport for access to remote areas.	• Include flexibility in the contract to allow reasonable variation in demand, with equitable adjustments. • Require tenderers to demonstrate capacity to meet surge requirements at short notice. • Allow tenderers to engage sub-contractors with equivalent skills to provide support in geographically dispersed locations.
Regulatory	• Legislative and regulatory constraints may limit the public sector's ability to negotiate commercial arrangements with contractors. • Laws or regulations may change in a way that affects the operation of the service being provided. These changes may be discriminatory, affecting a particular area of business, or affecting a whole sector of industry. • Over the term of a PF arrangement, there may be changes to taxation legislation that have material adverse effects on the contractor.	• Ensure draft contracts have the flexibility to provide for changes in law, including circumstances where contracts may be frustrated. • Include equitable price adjustment clauses within draft contracts to provide for changes to legislation that may impact upon the base contract price. • Determine whether the public sector will carry the risks associated with major tax changes, and include appropriate provisions in draft contracts.

TECHNICAL TOOLS AND TECHNIQUES

17

Chapter overview

- ### Purpose

  This chapter illustrates the use and application of several important tools for technical risk and hazard assessment.

- ### Rationale

  Appropriate technical analysis tools are used to augment the general risk management process and improve its effectiveness and efficiency in particular circumstances. They are generally used in the risk identification and assessment stages and often associated with safety and environmental risks.

- ### Method

  Specific techniques outlined in this chapter include:

  - hazard and operability studies (Hazops);
  - fault tree analysis;
  - event tree analysis;
  - rapid risk ranking; and
  - risk contours and threshold risk curves.

- ### Inputs, Outputs and Documentation

  The form of the inputs, outputs and documentation depends on the specific analysis tool to be used. Examples are provided through the chapter.

Risks and hazards

Technical risk and hazard assessment is a particular sub-set of project risk assessment that usually targets specific safety, environmental and associated regulatory requirements. The technical assessment techniques outlined here provide specific approaches to different parts of the general risk management process described in earlier chapters, applied in a technical framework. The intent of this chapter is not to provide a detailed description of all the tools that might be used in a technical risk assessment, as that is beyond the scope of this book, but rather to indicate some of the more widely used approaches that have broad application and the integration with general project risk management. Many sources provide more specific guidance; for example, see the excellent books by Tweeddale (2003) and Green (1982).

Employees, managers, unions and the public require a high standard of safety in projects and facilities, and good safety practice is often an enforceable requirement of regulatory authorities. Demonstrating a tolerable level of safety is part of obtaining necessary approvals from regulators, stakeholders and internal authorities. Technical risk and hazard assessments, studies and management plans often play a key part in obtaining these approvals. Safety and land-use planning legislation in many countries requires formal risk assessments to be undertaken for proposed and existing hazardous installations. Regulatory authorities often use quantitative risk assessments to assess whether the risks imposed by a hazardous installation on the public and surrounding land uses satisfy specified risk criteria, including criteria relating to individual fatalities and societal risk.

In his report on the Piper Alpha disaster in which 167 lives were lost, Lord Cullen (1990) recommended that the safety management system implemented by a facility should be a key component of the case being made that a facility is safe. His requirements referenced the six fundamentals for safe operation referred to by Hawksley (1987). These can be summarized as:

1. Hazards must be recognized and their risks must be understood by management.
2. Appropriate equipment and facilities must be provided to reduce the risks to a level as low as reasonably practicable (ALARP).
3. Systems and procedures must exist to operate that equipment in a satisfactory manner within the design intent and to maintain its integrity.
4. Appropriate staff must be provided and given sufficient information, instruction, supervision and training to operate the equipment, systems and procedures.
5. Adequate arrangements must exist to detect and control emergencies.
6. Effective systems must exist for promoting safety, auditing safety performance and progressing safety issues.

All six fundamentals are required, and effective technical risk and hazard assessment is essential to achieving Fundamentals 1 and 2.

In addition, the technical analysis undertaken for safety and environmental reasons, when applied correctly and at the appropriate stage of the project, leads to a better and more efficient design for the facility, and hence to better and more efficient facility operations and improved project economics.

Technical risk and hazard assessments

There are many kinds of hazard study techniques, most of which perform a part or parts of the hazard study process very well. The challenge is to understand the information requirements and deliverables of each technique and to match these with the current project status, resources and requirements.

Early in the life of a project, when there are few design and engineering details and the requirement is to identify issues that could affect the performance of the facility, the cost or the implementation schedule in a way that affects the validity of project estimates, coarse non-specific techniques are most applicable. These should address:

- hazardous materials;
- hazardous process conditions;
- hazards associated with energy sources;
- hazards associated with movement;
- hazards associated with failure of a utility or loss of control;
- hazardous operational and maintenance activities; and
- externally caused hazards or natural perils.

Later in the project more detailed, specific and often targeted techniques are most applicable.

Many projects require a series of technical risk and hazard assessments throughout their lives, in the areas indicated in Table 17.1 and Figure 17.1, often using progressively more sophisticated techniques. As always getting the early design right will minimize the overall effect on the project. Risks that can be eliminated early in the design phase may have a relatively minor impact on cost, schedule and performance, but to retrofit protection systems late in the design has the potential to cause delays, unbudgeted cost increases and reduced plant availability and performance.

Concept hazard analyses and preliminary hazard analyses are often completed as part of feasibility studies, when overall project economics and regulatory approvals are reviewed and a decision is made about whether to proceed to project implementation. These preliminary studies identify the main factors that may affect the project schedule and cash flows significantly. However, many of the detailed technical designs are not yet complete in a feasibility study, so these preliminary technical risk and hazard assessments form the basis for continuing and more detailed assessments as the technical design and the project plan are refined in later phases of the project.

The type and timing of technical risk and hazard assessments and management plans depends on the information available at the time and the requirements of the design, construction, operations and approval authorities. The staged programme depicted in Figure 17.1 is based on currently accepted best practice. Many of the stages generate risks that should be included in the risk register for the project.

Table 17.1—Detailed technical risk assessments

Assessment	Purpose, focus	Integration
Concept hazard analysis	To review the concept design and identify significant hazards, to provide an opportunity for their elimination or minimization by changes to the fundamental concepts, re-design or byincorporating protective measures. Depending on the re-formulations of the project this study may be performed several times until a feasible concept is accepted. An output of the concept risk analysis is a plan for further risk and hazard studies throughout the life of the project.	Normally performed as part of the concept design or pre-feasibility study phase. The hazard study is linked to the project risk assessment and risks associated with significant hazards are incorporated in the project risk register. Value improvement exercises may be conducted in this phase. The risks and hazards of proposed changes must be assessed and managed.
Preliminary hazard analysis (PHA)	To extend the concept risk analysis as the design develops and much more information on the materials, quantities, process conditions, mechanical design and operational strategies becomes available. The PHA includes more detailed technical and hazard analyses, with feedback into the design process to eliminate or reduce risks and hazards. It is also often a requirement of the approval authorities.	Performed during preliminary design and feasibility studies including bankable feasibility studies. Linked to project risk management with significant risks, in particular those defined as major accident events, being incorporated into the project risk register. Changes from value improvement exercises are assessed and managed.
Hazard and operability study (Hazop)	To examine the proposed process systems, equipment and procedures systematically and in detail, through the use of a structured brainstorming process using guidewords to prompt examination of deviations from the design conditions. The objective is to identify the potential hazards to people, the environment, the plant or operations. A control system Hazop (Chazop) study is a variant that is used where the complexity or importance of the control system warrants it. Many approval authorities require formal Hazop studies.	Performed when the detailed design information becomes available, such as piping and instrument diagrams (P&IDs) and control strategies. A preliminary Hazop study may be performed early if beneficial in large projects, but the full Hazop study must still be performed. Safety integrity level (SIL) determination may need to be incorporated with an effective hazard identification technique. A Hazop study is suited to feed into SIL determination.
Fire safety study (FSS)	To study the specific causes and impacts of fires, and the means of treating them, including fire safety design, equipment, systems and procedures for preventing, detecting and extinguishing fires. Many approval authorities require a formal FSS.	Performed when the detailed information on the hazardous inventories and storage arrangements has been finalized, including in-plant inventories. The FSS should follow from the earlier hazard studies. It concentrates on fire and explosion prevention, protection and mitigation requirements.
Construction safety study (CSS)	To review the construction plan, identify major hazards and specify changes or procedures to reduce the risks from those	Linked to constructability and general construction risks in the project risk register.

(Continued opposite)

	hazards to as low as reasonably practicable. Many approval authorities require a formal CSS.	
Construction occupational health and safety study	To review the project safety management plan in relation to agreed project standards, with a focus on HSE issues.	Linked to the size and types of construction risks and generally dictated by the owner's, engineer's and contractor's safety policies and the requirements of the authorities.
Safety management system review (SMS review)	To review the systems and procedures for monitoring and maintaining the integrity of the plant during commissioning, operations and maintenance. A satisfactory SMS is a critical part of a safety case, or a similar report required for licensing a major hazardous facility.	A safety management system should be developed as the design evolves, but involving the eventual operator closely throughout. This is generally dictated by the owner's and engineer's safety policies and the requirements of the permitting authorities.
Operations occupational health and safety study (HSE study)	To review the operations safety management plan in relation to agreed project standards, with a focus on HSE issues.	The HSE study should follow from the earlier hazard studies. It concentrates on hazardous materials and activities.
Emergency response plan (ERP) or emergency management plan	Plans for dealing with identified emergencies during construction, commissioning and operations, including major fires, explosions or toxic releases, with a focus on the safety of people and plant. Many approval authorities require a formal ERP.	The ERP is based on the major accident events identified in previous studies. The response plan is part of the mitigation of the consequences of these events. The ERP may be part of a contingency plan or an overall business continuity plan.
Safety report	To provide a written report covering the hazards identified, the controls and the safety management systems in place to manage the risks. It strongly emphasizes the management of potential major accident events and the maintenance of the integrity of the plant and the procedures for operating it. This report is often a requirement for approval of a major hazardous facility. In the off-shore oil and gas industry this study is referred to as the safety case.	The safety report is a formal compilation of the prior hazard studies and safety systems reviews. It also incorporates emergency response plans.
Environmental management plan	Plans for dealing with identified emergencies during construction, commissioning and operations, including major fires, explosions or toxic releases, with a focus on minimizing their environmental impacts. Plans for monitoring and controlling events and toxic releases with potential long-term consequences for the environment or people.	The environmental management plan is a treatment plan for those risks that can affect the environment. In many instances it will be linked to the FSS and the ERP.

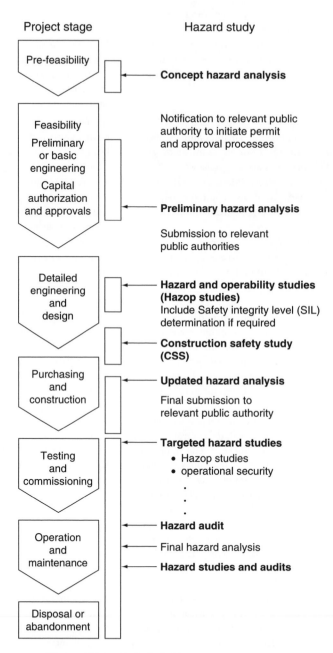

Figure 17.1—Technical risk assessment programme

Hazard study techniques

Most of the hazard study techniques are consistent with the basic risk management process, as outlined in Figure 17.2. Communication and consultation, and monitoring and review, all apply equally to both processes.

Table 17.2 lists some common hazard study techniques and provides an indication of when each may be applicable across the full chain of events associated with an initiating failure and discharge, from root causes at the top to the final consequences of an event at the bottom.

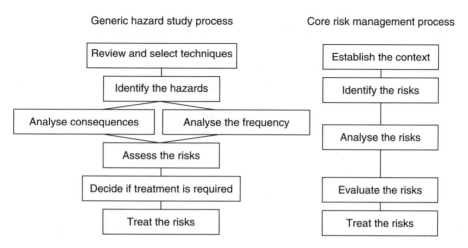

Figure 17.2—Hazard study and risk management processes

Table 17.2—Range of applicability of hazard study techniques

Event chain	Hazard study technique				
	Coarse techniques, what if and checklists	Hazop, Chazop studies	FMEA, FMECA	Fault tree analysis	Event tree analysis
Root cause of failure and discharge			✓		
Immediate causes of failure and discharge		✓	✓	✓	
Plant is in a dangerous state		✓	✓	✓	
Failure to control the situation		✓	✓	✓	
Unplanned release of material	✓	✓	✓	✓	
Escalating event and failure mitigation	✓	✓			✓
Consequences to people, plant, business and environment					✓

Hazard identification

There are many techniques for hazard identification, some of which are listed in Table 17.3. They range from coarse approaches for preliminary assessments to more detailed methods. Techniques for initial assessments include 'what-if' analyses, checklists and general reviews of hazardous materials and process conditions. More detailed tools include Hazop studies, Chazop studies, failure modes and effects analyses (FMEA), failure modes, effects and criticality analyses (FMECA) and safety integrity level (SIL) determination studies. As can be seen from the descriptions, many of these techniques (such as Hazop studies) take the process further than just hazard identification.

Hazard and operability study (Hazop)

A Hazop study is a common identification technique used to examine proposed systems, equipment and procedures systematically and in detail. Its objective is to identify potential hazards to people, the environment, the plant or operations and the proposed methods for their control. It particularly examines the effects of deviations from the design intent by asking a series of questions based on prompts or guide words: for example, 'High pressure, how might it arise? If it did arise, what would be the potential consequences?'

A Hazop study is usually conducted when the design for a proposed system, plant or production unit is at or nearing completion. Piping and instrument diagrams (P&IDs), sometimes termed process and instrument diagrams, are usually available, the control strategy including start-up and shutdown has been defined and the basic operating procedures have been specified.

Like the general risk management process described in earlier chapters, a Hazop begins by defining a set of key elements. Usually these are the main process lines or flow lines through sections of the plant, identified from the P&IDs, and the analysis begins as soon in the design process as they are available. Key elements could also be identified from process flow sheets if the Hazop is being conducted at an early design stage, as in a concept hazard analysis or preliminary hazard analysis.

Preferably the study is facilitated by an experienced independent person and includes appropriate management, design, operations and maintenance personnel with a direct involvement in the project. The process works systematically through the design, examining each item on each flow line in detail. For each item, the facilitator asks a series of questions based on guide words, such as those listed in Table 17.4. These are designed to stimulate the analysis team to think about how situations described by the key word might arise – possible causes or sources of risk. The flow line is examined for all possible deviations relating to each guide word.

For each potential deviation, the team identifies the cause of the deviation and its consequences for the plant as a whole. Assessments of the probability and severity of each potential deviation may be used to set priorities for management action.

Figure 17.3 illustrates the process. The elements are usually the specific flow lines, process flows, process steps or equipment items on the P&IDs. The process should be systematic and complete, addressing all the elements and all the guidewords.

Table 17.3—Common hazard identification techniques

Technique	Information required	Approach	Deliverable
What-if analysis	Preliminary design information such as basic process flows and conditions and a list of the main hazardous materials	Structured facility-specific list of what-if...? questions applied systematically across the facility	List of hazards inherent in the proposed process and materials
Checklists	Preliminary design information	Use generic checklists systematically across the facility	List of hazards, but may miss hazards specific to the particular application. More powerful when used in combination with a 'What if....?' analysis
Hazop study (IEC 61882)	Detailed design information including P&IDs or equivalent, control and safety system strategy	Detailed systematic review of each process step, process line or equipment item, explicitly examining deviations from the design intent	List of detailed hazards, their consequences and proposed rectification actions
Chazop study	Detailed design information including P&IDs or equivalent, control and safety system logic and sequences	Detailed systematic review of each control function, explicitly examining deviations from the design intent	List of detailed hazards associated with the control system and proposed rectification actions
Preliminary Hazop study	Preliminary design information including process flow diagrams and most P&IDs (but still in draft), combined with vendors' typical drawings	Systematic review of each major process step, process line or equipment item, explicitly examining deviations from the design intent	List of hazards and proposed rectification actions
SIL determination study (IEC 61508)	Basic design information including P&IDs or equivalent and control strategy	Often performed as an add-on to a Hazop study, rating the risk associated with each potential hazard without any proposed protection system	List of ranked hazards and the level of protection required to reduce each hazard to tolerable levels
FMEA	Basic design information including P&IDs or equivalent, controls and safety system strategy; if being applied to a single problem area, a detailed breakdown of the components	Systematically examines each item and determines how that item may fail and the consequences of a failure	Detailed list of the hazards caused from internal failures; may miss issues associated with human systems and external events, but can be applied with care to activities
FMECA	As for the FMEA, plus an agreed set of criticality (risk) rating scales	The hazards identified by the FMEA process are rated according to their criticality (risk)	Detailed ranked list of the hazards arising from internal failures

Table 17.4—A sample of Hazop guide words, adapted from Green (1982)

Guide word	Description	Examples
none	Nothing when there should be something	No flow, reverse flow
more of	More of the associated aspect than there should be	High flow, high temperature, high pressure, high viscosity
less of	Less of the associated aspect than there should be	Low flow, low temperature, low pressure, low viscosity
part of	Composition different from what it should be	Missing components, changed ratios
more than	More components in the system than there should be	Impurities present, extra phase
other	Other sources of deviation	Start up, shut down, different operating conditions, services failure, etc.

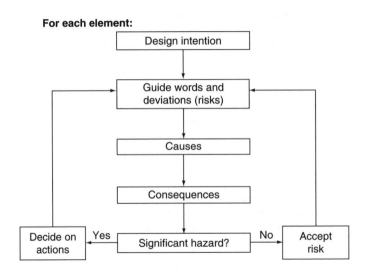

Figure 17.3—The Hazop study process

The process is iterative. Once all the guidewords have been studied for an element the next element is selected systematically and studied.

The Hazop study process must be documented in detail, to record the element or item being examined, the guideword and potential causes of a hazard, the consequences, existing safeguards and protective measures, the proposed actions to eliminate or reduce the risks and the responsibilities assigned.

Table 17.5 shows an example of a typical Hazop study recording sheet. This was developed as part of the initial hazard analysis for the coal handling and feed plant for a large kiln being constructed to expand the capacity of an existing facility. This Hazop study was part of a series of studies directed to improving safety and gaining regulatory approvals, including quantitative fire safety studies.

The Hazop study process should include formal design change and review procedures to monitor the status and progress of actions to implement the recommended modifications to

Table 17.5—Hazop record sheet: case example

Project: *Kiln Project*
Drawing: *123–1 Rev A, 456 Rev C*

Section: *Coal handling*

Date: *12 December*
Revision: *Draft*

Node	Guideword	Causes	Consequences	Safeguards	Action	Manager	Comments and status
1 Raw coal unloading	Position	Ignition from truck or front-end loader engine	Coal dust and explosion		Design means of controlling where dumping occurs. Western door must be closed at all times when coal is being delivered.		
2 Raw coal unloading	Movement	Coal left in corners for long periods	Undisturbed coal can self-ignite		Consider means of keeping corners free of coal for longer periods. Ensure no loader movement when there is a dusty environment.		
3 Raw coal unloading	High Temperature	Coal delivered hot and smouldering	Undetected coal fire		Consider thermocouples in the concrete to detect high temperature and/or a manual survey.		
4 Raw coal unloading	Low Temperature	Moisture content in coal freezes	Big lumps going into the plant	Front-end loader will break up some lumps	Screen on top of raw coal hopper.		
5 Raw coal unloading	Maintenance	No personnel doors in the roller doors and controls are outside	Person unable to egress from coal storage if doors closed		Consider operational philosophy of restricting access to the coal store.		
6 Raw coal hopper	Load	Overload	Spillage		Design some control to indicate when not to dump into the hopper.		
7 Raw coal hopper	Contamination	Rags, concrete, etc. in coal	Contamination of feed into the plant	Regular visual inspections of the hopper	Screen on top of hopper		

(Continued over leaf)

Table 17.5—(Continued)

Node		Guideword	Causes	Consequences	Safeguards	Action	Manager	Comments and status
8	Elevator	Movement	Friction and sparks, e.g. from broken buckets, combined with dusty environment as bucket tips over the top of the elevator	Explosion with missiles and fire ball		Ensure personnel clear of elevator during its operation.		
9	Elevator	Load	Spillage in boot will self-ignite over time if not cleaned up	Fire		Check elevator design for curved plating in boot or other means of controlling build-up.		
10	Mill feed system	Position	Low moisture content in coal increases dust content and explosion more likely	Coal dust explosion		Discuss with coal suppliers to provide coal with a minimum moisture content for safety reasons.		
11	Coal feed hopper	Movement	Hold-up in coal feed hopper	Coal left in hopper for long periods may self-ignite	Thermocouple to detect heating up of coal.	Determine optimum means of detecting hold-ups in coal feed hopper.		
12	Belt conveyor	Contamination	Metal in coal feed	Metal may damage equipment	Metal detector on belt conveyor	P&ID to show metal detector on belt conveyor.		

(Continued opposite)

No.	Component	Category	Cause	Consequence	Recommendation
13	Coal feed hopper	Process Control	Hold-up or rat holing in coal feed hopper and loss of coal feed means loss of air seal between feed hopper and mill	Loss of control of mill exit temperature due to excess air flow	Measure air pressure on the drag chain to detect air flow or provide other means of detecting loss of feed.
14	Drag chain	Electrical safety	Potential ignition source from the drag chain drive motor	Fire	Ensure the drive motor is rated to the appropriate area classification.
15	Coal mill	Movement	Excessive vibration	Mill damage over time	Investigate need for vibration monitoring.
16	Mill classifier	Movement	Broken classifier drive still running (when classifier not), but not detected. Will change the pressure drop across the mill.	Pressure drop change will mean that more coal will be fed into the mill and coarse product will be passed through the mill.	Check if zero speed switch is required for mill classifier.
17	Coal mill	Energy	Loss of power	Need back-up power for control systems and inerting system	Ensure back-up power provided in case of power failure of mill.
18	Coal mill	Maintenance	Existing personnel used to working with relatively unhazardous materials	Personnel unaware of hazards of liquified petroleum gas (LPG) and coal and may not handle these materials with appropriate care	Existing personnel need to be made very aware of hazards of coal and LPG and the importance of housekeeping. Formal operator training required.

19 . . .

the system. Additional Hazop studies should be performed as necessary to examine the effects of proposed and implemented changes.

Fault trees

Fault tree analysis is an important specialist technique for risk assessment, with significant extensions into quantitative aspects of risk analysis. It is a process, derived from systems engineering, for identifying and representing the logical combinations of causes, system states and risks that could lead to or contribute to a specified failure event, often termed the top event.

Fault tree analysis provides a structure for estimating the likelihood of the top event by tracing back the causes until it has identified simple events or component states for which the likelihood can be estimated. The analysis is continued until a set of base events is reached, sufficient to understand the nature of the failure processes and how they may be managed. Typically the top event is a system failure or undesired outcome, and the process attempts to identify the possible causes that might lead to the undesired outcome and its frequency.

Fault trees are constructed using two types of logical connection, 'AND' gates and 'OR' gates. Figure 17.4 shows a simple example of how a failure in a pressure vessel might arise and be represented as a fault tree. An AND gate is used when a fault tree component *and* another component must both be in the required state for the event to propagate; for example, the pressure vessel would only fail if there were both an over-pressure *and* the relief valve did not open. An OR gate is used if the failure event is propagated if either one component *or* another component is in a particular state; for example, the relief valve might fail to open if there were a failure of the safety valve itself in a closed position *or* if the isolation valve were closed manually by an operator.

Figure 17.5 shows a simple domestic example of a fault tree, based on an analysis of a particular undesired event: having to take a cold shower! The shower may be cold if there

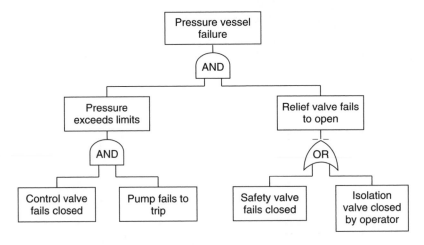

Figure 17.4—Example of a fault tree for a pressure vessel failure

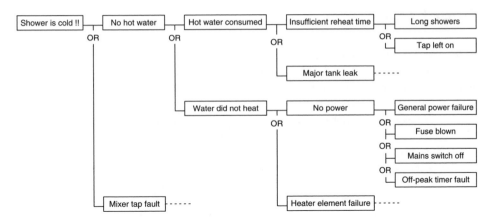

Figure 17.5—Fault trees: domestic example

is no hot water, or if the tap is faulty; lack of hot water may be due to excessive use or failure to heat; and so on.

Figure 17.6 shows an abbreviated fault tree for a cutter dredge involved in hydraulic reclamation of sand and gravel from a river. This diagram illustrates that fault trees need not be confined to examining technical hazards. They provide a logical way of decomposing a complex problem, in this case concerned with economic production rates for a class of dredge, and identifying areas of threat to the desired outcomes, in this case the production rate of the dredge measured in tonnes of solid material extracted in each period. All the relationships are 'OR' – a reduction in production rate occurs if any of the events on lower branches arises.

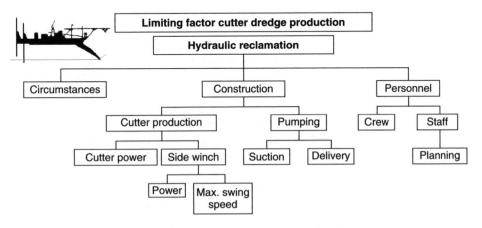

Figure 17.6—Fault trees: limiting factors for a dredge

Source: This diagram is based on information provided by Baggerman Associates, 1994. The dredge outline was also provided by Baggerman Associates.

Event trees

Event trees are used to show the patterns of events and consequences that may follow from one or more initiating events. The technique was developed in industries where individual and community safety was a key factor, such as the chemical or nuclear power industries. Here, the initiating events were typically failures in operating systems with the potential to lead to catastrophic explosions, fires or toxic releases to the air or the wider environment. The approach is now extended to many other areas in which an analysis is required of the potential outcomes of external events or failures in equipment or procedures.

The development of useful event trees requires a good analyst to generate the initial structure. It usually involves the key technical members of the project team, together with any specialists who can bring additional necessary expertise to the process.

Event tree analysis begins by listing and grouping the initiating events of interest. In many cases, the history of past failures provides an initial guide, supplemented by brainstorming and checklists as appropriate.

Initiating events are usually written at the top of the page. Next, events that follow each initiating event are written below. They are usually closely related to the safety systems and procedures that are in place to deal with the initiating event and the functions they are designed to perform, often in order of importance or chronological sequence. From each such event, branches are drawn corresponding to the success or failure of the associated safety system. The process is repeated for these 'first-layer' events, and so on, until a tree has been built to the level of detail necessary.

Each path in the tree corresponds to a specific accident sequence. If all the safety systems and procedures work as planned, the consequences are likely to be small. However, if the safety systems do not work fully, a range of more severe consequences may result. Probabilities and consequences can be quantified for the branches of the event tree, enabling the overall risk to the plant, its staff, the public and the environment to be assessed.

Event tree analysis has had wide application to any situation where the consequences of an initiating risk event are dependent not only on the event itself, but on the successful operation of safety systems or procedures, often through complex chains of intermediate events.

Figure 17.7 shows an event tree developed to examine the consequences of a catastrophic failure of a proposed tailings dam for a mine, to be located in a valley also used for farming. There are effects associated with the solid tailings material in the dam and the liquids. There may be physical effects – erosion, flooding, deposition – or there may be effects related to the particular tailings material in the dam, and particularly whether it is oxidized or acidified, or may become oxidized or acidified if dispersed by a dam failure. Specific impacts are related to loss of life and property, the environment and its use by the people who live nearby.

Figure 17.8 outlines in highly simplified form how fault trees and events trees were combined in the analysis of the costs of events and release modes for a set of options for an environmental remediation activity. The central 'hour glass' or 'bow tie' indicates the relationship between the fault tree analyses for determining the probability of initiating events and the event tree analyses for calculating their outcomes and impacts. In this case, event

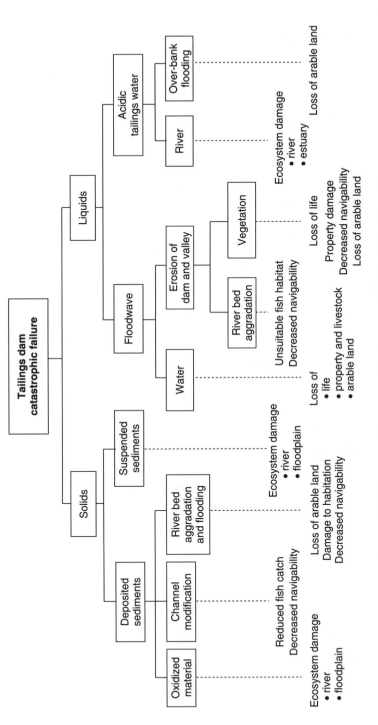

Figure 17.7—Case example: event tree for the catastrophic failure of a tailings dam

Source: This diagram is based on material supplied by Malcolm Lane of Lane Associates, Auckland.

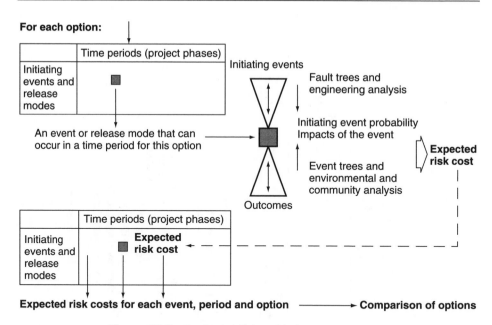

Figure 17.8—Combining fault tree and event tree analyses

probabilities were related to the durations of the relevant project phases, and the impacts were assessed as distributions of consequences.

Rapid risk ranking

Rapid risk ranking is a particular application of the general risk identification and assessment process described in earlier chapters. It was developed and is commonly applied to the identification of hazards and for determining their priorities for risk treatment. Applications and examples of rapid risk ranking are described by Tweeddale, Cameron and Sylvester (1992) and Tweeddale (2003).

Risk identification is a structured process (Figure 17.9):

- list the hazardous areas and potential sources of risk;
- list the possible kinds of incident or initiating events for each source; and
- list the specific consequences that may arise from each incident.

Risk analysis estimates consequences and likelihoods, commonly using qualitative or semi-quantitative scales. (What is described here is a typical method, but there are several other recognized rapid risk ranking methods.)

The severity of the consequences is often rated in terms of the effects of hazards on:

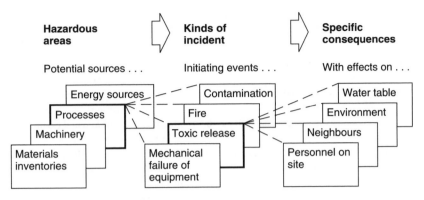

Figure 17.9—Risk identification

- people;
- property, plant, equipment and production; and
- the environment.

Likelihoods are based on estimates of the frequency of occurrence of the specific hazard and the probability that any controls will fail.

For each identified hazard, the level of risk is obtained by combining:

- the frequency of its occurrence;
- the probability the controls will fail; and
- the severity of the consequences.

For simplicity and speed, agreed scales and look-up tables or simple formulae are used. It is important that the scales be consistent. They must be appropriate for the hazards being examined, the objectives of the organization and the purpose of the assessment – refer to the discussion of the context in Chapter 2. Table 17.6 illustrates a typical consequence scale directed to safety and environmental impacts.

The outputs from a rapid risk ranking are a structured list of potential hazards, with priorities. The priorities can be compared against targets or other criteria to gauge hazard management performance, to identify hazards for which additional analyses are required, and to guide the development of action plans and the allocation of resources.

Representing the results of quantitative technical risk analyses

Some risk analysis approaches, like the rapid risk ranking described above, are designed to generate priorities or rankings that enable risks or hazards to be compared. Other tools

Table 17.6—Example of consequence scales

Rating	Description	People	Score	Environment	Score
A	Catastrophic	Multiple fatalities	##	Catastrophic long-term environmental harm	2 or more
B	Major	Single fatality	1	Major release of pollutants; significant environmental harm	1
C	Medium	Multiple serious injuries	0.5	Measurable environmental harm with medium-term recovery	0.5
D	Low	Serious injury requiring hospitalization	0.1	Transient release of pollutants; required to inform Environmental Protection Agency	0.1
E	Negligible	Minor injury	0.01	Brief transient pollution	0.01

Note: ## indicates the number of fatalities.

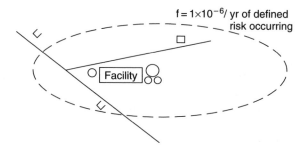

$f = 1 \times 10^{-6}/$ yr of defined risk occurring

Figure 17.10—Risk contour map

generate quantitative measures of consequences and the probabilities of those consequences arising.

There are many ways in which the overall risk from a quantitative technical risk analysis can be represented. For example, consider the risk of release of a hazardous material from a processing plant. Risk contours can be developed by combining all the consequence analysis results for each release scenario with the frequency of each scenario, and providing a combined expected risk value at each specific location. Locations of equal risk can be represented using risk contours on a plant layout, illustrated schematically in Figure 17.10.

More detailed and specific modelling may be required, according to the specific needs and circumstances. For example, analyses of gas cloud dispersion can be used to derive contours associated with specified levels of concentration or toxicity through time in the event of a toxic gas release. In some cases analyses of this kind may be very complex, requiring detailed modelling of such things as:

- the source and release rate of the gas;
- atmospheric dispersion rates;
- atmospheric stability, and wind speed and direction;

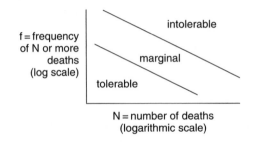

Figure 17.11—Threshold risk curves for regulatory use

- air flow turbulence (often linked to the physical site and structures) and entrainment of air;
- heating and heat transfer;
- density and gravitational slumping; and
- the effects of the gas cloud.

Models can be developed to show the effects of other hazards, for example the impacts of blast over-pressure as a consequence of an explosion.

Figure 17.11 shows a common form of risk threshold or f-N curve used to show the range of worker and public safety outcomes possible from a failure at a hazardous facility. The graph illustrates the frequency f with which a hazardous event will cause a specified number N of deaths.

Such diagrams are often used by regulators to determine whether a facility is 'safe enough' to receive an operating license. The axes commonly use logarithmic scales. The top-right region, with high frequencies of many deaths, is intolerable; the bottom-left region, where there are low frequencies and low impacts, is tolerable; the intermediate region usually requires treatment action to be undertaken if it is practicable. This central region is sometimes called the ALARP region, where the risk is reduced to as low as reasonably practicable. Even in the tolerable region, risk treatment actions should be considered as they may be worthwhile if they are cost-effective.

Conclusions

The tools and techniques discussed in this chapter support different stages in the general risk management process. For example, the following outline of a technical hazard process illustrates some of their applications.

- Identify all the initiating events or hazards that might cause a safety or environmental problem for the facility. Hazop studies provide a structured process for this.
- If required for each initiating event, construct a fault tree to model the interactions of the components and sub-components, how they might cause the initiating event to arise and the frequency of the top event.

- For each initiating event, use event trees to identify and model all of the scenarios or outcomes that might follow from its occurrence.
- Quantify the probabilities and the consequences of each outcome and thence determine the associated level of risk for each branch of the event tree. Combine the risks for the branches to determine the risk for each initiating event. Combine the risks for the initiating events to determine the risk for the facility itself.

There are many technical tools for risk and hazard assessment, all of which have their own strengths and weaknesses. The key is to use the most appropriate tools for the problems being addressed, and to involve technical experts when appropriate to ensure the tools are applied in the most effective way.

INTRODUCTION TO ENVIRONMENTAL RISK MANAGEMENT

18

Chapter overview

- ## Purpose

  This chapter summarizes general processes for environmental risk management.

- ## Rationale

  Many projects and associated industrial activities pose risks to the environment, and environmental issues present risks to the business itself if not addressed appropriately. Managing environmental risks is an important part of good project and business management.

- ## Method

  The recommended approach parallels the standard risk management approach except that there is more emphasis on the way in which an environmental exposure can develop. The concepts and processes are substantially the same, although the terminology differs in places.

- ## Documentation

  Documentation for environmental risks may be needed for several audiences, including managers, local communities and regulators. In some circumstances this may require more detail and different methods of presentation than that generated for other project risk management activities.

Benefits of environmental risk management

Project plans and appraisals should consider environmental risks, their impacts and their treatment. There are many reasons why organizations undertake environmental risk management as part of their project management activities.

- There is a regulatory requirement for it. In many jurisdictions, regulators require formal environmental impact studies and reports, to ensure environmental risks have been identified and adequate treatment measures to mitigate them have been included in project plans. Often the mitigation measures become a condition for project approval and licensing. Mitigation activities are likely to extend over all phases of a project and the whole life of the asset created by a project, from design and construction through operations and on to close-down and site rehabilitation.
- There is an ethical requirement for it. Many companies have codes of ethics and environmental conduct that require appropriate priority to be given to minimizing environmental damage and harm. This is part of the 'good citizen' role of companies. Environmental performance may also be included in the organization's triple-bottom-line and balanced scorecard reporting and monitoring systems.
- There is an economic reason for it. Identifying environmental risks and mitigating them early in the life of a project is usually far easier and cheaper than having to rectify problems and clean up a harmful environmental release. As well as direct financial benefits, avoiding environmental problems reduces the amount of management time and distraction involved in dealing with them, reduces disruption to operations and, in the extreme case, avoids regulatory penalties and costly litigation.
- There are social and community reasons for it. Most projects have many stakeholders with an interest in the project's outcomes and its wider effects. Sound environmental risk management promotes better communication with stakeholders, better community understanding of environmental costs and benefits and greater transparency of process. In some jurisdictions, explicit community consultation is a formal requirement, and in many projects it would be strongly recommended anyway without the regulatory imperative.

Overall, good environmental risk management makes good business sense. Systematic consideration of environmental risks as a component of business risk assessment helps identify key uncertainties and areas where lack of knowledge may be critically important to estimates of potential business performance. In extreme cases, environmental risks may be a reason for not proceeding with a project as conceived or at all.

Risk assessment may also be used to set remedial action priorities, where past activities may not have met current environmental guidelines.

Environmental risk

Risk may arise from an event, an action or a lack of action. Risk to the environment can be in the form of stresses caused by human activity, or inactivity. This risk might manifest itself as a threat, which can lead to degradation of the environment or loss of sustainability (see, for example, Gough *et al.*, 2000). Conversely, risk can also lead to the enhancement of the environment when a risk management process is used to identify opportunities and they are pursued.

When reviewing environmental risks and the actions that may be taken to manage them, the threats and opportunities that an activity, service or product may present should be considered. Opportunities and threats are both important parts of risk management, as assessing the opportunities on offer may influence the prioritization and subsequent treatment strategies.

Communication

Management of the environment is a complex and sometimes emotive process. There are typically many stakeholders in environmental management, many views on how risks should be managed and increased levels of public scrutiny. Therefore, communication and consultation are integral parts of the environmental risk management process. It is especially important that senior managers, operations managers and community liaison personnel effectively communicate the nature and significance of environmental risks between affected parties and stakeholders, and across different groups within the organization and the wider community.

Environmental risks can be managed effectively only if they are well communicated. The environmental risk management process must facilitate quick and effective communication of serious risks to the most appropriate level and individual within the organization. Risks may be communicated by written or verbal means, depending on what is most appropriate for the situation. However, a record should be kept for accountability purposes of any decision that arises from the communication or consultation.

Similarly, it is important that senior managers consult with other stakeholders and entities on the nature of the environmental risks, what is being done and what may be done to manage them. Such consultation is a part of good environmental management and facilitates a better understanding of the environmental challenges the organization faces. It may also assist in drawing together the resources necessary to manage risks effectively.

The major stake that communities have in environmental issues means that the boundaries between environmental and social risks are usually blurred or inseparable, and the major consequences may in fact be social ones, with the environmental outcomes providing the pathway from the initiating event. In addition, there are often major difficulties associated with communicating adequately the reality of the technical risk, as opposed to the apparent severity of the risk as perceived by the community. Hence with social risk, it is the perception that is real, as this is what motivates the community. These factors make good communication even more important, and in practice it is a critical feature of effective environmental risk management.

Research to measure the effectiveness of communication with stakeholders and the community will determine how successful the environmental risk management process has been and which audiences require more attention.

The process of communication between environmental stakeholders, and the benefits that good communication of environmental risks can bring, should be detailed effectively in a communications plan that includes risk management. This plan should show the lines of communication that currently exist, and perhaps should exist, within the environmental management community. Important stakeholders and their role in this community should be listed and detailed. Methods of communication, format and themes, and the objectives of good communications should be spelt out.

The communications plan, together with the environmental risk management policy and process, should provide a consistent structure, a standardized terminology, and a common reporting format that stimulate good communication of risks amongst stakeholders.

Other aspects of communication were discussed in Chapter 8.

Context

The context stage of risk management is similar to that for any project, although the criteria and consequence scales may be more specific to environmental matters, and the elements for structuring the process may be tailored to have a particular environmental focus.

Environmental management systems

The basis and much of the information for the context stage may often be found in the environmental management system (EMS) that many organizations maintain, consistent with the ISO 14000 series of environmental standards. An organization's EMS should contain a risk policy that incorporates some or all of the elements noted in Table 18.1.

Risk management is an integral part of such an EMS. ISO 14000 requires organizations to maintain an 'aspects and impacts register', which is equivalent to a risk register, and to maintain formal environmental risk management practices. Whether the EMS drives risk management or risk management drives the EMS may not matter much – the important thing is that the processes work together to generate better environmental and project outcomes.

Table 18.1—Elements of an environmental risk policy

Elements	Concepts that should be included
Principles	Possible environmental incidents must be anticipated, and managed. Proactive and diligent risk management is essential. Risk management forms a key part of responsible environmental policy. It is also good business practice.
Objectives	Identify and characterize environmental risks. Determine priorities for the introduction of effective risk management actions.
Responsibilities	Managers responsible for operations that may present a potential risk to the environment should review their operations to determine whether or not they represent a significant risk, and take appropriate risk management action to reduce both the organization's and their own exposure.

Criteria and consequences

It is common to think about environmental risks in terms of events with potential environmental consequences, and to restrict the assessment purely to consequences for flora, fauna and the natural environment. However, this is often too narrow a perspective, and business impacts may be as important as environmental consequences in many cases. An appropriate range of consequence criteria should be included in all risk assessments, including environmental risk assessments.

For example, Table 18.2 shows a holistic set of environmental consequence criteria adopted by the Australian Department of Defence as part of its defence EMS risk management framework (www.defence.gov.au/environment). In this case, environmental and related community and heritage criteria alone would be insufficient to reflect the range of consequences of interest to defence managers and environmental managers. Similar concerns arise in more obviously commercial businesses.

Key elements and environmental aspects

Except for very small projects or activities, it is useful to disaggregate the project or function into key elements for risk identification. In the context of environmental risk management, key elements are closely related to environmental aspects; an environmental aspect is defined in the ISO 14000 series of standards as an element of an organization's activities, products or services that can interact with the environment. Environment Australia (2000) expands on this:

> The organisation needs to identify the environmental aspects of its activities, products or services (over which it can be expected to have an influence) in order to determine areas where environmental impacts are most significant.

Table 18.2—Example of environmental consequence criteria

Criterion	Notes
Capability and mission	Impact on the ability of the Australian Defence Force (ADF) to protect Australia and fulfil its national security obligations. Impact on the ADF's ability to train and equip for war and for the conduct of peacetime operations. Impact on the ability of defence to develop its capability as detailed in the Defence White Paper.
Environment	Impact on the environment, including contamination, damage to flora and fauna, fire, noise, soil damage and erosion, green house gas emission. Environmental management in the strategic context of defence business.
Community and sustainability	Impact on our ability to create a sustainable environment for the future, including depletion of resources, excessive energy use, long-term damage to the environment
Safety (staff and public)	Impact on the physical well-being of military and defence employees, communities in defence regions and the public in general.
Compliance and reputation	Impact on defence's reputation as a world leader in managing the environment, political and media attention to environmental matters, community concerns or actions over defence environmental management. Compliance with environment and other regulatory requirements and the impact of failing to comply. Short-term cost of prevention vs. long-term cost of recovery.
Financial	Monetary impact on defence, the Government and other stakeholders.

Environmental aspects are determined by taking into account the inputs and outputs associated with current and, where relevant, past activities, products and services. The cause and effect relationship between environmental aspects and impacts means that once aspects have been determined, the impacts that result from these aspects can be assessed.

Often, a project, activity, product or service may be disaggregated in a number of ways or dimensions so that different but equally effective sets of key elements or environmental aspects may be generated. To illustrate, Table 18.3 shows a set of elements used in a recent environmental risk assessment exercise. Another entity used a comprehensive set of key elements structured on the organizations and sub-units located on a site, their locations on the site, and the activities in which they engaged. Yet another used a set of general functions (Table 18.4), each of which was divided in a set of relevant and more detailed activities.

Table 18.3—Elements based on issues and environmental aspects

Environmental issue	Environmental aspect (key element)
Sustainable management of ecosystems	Land use
	Interaction with marine environment
	Interaction with aquatic environment
	Flora and fauna interaction
Natural resource consumption	Energy use
	Water use
	Waste generation
Pollution prevention	Soil and water contamination
	Waste treatment and disposal
	Air emissions
	Noise, vibration and electromagnetic radiation generation
Climate change and ozone depletion	Use of ozone depleting substances
	Greenhouse gas emissions
Stewardship	Procurement and acquisition
	Infrastructure development and support
	Stakeholder management
	Business practices
	Heritage management

Table 18.4—Elements based on general functions

Functions	Functions continued
Ablutions and sewage treatment	Landfilling
Accommodation	Office administration and miscellaneous
Dangerous goods	Special functions
Dining areas and kitchens	Vehicle servicing
Engineering and building	Vehicle washing
Grounds maintenance	Warehousing
Hospital and first aid	

Risk identification

Risk identification for environmental risk assessment is often based on general structures relevant to the way in which hazards may arise and affect things in the surrounding environment. For example, it is often useful to consider that a risk exists if there is (Figure 18.1):

- a hazard or potential source of harm;
- one or more targets susceptible to the hazard; and
- one or more pathways for the source to affect the target.

This simple arrangement provides a basic structure for risk identification, in addition to those noted in Table 18.3 and Table 18.4, as well as a guide to thinking about how a risk might arise and the kinds of effects it might have. In addition, the pathway component is often an indicator of barriers that might be considered in the assessment and treatment process. Table 18.5 provides examples of sources, pathways, barriers and targets, and the kinds of potential environmental impacts that may result. Multiple interactions may also be important in some circumstances.

Two important categories of environmental hazards relevant to environmental risk assessment are chemical and physical hazards. However, it may be worth reviewing the list of energy sources noted in Table 18.5 for a more comprehensive list.

Sources may be identified by site reviews, process reviews, hazard inventories and incident monitoring, some of the tasks that may be mandated by regulators as part of environmental impact assessment processes.

- Site reviews should consider structures (buildings, surfaces, drainage systems), storage facilities for hazardous substances, including wastes, and process equipment.
- Process reviews should consider potential hazards associated with processes, process streams, materials and by-products, and transport and storage systems.
- Hazard inventories should list all potentially hazardous materials on or near the site.
- Incident monitoring should record and analyse previous incidents of non-routine releases of hazardous materials into the environment, or near-misses where a release was possible but avoided.

Chemical hazards are often classified according to their potential effects. It is often useful to distinguish between acute hazards (those where the event itself poses the primary risk directly) and chronic hazards (where there are long-term effects or long-term accumulations in the environment). Particular characteristics of note may include:

Figure 18.1—Hazards, pathways and targets

Table 18.5—Examples of sources, impacts and the relationships between them

Example	*Impact*
Source Hazard/Aspect	Energy sources • chemical • electrical • mechanical • pressure • noise • gravity • heat and cold • radiation • bio-mechanical • micro-biological Machinery Processes Activities Materials inventory
Event	Plant failure Toxic release Fire Contamination Land clearing Dredging activities Waste disposal
Pathway	Atmospheric dispersion and deposition Surface water • site drainage and run-off • streams and river systems Groundwater Soil Bio-pathways • ingestion • food chain • bio-vectors
Barrier	Physical Procedural Administrative Regulatory
Target (or receptor)	Human Social Economic Amenity Natural heritage Cultural heritage

(Continued opposite)

Environmental impact	Measures relating to
	• sustainability
	• human
	• social
	• economic
	• amenity
	• natural heritage
	• cultural heritage

- acute ecotoxicity – immediate impacts, e.g. death;
- chronic ecotoxicity – long-term damage, e.g. ability to reproduce;
- mutagenicity and teratogenicity – the potential effects on offspring due to mutations or congenital malformations;
- persistence – the length of time a release will remain hazardous before decaying;
- bioaccumulation and bioconcentration – the potential for material to accumulate and concentrate within components of the ecosystem.

Physical hazards are usually associated with the industrial operations presenting potential for harm to the environment. These may include fire, explosion, noise, flooding or dust.

To identify receptors, survey the environmental setting and neighbourhood to identify targets that may be at risk. Where appropriate, discuss the initial list with regulatory authorities and other groups with interests in potential receptor categories. Examples of receptors include:

- population areas;
- farm land and fisheries;
- water resources, including ground water and surface water;
- park land and recreational areas;
- specific ecosystems, particular species and the wider natural environment;
- rivers and lakes;
- geological features and features of scientific interest;
- historic buildings and ancient monuments; and
- sites of cultural or religious importance to indigenous groups.

Potential sources of risk should be considered systematically against each potential transport pathway to determine which are relevant to each identified hazard.

Sources, pathways and receptors are sometimes described in terms of the risk scenarios that may result in hazardous incidents. Tools for developing and classifying risk scenarios include:

- failure mode and effect analysis (FMEA);
- event trees; and
- project hazard studies.

These tools provide systematic approaches that are particularly useful for complex processes. Most work best if applied by a multi-disciplinary team of specialists.

Event trees provide a useful way of summarizing complex processes and pathways, where there are branching points representing alternative conditions that might arise. They were discussed, with an environmental example, in Chapter 17.

Environmental risks have other less direct business consequences too. For example, external stakeholders may pose significant threats to the business in some circumstances:

- adverse reactions from local community;
- adverse media interest;
- regulatory delay in gaining permits and approvals; and
- uncertainty in standards to be applied to rehabilitation.

Iterative risk analysis approach

Risk analysis considers the likely frequency of incidents and their associated environmental consequences to determine risk priorities. For complex environmental matters, an iterative risk assessment process is often used (Figure 18.2). This starts with a screening analysis, to eliminate risks that are obviously not relevant, followed by a detailed assessment for significant risks.

The screening analysis uses simplified scenario descriptions of potential risks. It avoids detailed calculations and modelling of events and uses pessimistic or worst-case assumptions to eliminate obvious low-risk scenarios and avoid wasting time and resources. For example, a screening assessment might assume that the total on-site chemical inventory is released, with minimal dispersion on pathways to the target and broad descriptions of impacts.

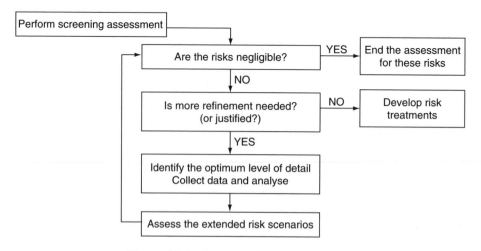

Figure 18.2—Iterative risk assessment process

The screening analysis process often uses coarse ratings of impacts and frequencies, and simple matrices, like the ones discussed earlier in this book, to combine them into an assessment of risk priority. Only those risks that are rated low in this conservative analysis are discarded – remaining risks are examined in more detail.

The next stage refines the preliminary analysis using more detailed, specific and realistic models with less pessimistic assumptions. Initiating events and pathways are examined more closely, to improve the frequency estimate and better understand the initial development of the incident. Site-specific and mitigating factors are taken into account, and consequences are analysed more precisely.

Environmental risk analysis may involve any of the qualitative or quantitative analysis processes and structures discussed in this book, according to the need and the decisions to be made. A semi-quantitative approach to setting priorities for environmental risks was outlined in Chapter 5.

Further iterations and more detailed modelling may be necessary, if they are appropriate in the circumstances. Uncertainty exists in any risk assessment, and it is necessary to balance the effort associated with more detailed analysis against the potential benefits it brings.

Risk treatment strategies

The same kinds of risk treatment options are available for environmental risks as for other project risks: avoidance, reduction of consequences and likelihoods, transfer and acceptance.

For environmental risks, examples of physical treatments include:

- design and engineering solutions;
- bunds, cut-off drains;
- reduced hazardous inventory; and
- removal of vulnerable targets from potential impact areas.

Examples of procedural treatments include:

- preventive maintenance;
- monitoring, sampling and alarms;
- risk-based inspections;
- emergency plans;
- formal operating procedures; and
- incident and near-miss reporting.

Approaches to environmental risk management

While the approaches to environmental risk management often have many similarities, the terminologies and underlying philosophies may vary. For example, Table 18.6 shows the

Table 18.6—Comparison of the base process with the US
EPA Guidelines

Reference process	US EPA Guidelines
Establish the context	Planning
	Problem formulation
Identify the risks	Analysis
Analyse the risks	
Evaluate the risks	Risk characterization
Treat the risks	Risk management decisions
Monitor and review	Iteration and monitoring

terms used in the US Environmental Protection Agency Guidelines, showing the similarity
in the basic steps. The approach to regulatory decision making in some jurisdictions seems
to envisage a clear separation of responsibilities between the risk identification and analysis
activities – viewed as a more-or-less scientific and value-free pursuit – from the risk treatment or risk management activities involved in making decisions, where a broader range of
political criteria and values are not only appropriate but necessary for policy setting.

Case study: iterative risk assessment for mine waste management options

The Ok Tedi mine

The Ok Tedi copper–gold mine is located at Mt Fubilan in the Star Mountains of
Papua New Guinea, approximately 15 km north-west of the mining town of Tabubil
(Figure 18.3). The mine is located at an elevation of approximately 1500 m in the headwaters
of the Ok Tedi, a tributary of the Fly River. Processing of ore to produce copper concentrate,
also containing significant amounts of gold and silver, is carried out in an adjacent mill
facility. Concentrate is pumped along a 156 km pipeline to the upper Fly River port of
Kiunga, whence it is barged approximately 820 river kilometres down the Fly to a floating silo
vessel for transshipment to ocean-going ships for world-wide copper smelter destinations.
The mine began production in 1984. At the time of the assessment outlined here, it was
scheduled to close in 2010.

The region is one of the wettest places on earth, receiving 10–12 m of rain annually, and it
is geotechnically and seismically unstable. The average water and natural sediment discharges
of the Fly River to its delta are approximately 6000 m^3/sec and 84 Mt/a respectively.

Annual mine production consists of approximately 30 million tonnes of ore and 50 million
tonnes of waste rock. Ore production is expected to continue at the same rate until closure,
whereas waste rock production is expected to increase to approximately 55 Mt/a, followed
by a gradual decline from 2007 to 2010. In addition, a considerable amount of limestone is
mined to maintain balance in the river system.

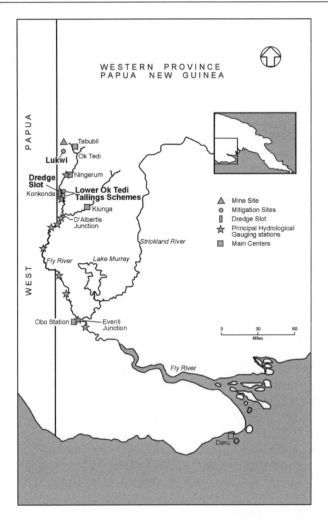

Figure 18.3—Ok Tedi mine site

The mine development was to have included waste rock dumps adjacent to the open-pit and a conventional valley-fill tailings dam in the Ok Ma catchment. Whilst under construction, a slow moving landslide entered the abutment key of the Ok Ma tailings dam in January 1984, forcing abandonment of the site. Following the Ok Ma landslide, an interim waste disposal scheme was approved, providing for the retention of coarse tailings in a dam adjacent to the mill, with sub-150 micron material being discharged to the river system. However this was only a short-term measure as the dam was soon filled.

Since 1988, all tailings have been discharged directly into the Ok Mani, a tributary of the Ok Tedi. Further sediment is added to the river system from valley wall erosion into the Ok Mani. Approximately 40% of the mined waste rock and valley wall erosion discharged to the Ok Mani since mining commenced, mostly coarser gravel, has been retained in the Ok Mani. The remaining 60%, plus all of the tailings, have entered the Ok Tedi. A portion of the discharged sediment has been retained in the Ok Tedi and the Fly River, with finer materials reaching as far as the Fly delta and beyond.

In August 1989, a major landslide of approximately 160 million tonnes, the Vancouver Ridge Landslide, occurred immediately to the north of the open pit, undermining the toe of the northern waste dump and resulting in an immediate increase in the river bed level in the upper Ok Tedi. Based on a 100-year landslide record, it is estimated that there is a 40% probability of another Vancouver-size landslide occurring in the Ok Tedi catchment during the life of the mine, raising issues of the long-term integrity of any permanent man-made structures in the catchment.

The annual quantities of mined waste rock, tailings, landslide material and valley wall erosion that have entered the river system since the commencement of mining have been considerably greater than the recorded pre-mine natural sediment loads. Deposition of mine-derived materials has caused environmental degradation, including increased river sedimentation, increased flooding leading to forest dieback, loss of gardens and agricultural land, loss of some amenities, and declining fish populations.

The mine waste management project

The company, Ok Tedi Mining Ltd (OTML), was subject to international scrutiny, and the board wanted to demonstrate clearly that it was doing its best for all the stakeholders, particularly the local communities.

In 1995, OTML began a review of all work previously conducted on alternative waste management methods to seek an acceptable method of managing mine impacts. In 1997 a detailed study led to the initiation of a dredging trial, with the aim of extracting solid material from the Ok Tedi and hence reducing the amount of aggradation in the river system. Further multi-disciplinary examinations of options for dealing with mine waste are continuing. Four mine waste management options were examined in the risk assessment in 1998 and 1999, identified and defined by OTML (Table 18.7).

The risk assessment

The risk assessment study objectives were to:

- identify the significant engineering, environmental and community risk events associated with the approvals, construction, operation and after-care phases for each of the schemes;

Table 18.7—Mine waste management options

Scheme	Summary
A Closure	Immediate closure of the mine
B Tailings	Continuation of the current dredging scheme to the end of 2001 to build an embankment in which to store tailings, and the piping and storing of tailings until the end of mine life in 2010
C No dredge	Demobilization of the dredge at the end of the trial period in 1999
D Dredge	Continuation of the current trial dredging scheme (nominally 20 Mt/a) until the end of mine life in 2010

- quantify the risk events associated with each phase of each scheme, i.e. quantify the frequency of occurrence and the financial consequences of the identified engineering, environmental and community issues that may occur during the life of the project;
- combine the engineering risks with the environmental and community risks to provide a total scheme risk for each phase of each scheme;
- quantify OTML's highest realistic financial exposure associated with each scheme; and
- present the base costs and the total risk costs in a way that enabled comparison of the schemes.

The risk assessment proceeded at several levels, outlined in Figure 18.4 and shown in more detail in Figure 18.5. At the highest level, the process followed a structure similar to the risk management processes described in this book. This was supported at lower levels by many detailed studies concerned with health and ecological risk assessment (HERA), engineering, and social and economic aspects of the mine and its impacts (Figure 18.6). OTML has made many of the individual studies available on its web site, www.oktedi.com

Each of the detailed studies conformed to good practice in its own discipline (for example, EPA, 1998). In particular, the scientific aspects of the work were subject to intensive review by an independent international peer review group (PRG) of eminent scientists appointed by OTML for this purpose. The HERA was itself conducted at two levels, beginning with a screening level risk assessment and followed by a detailed level risk assessment, according to accepted principles, and subject to detailed PRG scrutiny.

A key part of the risk management process was the construction and validation of a detailed quantitative risk model, which is outside the scope of this chapter. The model consolidated the risk information from all the individual studies to assist the OTML board in its evaluation of the four main mine waste management options.

The overall risk assessment process, managed by OTML, and the quantitative risk analysis model, were also subject to an independent audit, conducted by the first author.

One important feature of the process was OTML's instruction that the risk assessment be directed to a comparison of mine waste management options and information relevant

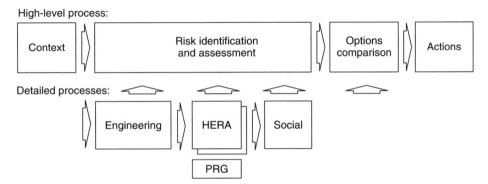

Figure 18.4—Case: multi-level risk management process

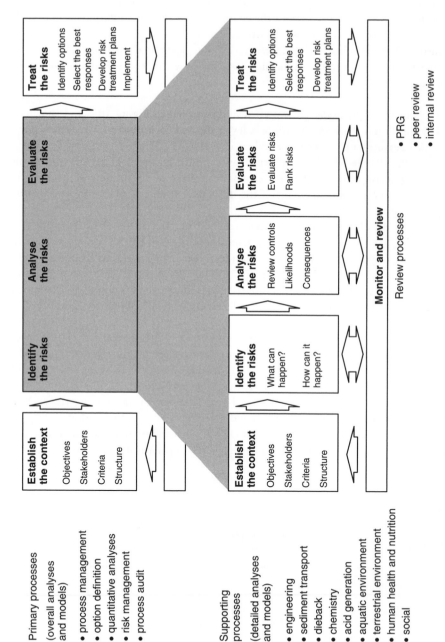

Figure 18.5—Case: detailed structure of the assessment

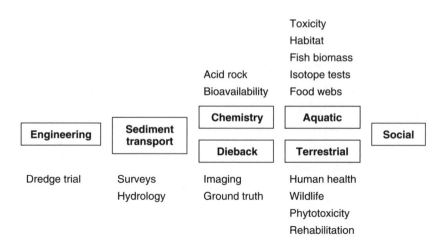

Figure 18.6—Case: supporting models

to decision making in this context. This affected the way in which some of the studies and activities were conducted, and they generated comparative rather than absolute assessments of risks in many cases. While this may seem an unnecessary constraint to some interested parties with other objectives, a key question is whether the risk assessment was adequate in its approach, processes and use of available data for the purpose for which OTML commissioned it; that is, for generating information to assist decision-makers to compare and select options.

Sources of risk

The engineering, environmental and social context of the risk assessment was very complex, with many linkages and interrelations. Figure 18.7 and Figure 18.8 provide an overview, based on five more detailed models shown in Figure 18.9 to Figure 18.13. The Agu is another river.

The risks in the quantitative model were based on the outcomes from a series of workshops and specific studies performed over a long period. They were consolidated, assessed and reviewed in detail by a large multi-disciplinary group of internal and external specialists at a combined risk workshop held in Tabubil over a four-day period. A risk register was established, detailing all the identified risks, whether they were included in the assessment and, if not, the reasons for their exclusion. The list of risks identified in the combined workshop was relatively complete, in the sense that no major issues are likely to have been omitted inadvertently. A further review was conducted as new scientific information was generated.

Data for the quantitative model were elicited at the combined risk workshop, supplemented by information from the detailed risk studies undertaken as part of this

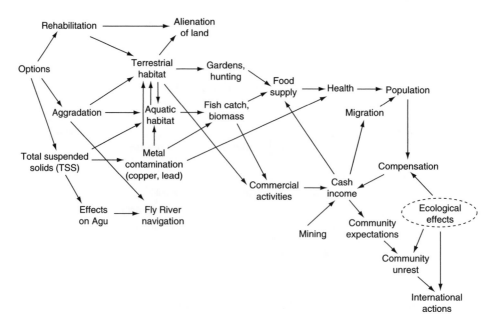

Figure 18.7—Overview of linkages

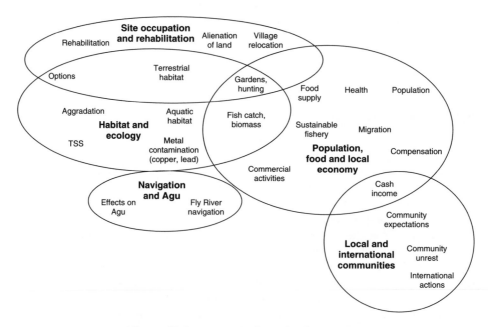

Figure 18.8—Key to the detailed linkage models

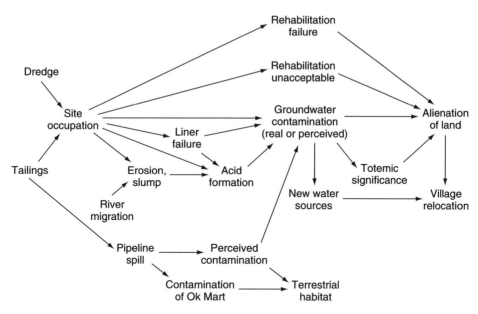

Figure 18.9—Site occupation and rehabilitation

project, the outcomes from earlier risk assessments, and additional data collected to fill obvious gaps.

Risk model outcomes

Several approaches were used to model risks quantitatively. The models generated quantitative measures of the level of risk associated with the main options for mine waste management. Results were presented in a variety of ways for the board and other stakeholders, in a way that provided as much information as possible and demonstrated the variability in the outcomes. The aim was to provide results that could be understood readily, without either over-simplifying or over-complicating them.

Figure 18.14 shows an example from an early run of the model, demonstrating that the Dredge option has the lowest risk cost at any specified level of confidence. Figure 18.15 shows another representation of the costs of the risks that might arise with each option, compared with their fixed or base costs, using different methods for analysing and estimating risk.

As noted earlier, the OTML Board was concerned to ensure the risk management was adequate and transparent, and could be justified to the wide range of key stakeholders. The overall process provided outcomes that were valuable for the board, management and shareholders in determining the most appropriate course of action, given the complexity and constraints in the operating environment. The audit report confirmed this.

More details are provided on the Ok Tedi website, www.OkTedi.com (search for risk), and in Bowden, Lane and Martin (2001).

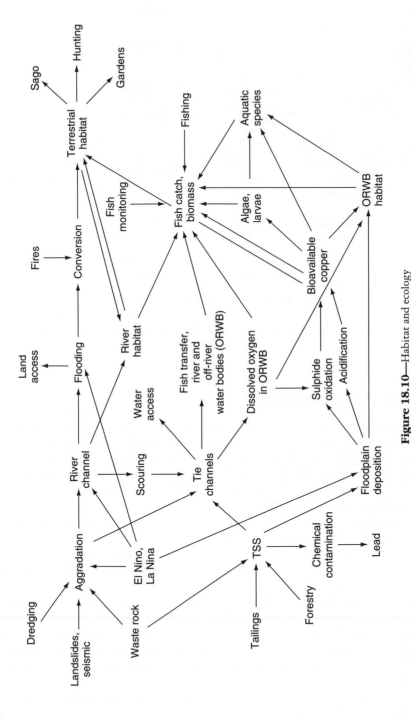

Figure 18.10—Habitat and ecology

Note: Acid rock drainage (ARD) may have widespread effects on many of the factors in the diagram. The effects of ARD have not been shown separately. 'Acidification' refers to acidification of existing floodplain sediments in the absence of significant new ARD problems generated at the mine.

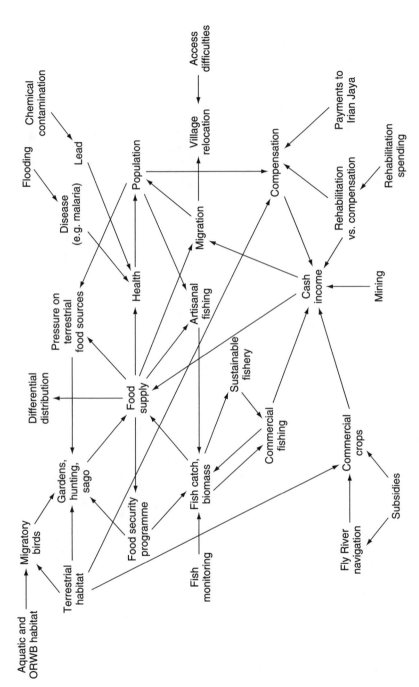

Figure 18.11—Population, food and local economy

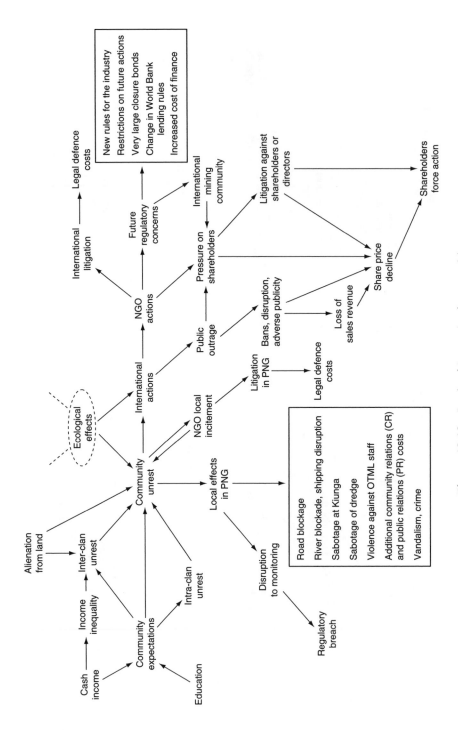

Figure 18.12—Local and international communities

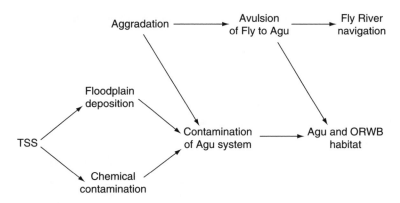

Figure 18.13—Navigation and effects on the Agu river system

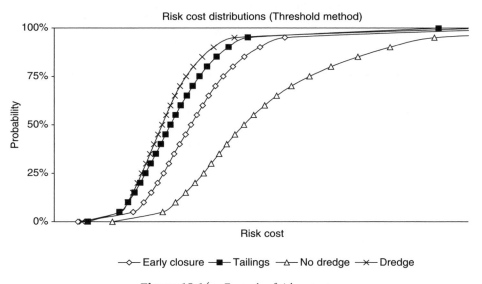

Figure 18.14—Example of risk outputs

Conclusions

Many projects have environmental implications, and many require explicit environmental risk management activities. Regulatory compliance is often an important driver, although many companies undertake environmental management as part of their own good corporate governance and triple bottom line reporting activities.

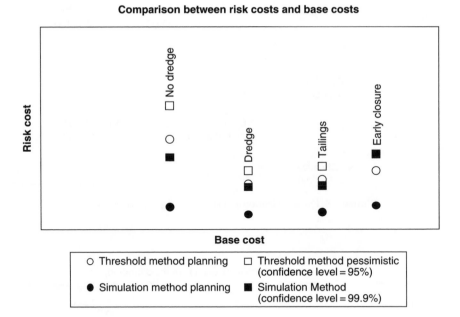

Figure 18.15—Risk costs and base costs for different calculation methods

Many of the general project risk management methods discussed in this book also apply to environmental risk assessment, and the iterative analysis approach outlined in this chapter has quite general application in many fields of risk management.

Part III
Quantification of project risks

INTRODUCTION TO QUANTIFICATION FOR PROJECT RISKS

19

Chapter overview

- ### Purpose

This chapter addresses quantitative risk modelling in which many component uncertainties, possibly interacting with one another, simultaneously affect the overall uncertainty and risk associated with a project. It deals with the purpose, development and evaluation of models as well as their use to support decision-making.

- ### Rationale

Quantitative risk analysis provides detailed information for senior decision-makers by evaluating the overall uncertainty in a project. It contributes to strategic decisions about acceptable project options, and to operational decisions about resource allocation and target and contingency setting, in a way that is consistent with the risks they are willing to accept.

- ### Inputs

Inputs to quantitative models include probabilities representing uncertainty in the occurrence of events, distributions of the model parameters, and the main correlations and other relationships between parameters.

- ### Method

Quantitative risk modelling involves establishing the context and boundaries of the model, structuring it to take account of the relationships between the risks and the project, executing it and validating it in an iterative process, and interpreting its outputs.

● **Outputs**

The outputs from a risk model include the realistically likely range of outcomes to expect, the risk of exceeding specified targets as a function of their values, the relative magnitude of different sources of uncertainty and the major risk drivers for the project.

● **Documentation**

Documentation of a risk model should record the process by which it was developed, its structure, parameters and outputs, its reconciliation with other views of the project, and the main conclusions and recommendations derived from it.

Introduction

The earlier chapters have set out a framework for managing risk. They describe risk management processes that are applicable to many forms of projects and different kinds of risk requirements.

While the early chapters set out detailed processes for implementing risk management in a qualitative or semi-quantitative framework, they do not address quantification in any detail. The following chapters show how the aggregate uncertainty associated with a project can be evaluated using quantitative risk models in a variety of circumstances.

Quantitative modelling provides a means of:

● describing the detailed mechanisms at work in a set of risks;
● evaluating the overall uncertainty in the project to which they relate and the overall risk that this places on stakeholders;
● establishing targets, commitments and contingency amounts consistent with the uncertainty the project faces and the risk the managers are willing to accept; and
● exploring the relationship between detailed instances of uncertainty and an overall level of risk, to inform risk management resource allocation.

The early chapters specify how to identify, evaluate and treat individual risks and groups of risks. However, an analysis of individual risks gives no indication of the combined effect of all the risks affecting a project.

Quantitative modelling provides a framework within which to integrate individual risks into an overall assessment to support decision-making and management control. In the case of large, complex or particularly sensitive projects, quantitative modelling may also play a role in the evaluation of individual risks.

General approach

Quantitative risk assessments extend the process described earlier to more detailed numerical analysis of uncertainty, usually in the context of a model of the project being examined. Often the model is implemented in a spreadsheet, incorporating the main cost or schedule aspects of the project and their interrelationships.

Quantitative analyses come into their own when a view of the overall risk associated with a project is needed, such as when:

- setting targets or accepting commitments;
- evaluating the realism of estimates;
- selling a project proposal on the basis of confidence in the forecast outcome;
- assessing the return on major investments at pre-feasibility or feasibility stage;
- choosing between alternative investments; and
- choosing between alternative technologies with different risk profiles.

Risk modelling may be viewed as an extension of conventional project and business forecasting and modelling (Figure 19.1). Generally, a conventional spreadsheet is the starting point, such as a simple cost estimate or a cash flow model of the net present value (NPV) of a capital investment. The main elements of the model are examined to determine what might cause the elements to vary, and the likely management responses to variations are considered. The elements of a model, risks and responses are used to develop quantitative descriptions of the variability in the model expressed as distributions that replace simple fixed values in the spreadsheet. Of course, this requires special software, often in the form of a simple spreadsheet add-in, such as @Risk. The distributions are combined through the model structure to generate distributions of the key variables need for decision making, such as the distribution of capital cost, NPV or rate of return (Figure 19.2).

Risk model parameters quantify uncertainty in the occurrence and the value of model components. Uncertainty in the occurrence of an event is described in terms of its probability of occurring. Uncertainty in the values of model components, such as their cost, duration,

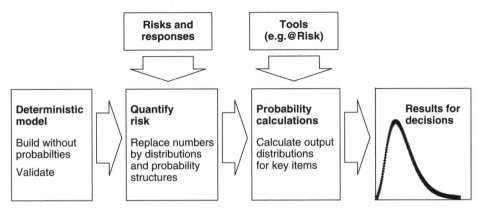

Figure 19.1—Outline of the quantitative risk analysis approach

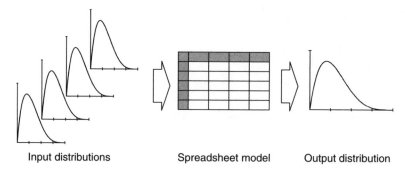

Input distributions   Spreadsheet model   Output distribution

Figure 19.2—Quantitative risk spreadsheet

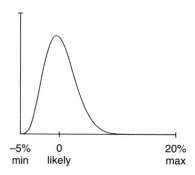

−5%   0   20%
min   likely   max

Figure 19.3—Input distribution, percentage variation about a base value (density form)

throughput or other characteristics, is described using probability density functions that are in turn defined by parameters such as minima, maxima, most likely or mean values.

For example, Figure 19.3 shows an input distribution in density form, in this case estimated as a percentage variation around a base value. Such a distribution might be used to represent the uncertainty in an estimate of a cost at some time in the future, where the base cost is linked to a standard cost-estimating process and the risks are 'standard' estimating variations.

Output distributions can be displayed in several forms. The one most people find immediately useful is the range of likely outcomes, and the risk of exceeding targets in that range. Figure 19.4 shows a typical example.

If Figure 19.4 represented the capital estimate for a procurement, for instance, it would help in setting an overall budget target, generally towards the right-hand end, and establishing how much to release initially to the project budget, usually somewhere nearer the middle. It would also make it clear if earlier expectations had been realistic. Anything falling to the left of the range would be seen as very risky for all concerned.

Risk models provide considerable information about the business or project being analysed. They can show:

- the realistically likely range of outcomes to expect;
- the risk (or probability) of exceeding a target as a function of the value of the target;
- the relative magnitude of various sources of uncertainty; and

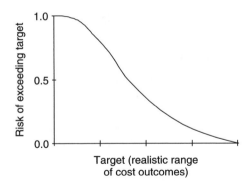

Figure 19.4—Output distribution, risk of exceeding cost target (reverse cumulative form)

- the sensitivity of the uncertainty in the output to uncertainty in each input, highlighting the major risk drivers (which might not be those expected!).

Quantitative risk assessment and modelling are described in detail by Grey (1995) and Cooper and Chapman (1987).

Application

Applications of the quantitative risk analysis processes described in this book include, but are not confined, to the analysis of project-related aspects of:

- project cost, schedule and cash flow;
- enterprise or business cash flow (for example, where the project is a stand-alone entity, or the dominant commercial activity of a company or joint venture organization);
- capital investment decisions;
- processing system throughput; and
- marketing and sales forecasts and project revenues.

Such analyses can have a multitude of uses including:

- go/no-go investment decisions;
- establishing or negotiating targets, commitments and contingency amounts;
- evaluating the realism of established targets and commitments;
- planning risk treatments that will reduce overall project uncertainty; and
- prioritizing sources of uncertainty and establishing the extent to which various stakeholders can control the overall uncertainty in a project.

The ability to make better decisions provides the justification for quantitative risk modelling activities. The chapters that follow provide examples of the kinds of models that may be used, the outputs they produce and the decisions they support.

Risk modelling processes

Establishing the context

The context of a risk modelling exercise must be clear if a model is to serve its purpose. The major features of the context that must be agreed are:

- the scope and boundaries of the project to be modelled, including the physical scope of project inputs, activities, assets and outputs and the time horizon to be considered;
- the project measures that are to be modelled, which could include financial quantities, schedule milestone dates, investment indicators, production and throughput characteristics and any other quantitative measures of performance;
- the basis on which the quantitative risk calculation is to be made, including any accounting, taxation and other conventions and standards to be followed;
- control mechanisms, including how deviations from plans will be recognized and treated in the project management process;
- risk treatment policies, including how risk events and deviations from plans will be responded to and how such responses should be incorporated in the project model.

Structuring the risk model

The structure of a quantitative risk model is a logical framework that defines the relationships between individual sources of uncertainty and the uncertainty in overall project measures. Risk models are often based on conventional planning and forecasting mechanisms, such as project activity networks, cost-estimating frameworks or process flow charts.

The detailed view of risks, such as can be generated using the qualitative processes described in earlier chapters, forms one of the foundations of a risk model. It identifies the issues that the model must address. Any model of the overall uncertainty in a project must be consistent with a detailed analysis of the individual risks affecting it. In the case of large, complex or particularly sensitive projects, quantitative modelling may also play a role in the evaluation of individual risks, being used to support the evaluation of the likelihoods and consequences of particular events.

The detail in a risk model may be less than in a conventional forecasting structure, and it is often distributed differently from a standard structure, with more detail in some areas and less in others. These structural differences reflect differences between the purpose of a risk model and that of a standard forecast. A risk model is concerned with the uncertainty in a measure, not just its base value, and attention is focused where the risks are greatest. This kind of model structuring activity is similar to that involved in developing a set of key elements for structuring a qualitative risk assessment, discussed in Chapter 2.

Conventional plans and forecasts are concerned with fixed values and possibly sensitivity analysis around these. Risk models are concerned with ranges of possible outcomes and the relative likelihood of values within those ranges. Representing uncertainty may require a different structure from that used to represent a conventional plan or estimate.

For example, in forecasting the capital cost for a project, the estimate structure typically includes unit costs for labour disciplines and for classes of plant and materials. These have common values across large parts of the estimate yet they appear in many individual estimating worksheets for specific activities or work elements. In a risk model, these common unit costs are drivers of risk across the project, as variability in any one of them will affect the cost of many elements in the estimate.

Because the unit costs in a risk model may be represented by distributions rather than simple numbers, the fact that one unit cost makes up part of several cost elements has a profound effect on the process and the outcomes that are obtained. If individual distributions are included each time a unit cost appears in the estimating spreadsheet, then appropriate levels of correlation must also be incorporated in the model to avoid underestimating the spread in the outcome of the total cost, as discussed in the next chapter. A preferred approach is to identify the uncertainty associated with each unit cost and apply it consistently through the model, usually by isolating the relevant unit cost and treating it as a model parameter.

It is important that the different model representations can be reconciled with one another. Conventional cost estimates and activity networks offer one view of the total cost and duration of a project. The relationship between these forecasts and the output of a risk model must be understood and be described in the summary of the quantitative analysis.

Figure 19.5 shows a typical cost estimate structure, in which the quantities and rates are combined for each element from left to right, and the element costs are summed to generate the estimate total. In Figure 19.6, where the items in the estimate are distributions rather than simple numbers, the common distributions for the unit rates have been extracted as model parameters. This allows the correlations between the elements associated with the rate parameters to be modelled explicitly and in isolation from other correlation effects. This is far simpler than trying to form an estimate where the drivers for correlations have not been separated in this way.

The tasks required to construct a risk model will depend on the modelling technique to be used and the tools that will support the process. They will typically involve the implementation of the structure discussed above in a computer-based tool such as a spreadsheet and the population of that structure with:

- probabilities representing uncertainty in the occurrence of events;
- probability density functions representing the model parameters; and,
- correlations and other relationships between parameters.

Project element	Discipline 1		Discipline 2		. . .	Element cost
	Quantity	Rate	Quantity	Rate		
Element 1	Q_{11}	R_1	Q_{12}	R_2		$Q_{11} R_1 + Q_{12} R_2 + \ldots$
Element 2	Q_{21}	R_1	Q_{22}	R_2		$Q_{21} R_1 + Q_{22} R_2 + \ldots$
. . .	. . .	R_1	. . .	R_2		
				Estimate total		Sum of costs above

Figure 19.5—Typical cost estimate structure

Rate	Discipline 1	dist R_1
parameters	Discipline 2	dist R_2
	. . .	. . .

Project element	Discipline 1 / Quantity	Discipline 2 / Quantity	. . .	Element cost
Element 1	dist Q_{11}	dist Q_{12}		dist $Q_{11} R_1 + Q_{12} R_2 + \ldots$
Element 2	dist Q_{21}	dist Q_{22}		dist $Q_{21} R_1 + Q_{22} R_2 + \ldots$
. . .	. . .	. . .		
		Estimate total		Sum of costs above

Figure 19.6—Revised structure when quantities and costs are distributions

Executing the risk model

The process by which a model is evaluated to produce outputs will depend on the technique selected to aggregate the individual sources of uncertainty into an overall view of risk. Simulation is the most commonly used technique, using Excel for spreadsheet modelling and packages such as @Risk or Crystal Ball to perform the simulation.

The simulation process is outlined in Figure 19.7. In each pass of the simulation, values are sampled from the distributions in the model, the model is evaluated and the calculated outputs for that set of values are stored. The process is repeated many times, and all the values that have been collected are used to estimate the distributions of the outputs and the ranges within which they might realistically fall. To obtain an accurate estimate of the output distribution, many hundreds or thousands of iterations are commonly made, with more iterations required if more accuracy is needed, particularly in the tail areas of the distributions.

Most modern simulation software samples values from the model distributions using a Latin hypercube process. This is a stratified sampling technique that spreads the sampled values across the full range of each model distribution, including the tails. The alternative is Monte Carlo sampling, which extracts values in proportion to the density of the distribution, and thus gives less weight to the tails than to the peak of each distribution.

Despite the routine use of the Latin hypercube technique, this form of simulation is still commonly referred to as Monte Carlo simulation. Latin hypercube sampling produces the same result as Monte Carlo simulation but reaches a stable result in fewer iterations, reducing

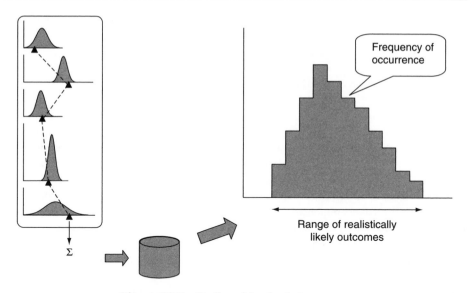

Figure 19.7—Outline of the simulation process

the processing time and data file size required to evaluate a model. Vose (2000) discusses @Risk modelling and simulation processes in detail.

Numerical integration processes, such as Chapman's Controlled Interval and Memory approach, may be used instead of simulation for combining distributions (Chapman, 1979; Chapman and Cooper, 1983; Cooper and Chapman, 1987). These usually require special-purpose software, which limits their practicability, but they have particular strengths where there are rare events or the tails of the distributions are important, circumstances in which simulation is less efficient.

The method of moments is an analytical process for combining distributions based on their mathematical form. It requires many simplifying assumptions, and so it is less commonly used. However, it is a process that may be applicable to simple systems, despite its limitations.

Validating the risk model

To ensure that the output of a risk model will be accepted and its conclusions will command the confidence of decision-makers, a model must be reconciled with other views of the project it represents.

It is not uncommon to find that the first attempt at a model shows that a safe cost or duration target is substantially higher than expected, indicating optimism in the original estimates or a failure to grasp the effects of complex interactions. Another common discrepancy between the first version of a risk model and a project team's understanding of their task is for the model to indicate much less uncertainty in the outcome than expected. This might arise from unwarranted optimism about the accuracy of forecasts or a failure to allow for correlations between linked distributions.

Discrepancies between separate views of a system must be understood and either:

- corrected, if they indicate an error in the risk model or the other system forecasts; or
- accepted with appropriate documentation, if they arise purely from the inclusion in the risk model of uncertainties that are not represented in the other forecasts.

Model validation and reconciliation is typically an iterative process. Figure 19.8 summarizes the modelling and review process developed for modelling the risk in a large resource project. In practice, the first phase of modelling went through three major cycles like this, with several additional iterations in specific parts of the model where it was important to confirm the accuracy of critical parameters and model features. (Additional case material relating to large resource projects appears in Chapter 22.)

The decision-makers responsible for the management of a project are the ultimate owners of the model and they must understand and accept its detailed content, its structure and parameters, as well as the conclusions drawn from it. Detailed estimates may be provided by technical and other specialists, but the decision-makers must live with the consequences of their actions based on the model. Because they must effectively take responsibility for the inputs to the model as well as the decisions based on its outputs, they should be closely involved in the validation and reconciliation process.

A further reason for careful validation lies in the nature of the inputs to a risk model. No two projects are ever identical and any particular project is a new activity, even if something similar has taken place in the past. Accordingly, even where historical information is available about similar tasks in similar projects, describing the probabilities and distributions will involve some degree of human judgement as the data is reinterpreted for the specific circumstances of a particular project. Just as the common aspiration to risk-free forecasts

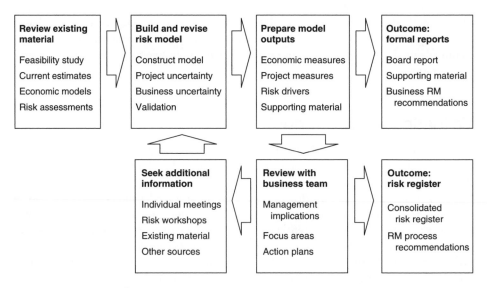

Figure 19.8—Iterative modelling and review process

and estimates is illusory and unattainable, the desire to produce an objective forecast, free from human judgement, is unrealistic.

Subjective judgement is often seen as an undesirable contaminant in the planning and estimating process. However, it cannot be removed, and it is imperative that the quantitative risk modelling process recognize the nature and role of human input and the way it affects the interpretation and utilization of the output of risk models. In particular, validation activities should pay particular attention to areas where judgement is poorly supported by data or experience, or where judgemental parameters have a particularly strong bearing on key outputs of the risk model.

Model documentation

Documentation of a risk model should record:

- the process by which the model was developed, including the names of those contributing to the exercise;
- the structure of the model;
- the parameters of the model;
- the output of the model and its reconciliation with other views of the project; and
- conclusions and recommendations derived from the model.

As circumstances change, a model must be kept up to date as far as it has a material effect on decisions about the management of the system it represents. The documentation should also be maintained up to date.

Organizational aspects of risk modelling

Quantitative risk modelling touches on two broad areas of organizational management and policy:

- the control systems by which deviations from plans are recognized and responses are initiated, including the way the organization manages the delegation of responsibility for risk to its personnel; and
- the organization's preference for taking risks and the way an individual project, process or operation fits into its overall portfolio.

Management review of quantitative risk modelling must address these two policy areas and consider:

- the detailed descriptions of individual sources of uncertainty and their interactions with one another; and
- the overall uncertainty they generate and its relationship to targets, commitments and contingencies.

Effective utilization of quantitative risk modelling requires that two distinct roles be filled:

- the analytical and modelling function that generates models and reports on their outputs and the insights that can be gleaned from them; and
- the decision-making function that uses the output to direct activity.

Sometimes these roles are undertaken by the same person, although this is not usual in large organizations or for large projects. Each role may be filled by a single individual or by a group.

The quantification of individual risks requires a clear understanding of the organization's control mechanisms. Policies on the control of key performance measures vary significantly from one organization to another and are closely linked to corporate culture. The opportunities to identify and rectify deviations from plans also differ markedly from one type of organization to another as well as being strongly dependent on the technical nature of the work being managed.

The interpretation and use of quantitative risk assessments must take account of an organization's preference for risk-taking. It is intimately linked to the relationships between levels of management, the role of other stakeholders, policies on allocating responsibility for risk and the mechanisms by which performance is rewarded. Ownership of the overall project risk strategy must ultimately lie with the manager or chief executive of the organization.

Summary

Any commitment or target places a risk on the person or organization that must meet it. The common aspiration to risk-free forecasts and estimates is illusory and unattainable. Because any meaningful target or commitment represents a risk, it is appropriate to seek to understand the level and nature of that risk and the mechanisms by which it might be controlled. The aggregate effect of a large number of component risks on a project as a whole is difficult to comprehend without support. Quantitative risk modelling is a means of describing these components and evaluating their aggregate implications.

COST-ESTIMATING CASE STUDIES

20

Chapter overview

> ● **Purpose**
>
> This chapter describes the application of quantitative risk analysis techniques to cost-estimating, a key task in the project planning process. It introduces basic techniques used in more sophisticated quantitative risk analysis processes discussed in later chapters.
>
> ● **Rationale**
>
> All cost estimates are subject to uncertainty. It is important for project managers, staff and end-users to understand this uncertainty, to plan for and source funding, to understand the kinds of responses and prices they might expect when tenders are invited, and to structure the allocation and pricing of risk in contracts. For suppliers, accurate estimates of costs and contingencies form a fundamental input to commercial bidding, price setting and negotiation.
>
> ● **Method**
>
> Estimates of the uncertainty in cost estimates are derived when the estimates are generated and described using distributions embedded in spreadsheet models. Simulation software is used to generate distributions of overall cost and assist in setting targets and contingencies.

Introduction

This chapter describes the quantitative risk analysis process as it is applied in cost-estimating using two simple case studies. The first case study describes the audit of a feasibility-stage cost estimate for a hydroelectric development. The purpose of this risk analysis was to provide an independent check on the reliability of the estimate for the owner, and to assess whether the contingency allowance was adequate. It did not involve a great deal of detail in the costs, although many sources of risk were considered.

The second case expands on the themes introduced in the earlier one. It is based on a cost estimation case study for a two-stage irrigation system, undertaken for a government agency on behalf of the end-user farmers. The application itself is similar to many other cost-estimation examples. The case demonstrates how a risk simulation package can be used in a cost-estimating spreadsheet, to derive a distribution of project cost. Different ways of specifying uncertainty and including it in the estimation model are presented.

The cases are extended into a consideration of cost-estimation processes in slightly more detail. It is shown that risk analysis can be integrated with an organization's standard cost-estimation procedures, without major additional effort or overheads.

The method illustrated in these case studies can be used as part of pre-bid contract evaluation, as a simple extension of standard cost-estimating procedures. It can also be applied in the same fashion to estimating the revenues and expenses, and hence the potential profit, from a project.

Hydroelectric development

Introduction and purpose

A large hydroelectric development had been proposed for an area with known hydro potential, and detailed preliminary studies had been completed. However, there was some doubt about the economic viability of the project, because the energy environment had become less certain than it had been: regional energy demand forecasts had been reduced due to the general economic recession; world oil and gas prices were unstable; and the general pattern of future regional energy production was unclear.

The owner, a consortium of utilities companies, saw a need to re-examine the capital costs. In particular, it was felt by the utilities involved that the original estimates may have been optimistic, and that the contingency allowances may have been too small. The critical factor of interest was the total cost of the development under 'normal' circumstances; that is, what the project might cost in the absence of catastrophic events and *force majeure* incidents. This is a very limited objective, as will be seen later, which had implications for the kinds of risks that were considered in the analysis.

The original cost estimate was derived from a traditional engineering analysis of preliminary design plans and drawings. It decomposed the project into a number of line items representing the main activities and items of equipment to be procured, with each item further decomposed into labour, material, equipment and indirect cost components.

Cost variability and risk were included in the estimate in the form of a single contingency allowance, calculated as a proportion of the total project cost. The proportion reflected past experience with projects of this kind, industry practice and the 'feel' of the estimating team. The estimate is summarized in Table 20.1 where the contingency is shown as 10% of the total cost.

Table 20.1—Summary of the hydro cost estimate

Item	Cost %
Preliminary works	11
Civil works	28
Electrical equipment	18
Total direct costs	**57**
Indirect costs	19
Clearing, seepage control	6
Engineering, management and owner's costs	8
Total cost before contingency	**90**
Contingency	10
Total project cost	**100**

Cost elements

Early in the risk analysis, the cost elements of the project were organized into a suitable structure. The objective of this step was to generate a structure that contained sufficient detail for adequate analysis, but was not so detailed that large amounts of resources and time would be required. The cost structure contained 24 base costs, representing the main activities and equipment items in the project, as shown in Table 20.2. Chapter 2 contains additional discussion on developing a list of the key elements.

Risk analysis approach

The risk analysis approach is outlined in Figure 20.1. For each element in the estimate, the risks that might cause its cost to vary were identified and, where appropriate, the responses to those risks were considered.

For each risk, the effect on the cost was quantified as a distribution of the cost expressed as a percentage of the base estimate for the relevant element. For each element, the percentage distributions for each risk were multiplied, to form a distribution of the cost of each element as a percentage of the base cost, taking account of all risks combined. This distribution was scaled by the estimate value to generate a distribution of cost for the element measured in dollars. Within cost elements, the risks were considered to be independent.

The cost distributions for the individual elements were added, taking into account the relationships and correlations between the elements, to generate a distribution of total cost for the project. This distribution was used to evaluate the adequacy of the contingency allowance.

Risk identification

The risk analysis considered a range of 'normal' risks for projects like this, concentrating on those risks that might affect the total cost of the project (Table 20.3). Quantity and unit cost risks have direct affects on the cost estimate. Schedule risks cause delays, and have

Table 20.2—Base costs (key elements) used in the risk analysis

Elements	Details
1. Preliminary works	1.1. Site development and associated works
	1.2. Construction camp
	1.3. Construction camp operation
2. Concrete structures	2.1. Common considerations
	2.2. Spillway
	2.3. Intake
	2.4. Powerhouse
	2.5. Concrete gravity structures
3. Fill structures	3.1. Common considerations
	3.2. Diversion stage 1
	3.3. Diversion stage 2
	3.4. Main dam
	3.5. Other fill structures
4. Electrical and mechanical equipment	
5. Indirect costs	5.1. Salaries, expenses, site expenses
	5.2. Bonds and insurance
	5.3. Contractors' financing
	5.4. Contractors' head office expenses
	5.5. Contractors' profit and contingency
6. Engineering, management and owner's costs	
7. Reservoir clearing	
8. Reservoir seepage control	
9. Global risks	
10. Escalation risks	

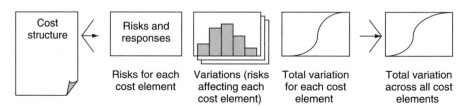

Figure 20.1—Outline of the risk analysis approach

effects on indirect costs as well as on the present value of future spending. Some risks that were common to all cost elements were identified explicitly in the structure as 'global risks'.

Note that the same process can be used for estimating variations in revenues where the objective of the risk analysis is to evaluate profit projections. A table equivalent to Table 20.3 might include sales volume and sales margin risks in place of quantity and unit cost risks, as well as schedule and global risks.

Abnormal or catastrophic sources of risk having the effect of *force majeure* were outside the scope of this cost analysis. They were treated as project conditions, in the sense that the analysis and outcomes were conditional on them not arising. They included:

Table 20.3—Risks for the hydroelectric project

Type of risk	Examples
Quantity risks	Design
	Engineering approach
	Definition
	Rock quality
	Ground contours
	Overbreak
	River bank characteristics
	Compaction
	Estimation
Unit cost risks	Engineering approach
	Weather
	Processing
	Formwork re-use
	Royalties
	Placement
	Dewatering
	Engineering and management rates
	Estimation
Schedule risks	Weather
	Seasons
	River levels (high and low)
	Equipment delivery
Global risks	Labour-related factors
	Bidding environment

- major design changes;
- site changes;
- water charges;
- labour problems;
- land acquisition;
- major floods; and
- jurisdictional and regulatory processes.

In this particular case the objectives of the risk analysis were limited to a consideration of the cost estimate and its more-or-less normal variations. In other circumstances and with wider objectives these risks might be central to the project and they would be analysed and assessed in detail.

Quantification

The consequences of individual risks were quantified as histogram distributions, like those shown in Figure 20.2 for variations in the quantity estimate for concrete. For each distribution, the horizontal axis shows the proportional variation in concrete quantity attributable

2.3   Intake

2.3.5   Concrete quantity variations

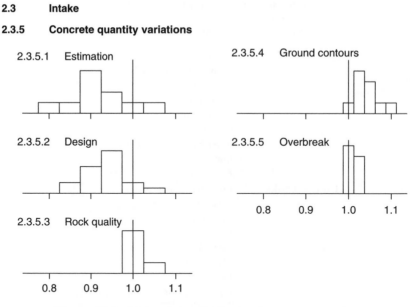

Figure 20.2—Risk variation distributions for concrete quantity

to the identified risk. The vertical axis is a probability axis. (The horizontal axes are the same in each case, but the probability axes use different scales to ensure the histogram areas sum to one, as required for distributions in density form.)

For example, distribution 2.3.5.1 in Figure 20.2 indicates that estimating has been conservative and that a more precise estimating process will lead to a lower value for concrete quantity. Specifically, the distribution for the estimating risk 2.3.5.1 has a peak at 0.9, indicating a reduction of 10% is most likely. Similarly, the estimator providing the information for this analysis thought that additional concrete would probably be needed when more precise quantity take-offs had been made from a design layout using closer ground contours: risk 2.3.5.4 has a peak at 1.025, indicating a most likely increase of 2.5%.

Histogram distributions of this kind can be very precise, because they can generate any shape required to represent the consequences of the risk. However, the precision comes at a cost, because they take time and resources to specify. In this case, the estimator started with a three-point estimate of the variation for each risk (minimum, most likely and maximum variation), which he interpreted initially as a triangle; he then adjusted the triangle to form a histogram that represented his more precise perception of the variation, taking into account his views on the way the original estimator would have derived the base estimate, the nature of the risk and the kinds of responses he expected to that risk. Simpler distribution forms are shown in the next case study.

Combining distributions

Distributions like those in Figure 20.2 were combined to form a cost variation distribution for each element, expressed in dollars. These were combined to form a distribution of total cost for the project.

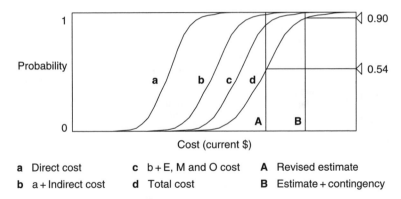

Figure 20.3—Results for the hydroelectric project

a Direct cost	**c** b + E, M and O cost	**A** Revised estimate
b a + Indirect cost	**d** Total cost	**B** Estimate + contingency

Graphical outputs were used to demonstrate the sources of variability. Figure 20.3 shows the final computational results from the risk analysis. The curves indicate the cost contribution of groups of elements. They are shown in cumulative form, so the graph indicates the probability (on the vertical axis) that the project can be completed within any given cost budget (on the horizontal axis).

Curves a, b, c and d successively incorporate groups of costs, with curve d representing the total cost distribution for the project. The vertical line A shows the dollar value of the most recent cost estimate: the results indicated slightly more than a 50% chance the project could be completed within this amount. Line B shows the estimate including the original contingency allowance: the results indicated a 90% chance of completing the project within this budget under normal conditions. (But remember, these results are conditional on catastrophes not arising.)

Irrigation scheme

Introduction

The second case study concerns an irrigation scheme serving a group of small farms, to be procured in two stages, with a far smaller budget than in the previous project (Figure 20.4). The first stage consisted of a pumping station to take water from the river to a secondary reservoir or balance tank. In the second stage the existing open-channel water distribution system was to be replaced with pipes and extended to cover more farms and outlets.

The end-users, the farmers' cooperative, were interested in assessing the accuracy of the costs, because that would govern whether they could irrigate a wider area.

Key elements

The objective of the initial steps of this analysis was to develop a structure that covered all the main elements of the project, but was simple enough to allow risks to be examined

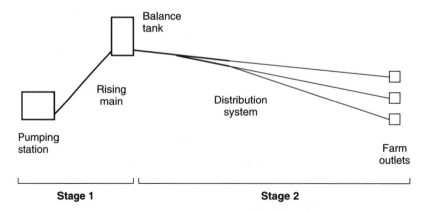

Figure 20.4—Irrigation scheme

in reasonable detail. The Stage 1 estimate used the summary structure included in the current management reports (Table 20.4). The Stage 2 estimate was based on the work breakdown structure developed for the most recent estimate. Several other costs and contingencies were considered in the risk analysis in addition to those in the initial estimates (Table 20.5).

Risk identification

The estimate numbering structure was expanded to incorporate risks. For example, the Stage 2 pipeline cost and risk structure involved 15 potential sources of risk (Table 20.6). These were relevant to the length of pipe to be procured and laid (2.1.1), the cost of procurement (supply rate, 2.1.2) and the cost of laying (construction rate, 2.1.3). There are

Table 20.4—Elements in the Stage 1 estimate

Number	Element description
1.1	Project feasibility studies
1.2	Project management
1.3	Design
1.4	Owner's costs
1.5	Construction management
1.6	Pump station construction
1.7	Mechanical/electrical supply
1.8	Gantry crane
1.9	Rising main pipe supply
1.10	Rising main construction
1.11	Balance tank
1.12	Electricity connection
1.13	Construction contingency
1.14	Site allowance contingency

Table 20.5—Summary of the cost estimate structure

Category	Number of elements
Stage 1	14
Stage 2	10
Other costs	7
Contingencies	2

Table 20.6—Sources of risk for the Stage 2 pipeline costs

Element		Sources of variation (risks)
2	Stage 2	
2.1	Pipeline	
2.1.1	Length (km)	2.1.1.1 Design, Phase 1
		2.1.1.2 Design, later phases
		2.1.1.3 Supply area
		2.1.1.4 Estimating variation
		2.1.1.5 Waste in construction
		2.1.1.6 Loops
2.1.2	Supply rate ($/km)	2.1.2.1 Estimating variation
		2.1.2.2 Aggressive ground
		2.1.2.3 Material selection
		2.1.2.4 Water hammer
		2.1.2.5 Rate correlation, RC pipe
		2.1.2.6 Rate correlation, UPVC pipe
2.1.3	Construction rate ($/km)	2.1.3.1 Estimating variation
		2.1.3.2 Bidding variation
		4.4 Contract claims

two design risks in 2.1.1, because the Phase 1 design was almost complete but only preliminary work had been conducted on the later phases. In 2.1.2, aggressive ground, material selection and water hammer all impacted on the pipe material selection and wall thickness requirement, and hence affected the procurement cost per kilometre.

Quantification

The effects of risks on the costs of the project elements were estimated directly as distributions. In the previous case study, individual variation distributions were estimated for each risk source. In this case, the approach shown in Figure 20.1 was simplified by assessing the combined effect of all risks that might affect an element, either indirectly in terms of distributions of percentage changes or directly in terms of costs expressed in dollars.

The following figures show several of the distribution shapes that were used, all in density form. For Element 1.8, the gantry crane, variations were expressed as percentage changes around the estimated value (Figure 20.5). The percentages were estimated initially

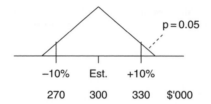

Figure 20.5—Cost distribution for the gantry crane, Element 1.8

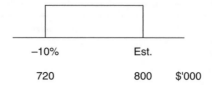

Figure 20.6—Cost distribution for the balance tank, Element 1.11

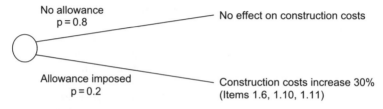

Figure 20.7—Probability tree for site allowance

as minimum, most likely and maximum variations from the estimate, and interpreted as a triangular distribution. In this case, there was a 5% chance of a variation less than −10%, and a 5% chance of a variation over +10%.

For Element 1.11, the supply and construction of the balance tank, variations were expressed as percentage changes from the estimated value (Figure 20.6). It was the estimator's opinion that detailed design would lead to a simplification of the pipes and valves under the balance tank, with a possible maximum cost saving of 10%. However, the saving could have been anything from zero to 10%, with no reason to believe any value in the range more likely than any other, and so a uniform distribution was specified.

For other risks, different structures were appropriate. For example, there was a 20% chance that a labour site allowance might be imposed on Stage 1 construction, which would have the effect of increasing the Stage 1 construction costs by 30%. Figure 20.7 shows the probability tree structure used to represent this.

Dependence and correlation

When distributions are added, it is important that any correlation or dependence between them be specified correctly. There are a number of reasons for dependence links between distributions.

- Common cause links. Two distributions may be linked because there is a common cause or driver that effects each in a similar way. For example, a poor choice of supplier can cause productivity to be low through several project elements, increasing costs for them all; two elements may both require skilled labour, and an increase in the labour rate may affect them both in similar ways. This form of common cause dependence is very common in projects.
- Cause and effect or cascade links. Two distributions may be linked if problems in one are likely to lead to problems in the other. For example, an equipment or transport breakdown in an early activity may lead directly to delays, and the replaced or repaired equipment may not be as efficient as the original, causing lower efficiency in the following activities.
- Compounding consequence links. If risks arise in two areas, their joint effects may be larger than their individual effects alone, so the consequences are multiplicative rather than additive. For example, a choice of less suitable equipment to save money may lower production, and inadequate staff training may also lower production, but poor equipment combined with poor training may lead to devastating effects if staff do not have the skills to cope with or work around equipment problems.
- Other statistical dependence links. Dependence can also arise for reasons that are not well defined or not well understood. This is referred to as statistical dependence.

The examples above all illustrate positive correlation, where two items move in the same direction so they are both small or both large together. In most projects, when there is correlation it is usually positive. Negative correlation, where problems in one area are offset by corresponding benefits in another, is rare in practice.

Ignoring positive dependence can underestimate risk significantly. For example, consider two elements with cost distributions as follows:

A   Expected cost $20 million, standard deviation $3 million;

B   Expected cost $20 million, standard deviation $4 million,

Assume for this purpose the cost distributions are normally distributed, and suppose we want to know the distribution for the cost of the two elements together:

- If A and B are **independent**, then A+B has an expected cost of $40 million, and a standard deviation $5 million;
- If A and B are **perfectly positively correlated**, then A+B has an expected cost of $40 million, and a standard deviation $7 million.

Recall that

$$\text{Variance } (A + B) = \text{Variance } (A) + \text{Variance } (B) + 2 \, R \, \sqrt{(\text{Variance } (A) \, \text{Variance } (B))}$$

where the variance is the square of the standard deviation and R is the coefficient of correlation between A and B. Positive correlation can lead to a significant increase in the variation as measured by the standard deviation. In other words, it increases the level of risk.

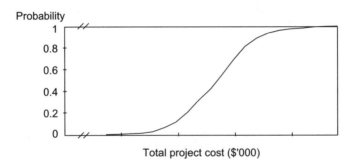

Figure 20.8—Results for the irrigation cost estimate

Detailed discussion of correlation and dependence is beyond the scope of this book. Two general rules should be kept in mind.

- When contemplating quantitative risk analysis, always check each pair of identified risks for the presence of any of the forms of dependence links noted above. If there are no dependence links that might lead to significant correlations, then proceed with care.
- If you identify dependence links that may be sources of significant correlation, seek assistance from a risk analysis expert. Ignoring correlation in quantitative risk analysis can lead to significant numerical errors.

Results

Figure 20.8 shows the form of the results obtained from the quantitative analysis. The kind of output is similar to that generated for the previous case and shown in Figure 20.3.

Software for cost risk analysis

The risk analysis package @Risk provides a convenient way of performing quantitative risk analysis calculations. @Risk is a simulation package that embeds within a standard Excel spreadsheet. @Risk has several useful features.

- It allows distributions and probability trees like the examples shown in Figure 20.5, Figure 20.6 and Figure 20.7 to be specified and incorporated in an estimating spreadsheet.
- It allows simulations to be run, taking samples from the input distributions and generating output distributions for the cost totals of interest.
- It facilitates graphical display of output distributions and allows sensitivity analyses to be performed. Figure 20.8 was generated using an @Risk simulation.

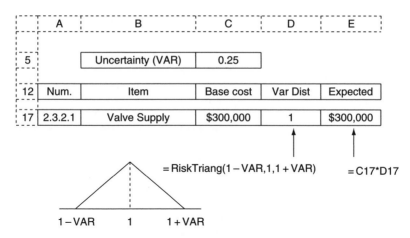

Figure 20.9—@Risk representation of the uncertainty in valve supply cost

As an example, Figure 20.9 shows how the distribution for valve supply, Element 2.3.2.1 in the irrigation case study, was represented in an Excel spreadsheet using @Risk. The element valve supply has a base cost estimate of $300 000. The @Risk function RiskTriang was used in cell D17 to represent a triangular variation distribution, with a most likely value at the estimate and a range from 0.75 to 1.25, i.e. a range of plus or minus 25% specified in cell C5 named VAR. The expected value of the cost distribution is displayed on the screen in cell D17. The distribution for the valve supply cost is in cell E17.

@Risk can also incorporate sophisticated dependence links if required. If software like @Risk is required, project and estimating staff are advised to get expert help in the first instance.

Risk and cost-estimating processes

Estimating procedures

Many organizations have guidelines or procedures for cost-estimating, often as part of their general project management procedures. The topics covered in such estimating procedures may include:

- Work Breakdown Structures, how they are constructed and their use in estimating;
- approaches to estimating time and resource requirements, to form the basis for estimating the cost of the project;
- the use of parametric estimating approaches to provide a benchmark for comparison with the detailed estimate, and to test the veracity and 'reasonableness' of preliminary cost data provided by suppliers;
- the definitions of costs to be incorporated in an estimate, including direct costs, indirect costs, management costs and overheads;

Table 20.7—Estimating accuracy

Estimate	Accuracy	Notes
Order of, back-of-envelope	+/− 50%	Based on limited calculations, to gain a feel for the project and eliminate options that are totally impractical
Preliminary, approximate, comparative	+/− 25%	Based on comparison with other projects, industry standards, or preliminary planning and design, to compare options broadly and identify those for more detailed assessment
Detailed, design	+/− 10%	Based on detailed plans and designs, using good data, to support economic appraisals and make decisions about implementation
Definitive, final, work-as-executed	+/− 2.5%	Based on implementation of the project, with actual cost data, to support estimates for future projects and for post-completion audits

- rules for incorporating the effects of inflation and guidance on the appropriate interest rates to be used;
- contingencies, what they are intended to cover and how they are to be estimated;
- the use of estimates for management decisions, including the relationships between cost-estimating and other appraisal techniques, such as cost-benefit analysis; and
- guidance on improving the quality of estimating, including 'best practice' notes and ways of avoiding common estimating errors and biases.

In many cases, different levels of estimating accuracy are expected for estimates at different stages of the project cycle. Table 20.7 shows some examples.

As a general rule, notes on accuracy should be included in estimating worksheets. For an estimate at a particular stage, the estimator will have a feel for the relative accuracy of the items. It is unlikely that the accuracies will all be the same, or the same as those noted in Table 20.7. The estimating worksheets should be annotated with assessments of the accuracy of each estimated item.

For large items, or those where the uncertainty is large, more detailed analyses of sources of risk and variability should be conducted. These might use an additional risk worksheet, like that shown in Figure 20.10.

Spreadsheets and risk simulation

Most estimators use spreadsheets as a matter of routine. Spreadsheets provide:

- ease of use;
- good presentation facilities;
- flexibility and adaptability for different tasks and different projects;

Element:			Ref:
Potential Risk	Responses	Assumptions	Accuracy
Compiler:	Date:	Reviewer:	Date:

Note: This is to be used in conjunction with standard estimating worksheets.

Figure 20.10—Estimating risk worksheet

- ease of modification as new information becomes available;
- backup facilities; and
- ability to incorporate risk and uncertainty.

For risk purposes, the ability to incorporate distributional information in the spreadsheet and evaluate the net effect of multiple distributions are the main features of interest.

Uncertainties can be included in estimating spreadsheets, with the accuracy set as a standard parameter in the absence of more precise information. An example of this was shown in Figure 20.9, where cell C5 contained a variation parameter.

Dependence should also be included in the spreadsheet, with high positive dependence assumed for early estimates in the absence of more precise information. Using @Risk, the level of dependence may also be set as a parameter.

If uncertainty distributions and dependence linkages are built into the estimating spreadsheet in this manner, the risk software can be used to simulate the uncertainty in the total cost. The total cost uncertainty, or the uncertainty for any sub-total, can be displayed graphically. The graphs can be used to assess the appropriate contingency allowance for the cost as a whole, taking into account the individual uncertainties and linkages.

The results from the risk simulation can be compared with the contingency assessed by traditional methods. The sensitivity of the estimate to key assumptions can be tested.

The process of estimating need not change much with the inclusion of risk and uncertainty information. For most organizations with a sound process of cost-estimating, no fundamental changes are needed although additional information may have to be gathered or examined more formally during the estimating process.

Estimators already think about risk and uncertainty, but they do not always do so explicitly. Recording the assumptions about uncertainty built into the estimate is an important first step towards doing so. If spreadsheets are used for estimating, then information about uncertainty in estimates can be included in the process without difficulty.

Conclusions

- Each organization involved in estimating should have sound guidelines and documented processes.
- Assumptions about risk and uncertainty should be recorded at the time estimates are formulated, using a risk worksheet where appropriate.
- High-risk items should be managed explicitly to reduce uncertainty and risk.
- Spreadsheets should be used for estimating as a matter of routine. Uncertainties can then be incorporated into the estimating spreadsheets as distributions.
- With uncertainties included in the estimating spreadsheet, a risk simulation can be run to generate distributions for key sub-totals and totals. These distributions can be used to set the levels of contingency appropriate for the project, or at least to check the contingencies generated by more traditional methods.

Summary

The general approach to cost estimation discussed in this chapter has wide application in substantially the form described here. The treatment actions implemented in response to identified risks provide important inputs to the design process, as well as to project planning and contract negotiation. The approach has also been applied to revenue and expense estimation in the same form.

This form of cost estimation can be integrated with an organization's standard cost-estimation procedures, with little extra effort or overhead. The benefits can be substantial:

- sensitivity analysis is facilitated;
- result distributions can be used directly in economic or cost-benefit analyses; and
- feedback to the design, tendering and contract negotiation processes is enabled.

As a key part of the procurement process, an analysis like this contributes to decisions about the form a contract should take (which party is best able to manage or bear the risk?) and the appropriate price (how much might it be worth?) assessed in probabilistic terms.

CASE STUDY: PLANNING A TIMBER DEVELOPMENT

21

Chapter overview

- ### Purpose

This chapter describes how quantitative risk analysis techniques were integrated with traditional approaches to project management in the pre-design evaluation of a timber development project.

- ### Rationale

Risk management can make important contributions to successful project management at all phases of a project, from the earliest concept phase through to the operation of a plant and the marketing of its products. This case provides an illustration of the process being applied throughout the life of a project.

- ### Method

The project's profit structure was used to provide a framework within which to combine quantitative risk analysis with other forms of analysis. A detailed example of a quantitative analysis of the capital cost estimate for the timber development is presented.

Introduction

This chapter describes how quantitative risk analysis can be integrated with traditional approaches to project management. Risk is interpreted as undesirable uncertainty about the project and its environment, and risk management is directed to developing the insight necessary to change risks for the better through effective and efficient decisions. In this decision-making context, risk management is just one facet of good project management.

The formal approach introduced by the discipline of risk analysis makes an important contribution to project management. It forces project managers to consider information inputs, as well as analytical outputs, in terms of the distributions of values they could face instead of average or most-likely quantities. One of the most costly consequences of the traditional attitude to project management based on 'best estimate' values, rather than on distributions, is the lack of a methodical analysis of the risks that might impact on the project and the associated probabilities of failing to achieve time and cost targets. This in turn leads to a lack of definition of the interdependence relationships between factors that affect the project, and a lack of analysis and understanding of the real 'disturbance' potentials in the project and their degrees of influence on the project's ultimate success.

Even though some degree of probabilistic analysis has been used for project scheduling, with approaches such as project evaluation and review (PERT), this provides only a partial view of the project. Risk is treated in a very rudimentary fashion in traditional PERT analysis, and the analysis is restricted to the project design, procurement and construction phases, with little or no regard for the concept and feasibility phases on one side, and for operations on the other. This chapter argues that risk analyses can provide valuable guidance for project managers at all stages of a project.

The timber development

The discussion here is based on the post-feasibility, pre-design evaluation of a timber development project. The project was situated in a small, independent nation in the Asia-Pacific rim. Large areas of forest, principally Pinus plantations, were nearing maturity. Initial investigations had shown that there was a regional demand for wood products, including sawn timber, wood chips and plywood, that would make a processing plant economically viable.

A site adjacent to good port facilities was available, and there was a pool of unskilled and semi-skilled labour in the vicinity. However, the processing plant equipment would have to be imported, probably from western Europe, and substantial foreign capital would be necessary. The project was not large by world standards, but was significant for the country concerned given its financial, economic and social implications. The initial acceptance decision was therefore made on the basis of a range of criteria. It was important that the planning for the construction and operation of the processing plant was undertaken with close regard for a variety of risks and constraints, some of which were financially, culturally and politically sensitive.

Determining the project strategy

A staged routine for optimization of the timber development project is set out in Table 21.1. The activities in Stage 1 were carried out by the project owner or sponsor in

Table 21.1—Stages in project optimization

Stage	Activities	Outputs
Stage 1	Market appraisal Market requirements study Resources appraisal Resources use strategy	Project feasibility decision Outline production targets
Stage 2	Production flow analysis Capital cost estimation Operating cost appraisal Financial and economic analysis	Set of 'best' production flow diagrams (PFDs)
Stage 3	Schedule analysis (time and cost) Cost-benefit analysis Detailed project optimization	Project implementation strategy

the pre-feasibility or feasibility stages of the project's life, leading to the decision about whether or not to become involved in the project at all and, if so, what the production targets should be. Stage 2 produced a set of the 'best' three or four ways of undertaking the project. Detailed analysis of these options in Stage 3 led to project optimization and the project implementation strategy.

In this case no explicit risk analysis was undertaken by the project sponsor during Stage 1 of the project, and the project management team became involved only early in Stage 2. An initial outline risk assessment was undertaken immediately, to avoid the possibility of project management being locked into product quality and product quantity expectations set out in the sponsor's brief. If such a risk assessment is not done quickly in circumstances like these, it may be too late by the time the management team is appointed to avoid optimism built into the initial view of a project.

The discussion here centres on Stages 2 and 3 of the project optimization and the role of risk analysis in the process. Nevertheless, we would draw the reader's attention to the desirability and usefulness of extending the application of risk analysis from the concept and pre-feasibility phases of the project through to the operation of the plant and the marketing of its products.

Stage 2

Production flow analysis

Alternative production methods and technologies were evaluated and compared, in the form of production flow diagrams (PFDs). Each PFD was structured so it was technically feasible, and capable of comfortably and safely achieving the required production outputs determined in the first stage. Each PFD had its own characteristics, in terms of:

- the number and kind of parallel lines and units of standby equipment, and their associated reliabilities and outage risks;

- production flexibility, product range and ability to adapt to changing market and budget conditions;
- production phasing, and the timing of capital requirements and revenue generation;
- the relative importance of capital equipment, compared with the need for skilled and unskilled labour; and
- energy requirements and the use of internal power generating capability or external energy sources.

Capital cost estimation

A capital cost estimate was derived for each PFD. The techniques used in this process differed according to the degree of refinement required in the estimate. They ranged from standard quantity take-off and estimating methods for producing line item costs to detailed risk analyses for determining probabilities of achieving capital cost budgets and setting appropriate contingency allowances. An extensive example from the timber development is presented later in this chapter.

Operating cost appraisal

The plant configurations resulting from the alternative PFDs were evaluated and compared in terms of operating costs. Factors considered here included: labour intensity or capital intensity; internal power generation or power acquisition; single- or multiple-shift operations; average cost curves; plant repair and maintenance requirements; and differential production distributions, productivity and efficiency rates.

Financial and economic analysis

Alternative cash flow streams were constructed by considering alternative implementation cost curves, project financing systems, export credit and other credit facilities, operating costs, marketing and other costs, and expected revenues. A staged completion of the whole project was determined to optimize cash flows in relation to capital requirements, debt repayments, taxation and export investment incentives, and a detailed financial assessment was prepared for each project implementation phase. The best three or four PFDs were selected for further analysis in the third stage of the project optimization process.

Stage 3

The third stage began with an analysis of project time schedules and cost profiles for each selected PFD. Standard techniques were used here, including critical path analysis and project costing. These were augmented as necessary by risk analysis of the development schedule, to derive detailed distributions for project milestones and to form the basis for revisions to the project plan to reduce overall risk exposure. Specific revisions included an assessment of potential plan improvements attributable to such factors as using more efficient equipment or standby equipment, and balancing labour productivity if a labour-intensive approach were adopted.

Specific amendments to the three or four basis PFDs were evaluated using cost-benefit analysis. Risk analysis provided important inputs here, particularly in the form of distributions of benefits and costs, and it assisted in comparing the marginal benefits and marginal costs as the base plans were revised. This led to detailed project optimization, and ultimately to the selection and specification of the project implementation strategy.

Quantitative risk analysis in project and operations management

Today's attitude by lenders and sponsors towards project financing is such that both the lender and the sponsor must be able to measure individual areas of risk and to assess an overall risk rating for the project. This overall measure might be derived in the form of a distribution of the annual profit for the completed project, or a distribution of the net present value of the capital investment. It is important that the effects of each major variable are considered carefully and their impacts on the project are measured. Relationships between variables can be of particular importance.

The basic analysis for the timber project began by considering risk sources in various categories, to form an integrated risk source summary table (Table 21.2). This was used as a simple check-list for items affecting the whole project. It became more useful as it was extended to include definitions and descriptions of what was involved in each risk, and the impact of each risk, if it occurred, on the project. The combination of resource, construction, operation, market and financial risks in the same summary, together with the descriptive material, provided the sponsor and the project manager with a comprehensive and easy to access informative instrument for periodic assessment and review. (Table 21.2 is a combination of a key element structure and an initial risk list, as discussed in Chapters 2 and 3.)

The descriptions associated with the risk source summary table became an important tool for risk management decision-making when expanded to consider possible responses to risk sources that did arise, the consequences of those responses, and recommended responses. Together with the project management master plan, this extended planning basis enabled the project manager to look ahead in the project's life, to identify and, as necessary, quantify critical features and potential problem areas. From this, it was possible to develop detailed contingency plans for preventing risks from arising or for mitigating their effects.

For the quantitative risk analysis to be manageable, it must be based on a relatively coarse breakdown of the project, typically between 10 and 50 major activities or components. Together with the more detailed breakdown in the project schedule appraisal, a risk model provides a project manager with a comprehensive planning and control tool for achieving levels of project performance which meet or exceed the time, cost and quality expectations of the client.

Table 21.2—Risk source summary table

Risk category	Risk source
Resource and technical	Quality of reserves
	Reserve coverage
	Silviculture risks
	Reliability of logging methods
	Other technical risks
Capital cost estimation	Project manager's experience
	Estimation standards
	Equipment supply
	Equipment erection
	Construction materials
	Construction labour
	Construction equipment
	Climatic effects
Production cost estimation	Training
	Operations management skills
	Labour productivity levels
	Industrial climate
	Equipment outage
	Equipment performance levels
	Consumption rates
	Wage and salary inflation
Market	Price volatility
	Volume variations
	Substitution and competition risks
	Transport and delivery risks
	Quality and reliability image risks
Investment climate	Currency risks
	Economic climate
	Government taxes and charges
	Foreign government tariffs
Security and support	Completion
	Security
	Support by sponsor

The purpose of the quantitative risk analysis was to provide new insights into the risk structure of the project, leading to more creative, effective and efficient risk management. This was achieved by structured analysis of the kind described above, augmented as necessary by quantitative probabilistic analysis, and traditional systems such as cost control, project scheduling and master planning charts. As the nature and degree of dependence between items was analysed and taken into account for computation, risk-response influence diagrams were used to investigate the major components of the risk assessment. The combination of these techniques formed a sophisticated and flexible planning and control system, suitable for assisting the project manager to determine the best course of action for project implementation and optimization, at each stage of the project's life.

It must be emphasized that this approach to risk management is not limited to planning and control during the design and construction phases of the project. It applies also to the operations management of the completed plant, as well as to marketing and financing. The level of detail of the analysis can be adjusted according to its purpose, the phase of the project to which it is applied, and the resources available.

Profit structure risk analysis

To examine the potential contributions of different forms of risk analysis to the timber development, it was useful to think about the total operating profit for the project, formed as the sum of operating profits for each of several product groups (e.g. sawn timber, wood chips, plywood), in each of several market areas. Operating profits were examined in terms of revenues and costs, which were treated more-or-less independently as they arose in different ways, revenues being dependent on international marketing issues, while costs were related to the engineering design and production operations in the home country. Revenues and costs were themselves subdivided into components, in the structure shown in Figure 21.1 and Table 21.3.

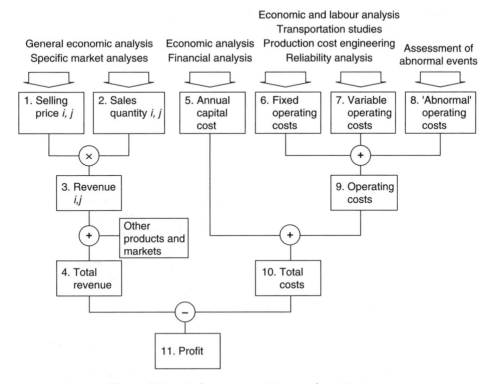

Figure 21.1—Profit structure, with areas of specialist input

Table 21.3—Relationships between contributors to profit, for a specific option

Item		Definition	Notes, linkages
1.	Selling price i, j (product i, market j)		Price in other markets, competition
2.	Sales quantity i, j		Item 1, plant capacity, sales in other markets, product substitutability, competition
3.	Revenue i, j	1×2	
4.	Total revenue	3	Sum Item 3 over all products i and markets j
5.	Annual capital cost		
6.	Fixed operating cost		
7.	Variable operating cost		Total sales (Item 2, over all products i and markets j), total throughput
8.	Abnormal operating cost		May be a project condition (see text)
9.	Total operating cost	$6 + 7 (+8)$	
10.	Total costs	$5 + 9$	
11.	Profit	$4–10$	

This was a simple static analysis, in which revenues, costs and profit were estimated over a fixed period of five years. This kind of analysis was adequate for initial appraisals and comparison of PFDs, but it is too simple for many other purposes. Later chapters deal with more sophisticated analyses of discounted cash flows through time, where net present value rather than profit is a more appropriate criterion for investment decisions.

Revenues

Determination of revenue from sales is a marketing issue, and is not treated in detail here. The discussion that follows is a simple framework for thinking about some of the most important aspects.

Revenue from a product group is derived from a number of market areas. Within each area, the sales receipts are the product of sales quantity and unit selling price. These factors (quantity and price) are not independent: quantities will change in response to price changes. To estimate revenue, it is necessary to estimate the relationship between quantity and price; first in order to determine what the selling price should be for that product in that market, and then to determine the quantity likely to be sold once the price has been set.

A number of factors complicate this simple analysis. The relationship between the sales quantity and the selling price depends on the total demand for the product in the market, alternative sources of supply, product substitution and competitive pressures. Quantity and price are uncertain and so appear as probability distributions rather than as simple numbers. In addition, there are constraints that may influence the quantity–price relationship: there may be a need to maintain relative price structures across different markets, which limits the ability to set prices independently in each market area; and there may be limitations to the operating capacity, which effectively provide a ceiling on the total sales quantity for the product across all market areas. A similar constraint may apply across product groups: for example, the debarking capacity of the plant, or the availability of logs, may set a limit to the total output of all products that is not specific to a particular product group.

Costs

Total cost consists of capital costs and operating costs. Capital costs on an annual basis depend on the financial structure of the venture (an issue beyond the scope of this chapter: see, for example, Merrett and Sykes, 1973, or Chapman and Cooper, 1985, for more detail, or Chapter 22 for an abbreviated outline) and on the actual construction and commissioning cost (as opposed to the budget cost).

It was useful to estimate construction cost in the form of a probability distribution. Quantitative risk analysis has been used successfully for this kind of capital cost estimation in many areas. Not only does it produce a distribution of capital cost for project feasibility evaluation, but it also integrates with project management to provide better risk management and a reduction in potential risk during the construction phase.

The operating cost consists of fixed costs and variable costs. Fixed costs are those costs that are independent of the quantity throughput of the plant. They depend on the kind of plant, the requirements for routine maintenance, operating management overheads, and so on. Variable costs depend on the plant throughput, and so are related to the total sales quantity. Variable costs are usually estimated on a per-unit basis, plus a variable overhead contribution, depending on the accounting and tax conventions used.

Operating costs can vary for a number of reasons. All plants have a spread of operating costs in 'normal' operation, due to uncertainty in the prices of such inputs as labour, energy and spare parts, as well as in the reliability of equipment. There are also 'abnormal' variations, due to such disparate factors as natural events (storms, fires), economic conditions (unexpected changes in inflation rates, unanticipated large changes in the real cost of energy), social issues (major industrial disputes), or technological aspects (catastrophic plant failures).

Risk analysis can provide some insight into each of these aspects of operating cost estimation. Risk analysis has been used to assess the reliability of production systems, as opposed to the reliability of the individual components. Together with standard production cost engineering methods, this approach can be used to estimate the 'normal' spread of operating costs. Variations due to 'abnormal' factors can also be assessed; similar applications have been successful for examining abnormal operating risks in a range of production environments.

An integrated approach

The issues that have been noted above can be integrated into a combined project analysis and management approach. This provides several important benefits.

An assessment of the capital cost of each production flow diagram can be obtained, as a distribution of total cost. This gives an indication of the appropriate level for the contingency allowance on the construction budget, as well as guidance for the project risk management process during actual plant construction. Both general economic analyses and specific financial analyses are amenable to quantitative risk analysis.

An assessment of the operating costs of each PFD can be used to derive distributions of 'normal' and 'abnormal' operating costs. This provides an indication of any insurance or self-insurance arrangements that may be necessary to avoid or mitigate excess costs; for example, by obtaining government guarantees or by providing stand-by systems or spares. It can also lead to outline contingency plans for dealing with production outages during the operating phase of the project. A range of different evaluation methods normally used here are amenable to quantitative risk analysis, including production cost estimation, reliability analysis, abnormal event analysis, transportation analysis and economic analysis.

The revenue potential of the project can be examined by product lines and market areas. This is constrained by product quality requirements, the relationship between demand and price, and the capacity of the plant option being considered. This is the realm of specific market analysis and more general economic analysis, both amenable to risk analysis approaches.

A combined approach permits the evaluation of options for different kinds of plant and equipment, and the feasibility of each, in terms of profitability and other aspects. Each of the factors discussed above contributes to this.

The overall structure and requirements for an integrated approach are illustrated in Figure 21.1. Notes on the linkages and dependencies between items are given in Table 21.3. In Table 21.3, Item 8 (abnormal operating cost) may be treated as a project condition if it involves unlikely but potentially catastrophic consequences, i.e. the evaluation of the project is conditional on the catastrophic event not occurring. Such project conditions may be the subject of separate risk analyses and risk management actions.

The capital cost estimate

This section illustrates the use of quantitative risk analysis for the evaluation of the capital cost estimate for the timber development. The base estimate at the preliminary design stage is summarized in Table 21.4.

The first stage of the analysis estimated a proportional variation about the base value for each major item. This was estimated as a probability distribution of percentage changes from the base, as shown in Figure 21.2 and Figure 21.3. Detailed documentation extended the form in Figure 21.3 to include a statement of data sources, major assumptions and the reasons for the particular numerical values.

The variation distributions for items in the estimate were converted to cost distributions by multiplying by the base cost values. The cost distributions were then added, to form a distribution for the total budget cost (Figure 21.4). The additions were performed using the @Risk simulation package embedded in a standard Excel spreadsheet. The analysis indicates a very high likelihood (better than 99%) of achieving the budget with contingency, and a 95% likelihood of achieving a cost less than 105.

In the addition process, substantial positive dependence was assumed between most items: if the cost of one item is higher than expected, the costs of other items are likely to

Table 21.4—Capital cost estimate, normalized

Item		Base cost
1.	Log handling	17
2.	Saw mill	15
3.	Drying	8
4.	Dry mill and planer mill	7
5.	Pressure treatment	3
6.	Boiler	11
7.	Turbo-alternator	6
8.	Fresh water system	4
9.	Offices	1
10.	Workshop	2
11.	Mobile equipment	4
12.	Mill site	3
13.	Port facilities	5
Total civil and equipment		86
14.	Construction overhead	3
15.	Project engineering	6
16.	Construction management	1
17.	Start-up costs	1
18.	Training	3
Base estimate		100
19.	Contingencies	10
Total capital budget		110

be high also. Relationships of this kind arise due to common dependencies on such factors as imported equipment, local labour rates and productivity, or an overall conservatism in the generation of the estimate. Failure to account properly for dependence can lead to serious underestimation of risk: Figure 21.5 shows the effect of interdependence on the cost variation associated with the four most expensive items, Items 1, 2, 3 and 6. (The 'kinks' in the curves in Figure 21.5 are associated with asymmetries in the underlying distributions, as seen in Figure 21.2.)

Figure 21.4 showed the build-up of cost components to form the total construction cost. 'Sliding' the curves in Figure 21.4 to a common zero-probability point allows the variations attributable to groups of cost items to be identified and compared (Figure 21.6). Here, the four most expensive items – the log handling plant, the sawmill, the dryer and the boiler – appear to contribute the major part of the overall variability. Analysis of this kind facilitated assessment of those areas to which management effort might usefully be directed to provide better estimates, to obtain more precise forecasts or to monitor more closely. In our experience, risk analysis and cost control processes during preliminary design, final design and project implementation contribute significantly towards capital cost reduction and cash flow optimization.

Financing charges and interest during construction were not included in the capital cost breakdown. However, for optimization purposes, they were taken into consideration when

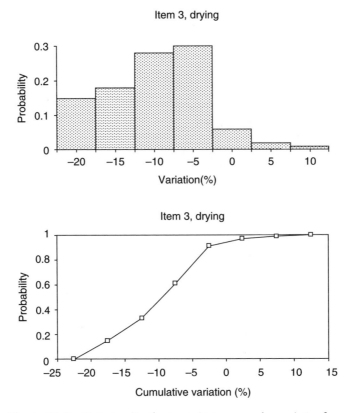

Figure 21.2—Variation distribution in histogram and cumulative forms

3. Drying							
Description	*... Description of the item, including references to preliminary designs, equipment lists and estimates, other data sources, major assumptions ...*						
Base cost	8						
Sources	*... Sources of variation in the base cost ...*						
Variation (%)	−20	−15	−10	−5	0	+5	+10
Probability	0.15	0.18	0.28	0.30	0.06	0.02	0.01
Discussion	*... Notes on risk treatment and management actions ...*						

Figure 21.3—Uncertainty about the base cost for Item 3, drying, illustrated in Figure 21.2

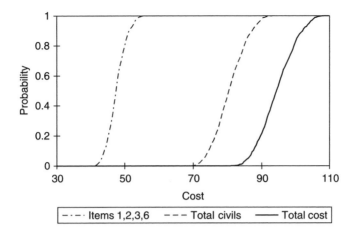

Figure 21.4—Preliminary estimates for costs excluding contingency

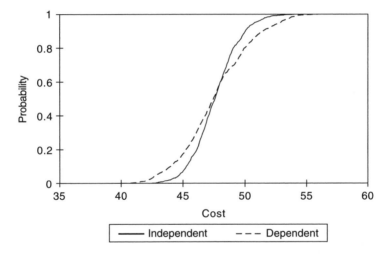

Figure 21.5—Effect of dependence on the combined cost of the four largest items

preparing the project time schedule. In this respect, the influence of phasing, completion time reduction and delayed or reduced financial exposure was further analysed for improved robustness.

For some purposes, the individual lines of the cost estimate might be sub-divided into component costs, or into quantities and unit prices, or a range of separate sources of variation might be estimated. Such refinements are useful at later stages of a project, when they provide the project owners and management with detailed guidance for contingency planning and control, for setting contract terms and conditions when tenders are let, and for allocating risks, costs and rewards between owners, contractors, suppliers and insurers. A detailed analysis of this kind was not necessary for evaluating the preliminary design estimate for this project.

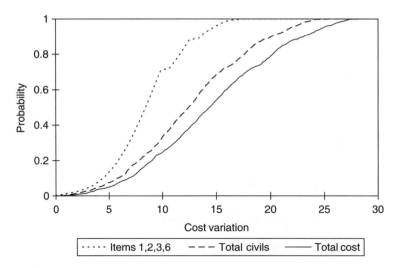

Figure 21.6—Cost variation contributed by Items 1, 2, 3 and 6, civil items, and all other items
excluding contingency

The risk analysis yielded a distribution of estimated capital cost in Figure 21.4, rather than the single value in Table 21.4. This enabled realistic figures to be given for the capital budget and contingency allowances, and it allowed the probabilities that the actual construction cost would be within these targets to be assessed. This is particularly important for projects that are unique in some way, are in new areas, or have special risks associated with them, where the use of a rule-of-thumb percentage contingency, based on experience in a stable environment, may not be appropriate. As Figure 21.4 indicates, the capital cost targets for this project were conservative, with a high probability of achievement, which is unusual.

Discussion

This chapter has outlined an application of risk analysis that can contribute to improved project management at all phases of a project's life. Similar approaches can be used for many different purposes, from economic viability and financial feasibility assessments when the project is still as the concept stage, to detailed optimization of the project schedule before construction begins, and review of the project at major milestones.

The quantitative risk analysis methods discussed here do not merely perform passive risk measurement. Because risks and responses are examined in detail, the emphasis is on robustness, communication, control and an active approach to risk management. Risk management should be integrated with project management, and the project management team should be closely involved with the risk analysis process. In this way contingency plans can be generated, and project managers can ensure they have an appropriate organizational structure, capable of coping with potential risks as they arise. The major benefits of risk management include greater insight, knowledge and confidence, leading to better decision-making and improved project management.

Acknowledgement

This chapter was written in conjunction with Dr Alessandro Bignozzi, who at the time was the Project Director for the timber development described here.

CAPITAL EVALUATION FOR LARGE RESOURCE PROJECTS

22

Chapter overview

- ### Purpose

This chapter describes the application of quantitative risk analyses in the evaluation of large mining and minerals processing projects, to illustrate some of the ways in which risk management processes can be adapted for large projects. It also outlines some of the wide range of extensions to the basic approach that can assist managers make better decisions in the early stages of resource developments.

- ### Rationale

Large projects, including large resource projects, have large uncertainties associated with them and involve very large up-front investments to be committed before many of the risks have been resolved. The processes and models discussed in this chapter provide an important information source for decision-makers as they determine whether a project is a worthwhile investment and in what form it should be undertaken.

- ### Method

This chapter builds upon and expands the quantitative risk analysis processes discussed in previous chapters. It uses discounted cash flow models, combined with detailed estimates of the effects of risk and uncertainty, to develop distributions of key decision criteria, such as net present value and rate of return.

Introduction

There are a number of reasons for undertaking risk assessments for large resource projects. Some of the typical reasons and the questions that are asked include:

- economic evaluation: Is the project worth doing?
- financial feasibility: Can we pay for it?
- project optimization: What is the best contracting strategy? Can we design and plan the project better?
- project management: What are the major risks and opportunities that must be managed to ensure effective and efficient project delivery?

Project capital evaluation is usually based on some form of discounted cash flow analysis. The project cash flows are estimated, often over an extended time horizon, and discounted to present-day dollars. The criteria for decisions about the acceptability or otherwise of the project are often the net present value (NPV) of the investment and its rate of return (ROR), also called return on capital employed (ROCE).

The inputs to the discounted cash flow models include cash inflows, primarily revenues from sales; and cash outflows, that may include capital cost, operating costs, capital maintenance and upgrades and financing costs. The calculations are usually performed, at least initially, on a pre-tax basis, with depreciation and amortization excluded.

For resource projects, there are several major kinds of risks and uncertainties.

- The quality and ease of processing of the resource are often dominant factors.
- The nature, location and availability of the resource is a related matter, including the ease with which it can be extracted and transported to processing facilities.
- Resource characteristics are often closely linked to the characteristics of the mining and extraction equipment and the processing technologies that are to be used.
- Product quantity and quality may be variable and influenced by the resource and the technology that is used.
- The productivity of the technology and the speed with which it is commissioned and ramps up to full production will affect the cash flows of the project.
- The future selling price of the product is usually a major uncertainty, and this may be compounded by foreign exchange variability in some circumstances.
- The project's contract and risk allocation arrangements may introduce new complexities and risks.
- The financial structure may impose new constraints and risks, particularly if there are financial restrictions and covenants.
- Delivery involves a wide range of risks to cost, schedule and the quality of the delivered project assets.
- Country, political and security risks may also be a factor, depending on the location of the project.

This chapter illustrates some of the ways in which quantitative risk analysis models can be used to aid decision-making in large resource projects.

Discounted cash flow calculations

Discounted cash flow (DCF) calculations are based on the notion that it is better to have a dollar today than to receive it next year. By the time you get your dollar at some point in the future, inflation will have eroded part of its value, and you will have lost the opportunity to use it productively yourself over the period until you receive it.

In its simplest form, the value now of $\$X$ received in one year's time is $\$X/(1+r)$, where r is the discount rate. This value, $\$X/(1+r)$, is the net present value or NPV of $\$X$ in one year's time. If the $\$X$ is to be received in two years' time, it must be discounted twice, so the NPV is $\$X/(1+r)/(1+r)$, or $\$X/(1+r)^2$.

For an annual cash flow stream $X_1, X_2, \ldots X_n$ in years 1 to n, the NPV is the sum of the net present values of the individual cash flows:

$$NPV = \Sigma_i X_i/(1+r)^i \text{ where the sum is over all cash flows.}$$

If the cash flows are all expenditures, the NPV is sometimes called the net present cost (NPC).

The NPV depends on the cash flows and the discount rate r. As a general rule, the discount rate should be set to the appropriate corporate cost of capital, as this represents the price the company would have to pay for additional funds to invest instead of those funds it does not have but will receive in the future.

If a project has a positive NPV, then it is generally worth pursuing, in the absence of risk. The justification for this is that the company could borrow the necessary funds for investment, at the appropriate corporate cost of capital, the discount rate, and the project's returns would exceed the borrowing costs.

The rate of return of an investment is that discount rate at which the NPV of the project's cash flows is equal to zero. If the rate of return exceeds the company's cost of capital, then in the absence of risk the project is worth pursuing as the return would exceed the borrowing costs. In practice, ROR is less commonly used than NPV, in part because NPVs are additive and thus more flexible to use.

Where there is risk and uncertainty in the cash flows, two approaches can be adopted.

- The discount rate may be increased by a risk premium. This has the effect of raising the cash flows that are needed for the project to be worthwhile.
- Cash flow uncertainty can be modelled explicitly, in a manner similar to that discussed for modelling cost uncertainty in the previous chapters, and a tool like @Risk can be used to generate a distribution of NPV or ROR that can be used for the investment decision.

The risk premium approach is very simple, but it is not always clear what level of premium is appropriate, particularly for a large, complex or innovative project, and it ignores all the information that is available about the specific risks that might arise in the project.

Our strong preference is to model the risks in the cash flows explicitly, and to use the distribution of the NPV (or ROR) to guide decision-making. This allows the decision-maker to make an explicit choice about the level of risk, or the probability of failure, that can be tolerated in the project investment. This approach also provides a wealth of additional information about the risks and the responses to them that is invaluable in many aspects of project planning and project management. It can also play a major role in developing project funding arrangement and negotiating risk allocation.

Capital evaluation of a new processing plant

This case study concerns an assessment of a large capital investment in the pre-approval stage for a major resources company. The project consists of a complex processing plant that converts feed stock (dirt with valuable impurities!) to a value-added product, with associated supplies and services. The objectives of the risk assessment were to identify the key factors that could affect the profitability of the plant, and to determine the key sensitivities. It differs from the cases in previous chapters in that it involved not only capital costs, but also operating costs and revenues through what was expected to be a long life for the new asset. The initial criteria for the decision to proceed with the project were the pre-tax NPV of the investment and its ROR.

The risk assessment involved two aspects:

- identifying the risks that might affect plant profitability and their impacts, for incorporation in risk models; and
- modelling the capital cost, operating profitability and cash flow characteristics of the plant with their associated risk impacts.

Risks were identified initially in a structured workshop assessment involving key members of the project team. The focus was on the main items with potential for major effects on the profitability of the plant: the largest items of capital or operating expenditure or operating revenue, or those items with the greatest potential variability. The approach was similar to the structured brainstorming discussed in Chapter 3. Later steps involved detailed discussions with the specialists in each area of the plant and those preparing the capital and operating cost estimates.

The workshop assessment followed a similar pattern for each item examined:

- the item was described briefly, and the key assumptions and risks were noted;
- a 'worst-case' or pessimistic scenario was discussed, and the associated pessimistic value for the item was estimated;
- a 'best-case' or optimistic scenario was discussed, and the associated optimistic value for the item was estimated; and
- the most likely scenario was discussed, and the likely value was estimated for those cases where it was different from the value in the most recent financial model.

The evaluation required a set of linked operational and financial models, outlined in Figure 22.1. The main risk model integrated capital spending, revenue and operating cash flow profiles into a combined cash flow profile for the project. These profiles were developed from a variety of supporting models and analyses of varying degrees of sophistication. In practice, the main model took several different forms, with differing levels of accounting and taxation complexity.

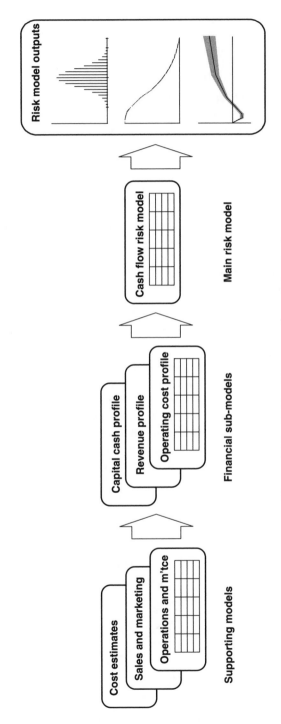

Figure 22.1—Risk model structure for capital evaluation

The purpose of the capital expenditure model was to assess the overall variation in capital cost due to variations in the main items in the estimate. The initial model underwent several iterations as new information became available. Further levels of detail were added where necessary, for several reasons.

- There was a desire to obtain a reasonably uniform treatment of the estimate, so there would not be any very large items that were not disaggregated.
- Where there were large potential variations, additional detail was sought in order to better understand the underlying mechanisms and risks.

Two categories of sources of uncertainty were included:

- uncertainties associated directly with individual items in the estimate, as identified in the risk assessment workshop; and
- estimating uncertainties, applied to the overall estimate to allow for the early stage of development of the project and the relative lack of detail.

The capital cost risk model incorporated uncertainties in the estimate. Three-point estimates were assessed for quantities and rates:

a Minimum, based on a credible best-case scenario;
m Most likely, based on the estimate;
b Maximum, based on a credible worst-case scenario.

In the initial models, the three-point estimates (a,m,b) were interpreted as defining triangular distributions (Figure 22.2). This was a simple assumption for modelling, but it gave appreciable weight to the extreme values within distributions where there was a long tail, i.e. where there was a chance of a large deviation from the most likely cost outcome. Figure 22.2 also shows the effect of using a smooth-curve distribution like the Beta distribution common in PERT analyses: the distribution is weighted more towards the most likely value than the triangular form and gives less weight to values near the extreme ends of the distribution. In later modelling, the Beta form was used for most distributions.

The risk assessment used a range of different shapes for Beta distributions, to reflect the different levels of confidence in the estimated ranges of key values. These were established

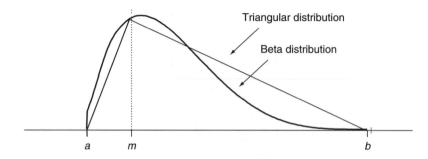

Figure 22.2—Comparison of the triangular and Beta distributions

in discussions with the individuals involved. Where appropriate, other distribution shapes were used in the models.

The operating revenues and expenses were modelled initially on an annual 'average year' basis, assuming the plant was running in a more-or-less steady state. There are many issues associated with the commencement of operations, such as the imbalance of expenses and revenues in the early stages, process inefficiency and wastage of process consumables as the plant is tuned to peak efficiency and as stockpiles are formed before any product is sold. These were not treated in the basic operating model, but were included in the cash flow analysis later.

The operating model followed, in outline, the structure of plant maintenance and feed stock processing.

- The cycle length, and the durations of scheduled maintenance and other unscheduled shutdowns, were used to determine the available days of production for the plant.
- The production efficiency of the plant, with the available production days, determined the output of product available for sale, and the energy requirement.
- The yields of the individual elements of the plant determined the tonnage of feed stock required to meet the output, and hence its cost.
- It was assumed that all product would be sold. The selling price and the exchange rate determined the sales revenue.

Uncertainty estimates for key parts of the operating model were developed during the initial risk assessment workshop. They were then revised following discussions with specialists after test results became available. The operating model was compared with other detailed estimating models for individual parts of the facility. The models achieved a high level of reconciliation.

Capital expenditure and operating revenues and costs were incorporated into a cash flow model, to enable rates of return to be calculated. The capital spending was 'spread' over the construction period on the basis of the preliminary master schedule using a standard S-curve. The base costs were escalated according to the construction index to determine the spending in nominal dollars.

Operating costs were escalated at the rates appropriate to the items being considered, to determine the notional operating expenditure in nominal dollars. They were adjusted during the initial years of the project life to reflect the build-up of capacity as the production trains are commissioned and begin operating.

Operating revenues reflected the forecasts of product sale price, yields and exchange rate variations. They were adjusted to reflect the build-up of production and the increase in operating efficiency in the initial period after commissioning.

In practice, working capital is required to fund the accumulation of stockpiles, work-in-progress and the delays in payments for sales. Working capital requirements for this project were included indirectly, as a side-effect of the build-up of revenue, on the basis that delaying the recognition of revenue has the same effect as increasing working capital from sales receipts. No attempt was made in this risk assessment to model the project's balance sheet and working capital requirements explicitly, although we have done so in other cases.

All the models were constructed in the form of Excel spreadsheets, with the @Risk simulation package used to represent the distributions for uncertain quantities, to perform the quantitative risk calculations and to generate simulation results.

Outputs from the risk model included distributions of the financial criteria (particularly the post-tax real NPV and ROR) and key operational measures (for example, physical production and energy consumption per unit of product). These were generated in the familiar density form, and also as profiles through time where appropriate (Figure 22.3).

The range of returns was associated with the uncertainty in technical plant performance and the margin between sales revenues and operating costs. There was a small chance the return would be negative.

The time-based profile for cash flows illustrated in Figure 22.3 shows the uncertainty in forecasts increasing further into the future. The central line is the mean outcome forecast by the model; the band on either side is the range in which the outcome is expected with 90% chance. This shows the realistically likely ranges of:

- the maximum working capital requirements, the lowest point of the profile;
- the payback period, the range across which the band crosses the time axis; and
- the closing position at the end of any period in the project's life.

Large projects are usually subject to large cash flow uncertainty, and hence the payback period may span a wide range. Figure 22.4 shows a similar cash flow profile from a different resource project with a forecast total capital cost of the order of USD 750 million. A large part of the cash flow uncertainty in this project was associated with future sales prices for refined metal and the foreign exchange rate. (The exchange rate was a factor here because the product was priced in USD in international markets, but this was not the base currency for the company's accounts.) This project was at the feasibility stage at the time this analysis was undertaken. While the ultimate profitability and return looked good, there were problems in funding the capital requirements and it did not proceed.

Risk analysis packages like @Risk permit sophisticated sensitivity analyses of the form illustrated in Figure 22.5. This shows the main contributors to uncertainty in the NPV, taking into account all the input variations in the risk model. Figure 22.5 indicates that the market price of refined product is the most important source of uncertainty in determining the value of the project, something that will not be a surprise to anyone involved with mining, and a similar result to the outcome in the project that gave rise to Figure 22.4. Almost all of the other drivers of uncertainty were linked to achieving the design performance

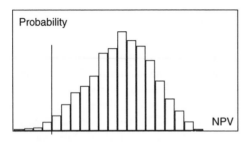
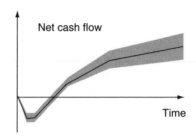

Figure 22.3—NPV distribution (density histogram form) and risk profile through time

Cumulative project cash flow

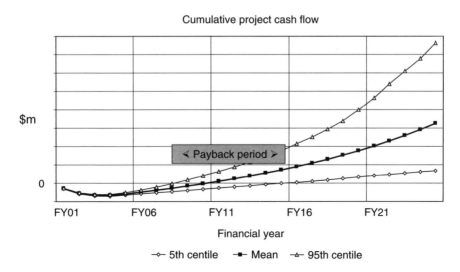

Figure 22.4—Cash flow profile and payback range

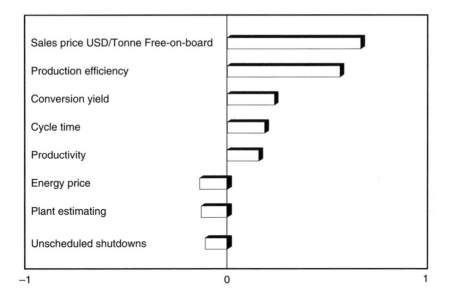

Figure 22.5—Sensitivity of NPV to project uncertainties (tornado diagram)

of the technology: the productivity and efficiency of the plant had relatively large uncertainties associated with them, an obvious reflection of the uncertainty in the performance of technology itself under different operating conditions. Capital cost uncertainty, as represented by plant estimating variation, was comparatively insignificant.

More detailed analyses were used to elaborate on the effects of risk on the overall project evaluation results. They confirmed that operating revenues were affected strongly by commercial factors and the production of the plant.

- Sales price uncertainty dominated the revenue uncertainty as well as uncertainty in the overall project return.
- Technical factors related to the production of the plant were significant. These included the productivity of the plant itself, the cycle time and the durations of scheduled and unscheduled shutdowns.
- Operating costs were affected by the productivity of the facility and the prices of key inputs to the process, particularly the energy price.

Although the capital cost was not a major driver of uncertainty for the project as a whole, it was important to understand where the main risks were so they could be managed as far as possible. The main contributors to the variability in the capital cost were identified.

- The foreign component of the mechanical equipment was the major driver for uncertainty.
- The plant contained risks associated with the complexity of the structure and the design and construction of the facility. The variability thus introduced was also a major driver.
- The project labour component was also significant because there was potential for a shortage of labour with the skills required for the construction. This arose due to the effects of potential parallel projects in the area.

Additional risk scenarios were also considered in outline and their associated effects on the rate of return of the project were calculated. Scenarios covered:

- delay in start-up due to problems with technology;
- delay in start-up due to engineering and construction delays;
- delayed capital spending and corresponding start-up delays;
- reduced capital cost, for example to include the benefits of project value analysis; and
- increased capital spending to ensure production start-up schedules are achieved.

Apart from the base case, a further set of technical options for the project was considered in outline and assessed using the base models, after appropriate adjustments to key parameters. Risks introduced by these options were considered and taken into account in the analysis as appropriate.

In many of the resource projects in which we have participated, quantitative analyses like the ones outlined above have formed an important part of the information used to plan the project development strategy. They have also formed an important part of the project funding proposal provided to the board for its decision on whether or not to proceed with the investment, in what form and with what financial structures.

Project financial structure

Cash flow planning, financial structuring and risk allocation must be integrated carefully. Simple quantitative project risk modelling is unlikely to be sufficient for large projects, and it is often necessary to model financial structures and view the project on a business or enterprise basis. Further extensions to include tax and accounting matters are common.

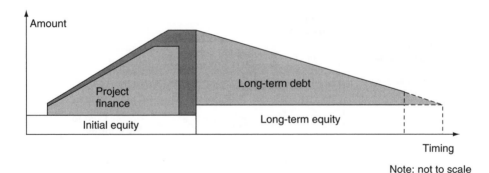

Figure 22.6—Indicative project financial structure

Financial structures for projects include short-term and long-term equity and debt, illustrated schematically in Figure 22.6.

- Initial project planning and preparation is likely to be funded from equity.
- Construction is commonly funded on a project finance basis, in which short-term debt is provided with the project itself as the debt security. The requirement for project finance may be faster, larger and longer than planned, so top-up facilities are often required. Project finance tends to be expensive, as the risks are large in this phase of the project life.
- Once the project has been commissioned and achieved stable operation, much of the risk has been dissipated. It is now possible to sell the project to equity investors and the long-term bond market, to pay back the construction debt and recompense the initial equity providers for the risk they have taken.

The quantitative models discussed in this and previous chapters can be extended to include project financial structures of this kind. Debt draw-down can be linked to the (uncertain) project schedule and key milestones, and the debt servicing costs can be incorporated in the cash flows. Such models can become complex and unwieldy unless they are constructed with care, usually by moving the financing aspects to a separate part of the spreadsheet. Models of this kind are also commonly used when evaluating potential public–private partnerships and private financing arrangements of the kind discussed in Chapter 16.

Incentive contracts

Incentive contracts can be used to focus the attention of the contractor on performance delivery outcomes, as well as limit the risk to the owner.

In a complex, high-technology acquisition in the resource sector, a quantitative approach to project delivery risk was adopted to estimate the cost of an incentive contract to the project owner. It was intended that the incentive contract operate under an open-book arrangement between the owner and the principle contractor, a large engineering and

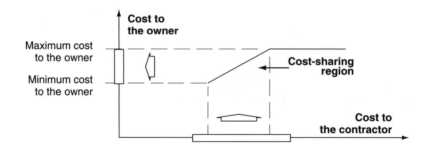

Figure 22.7—Cost allocation between owner and contractor in an incentive contract

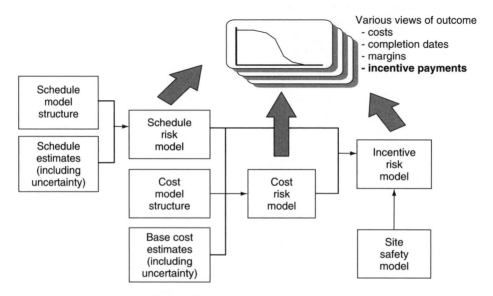

Figure 22.8—Incentive model structure

construction company. Figure 22.7 shows the structure of the proposed payment approach: above a designated maximum cost, the contractor would bear any overruns; below a designated minimum, the contractor would keep all profits from innovation and efficient delivery. Costs and savings would be shared according to an agreed ratio in the intermediate zone where the actual cost was expected to fall.

In practice, this simple representation was complicated by the inclusion of specific criteria related to minimum acceptable standards of site safety certification and safety incidents. The model, illustrated in Figure 22.8, was an extension of the evaluation models discussed earlier in this chapter; for example, compare Figure 22.8 with the general model form shown in Figure 22.1.

An analysis of the risks and their effects on cost uncertainty, in a form similar to that in previous chapters, was combined with the incentive targets and the agreed share ratio, to model the cost to the owner. This analysis was undertaken for each submitted tender, to contribute to the commercial evaluation of the tenders and allow a funding submission to be developed and justified. The model was used subsequently when negotiating specific contract terms.

However, it is worth noting that if the contractor's performance starts to fall outside the acceptable limits (e.g. at the right-hand end of the range in the diagram in Figure 22.7), the incentive structure may break down. The contractor can be left with no incentive to co-operate with the owner and resort to claims and litigation. In such circumstances, overall performance may deteriorate rapidly.

Technology choice

A cautious approach to technology risks is often prudent if technology is central to project profitability. Sometimes the choice is simple, between equipment that has a high capital cost but is efficient and low-maintenance in operation, and low-cost but inefficient equipment that has a high life-cycle cost. In cases like this, simple discounted cash flow analysis to calculate the NPV of each option often provides a useful guide to selecting the preferred equipment. If there is additional uncertainty, models like those described earlier in this chapter can be used to generate NPV distributions to assist in selecting a preferred option.

Risk may play a more important role in the selection process in some cases. For example, the choice might be between high-cost processing plant that is robust and has known productivity across a range of ore grades, and low-cost plant where there is significant uncertainty about the production rates that might be achieved in practice with variable run-of-mine ore grades.

Quantitative models like those that have been discussed in this chapter provide a means of incorporating this kind of uncertainty into the decision process. A model of the cash flow forecast for each option and the effects of major risks will indicate which one is preferred on simple financial grounds.

In other circumstances, a staged approach that takes account of the value of flexibility may be useful and a risk model can help estimate that value by simulating the outcome with and without various options. For example, Figure 22.9 is a probability tree for a minerals processing project, showing sequences of staged activities and decisions associated with pilot-testing potential new refining and smelting technology.

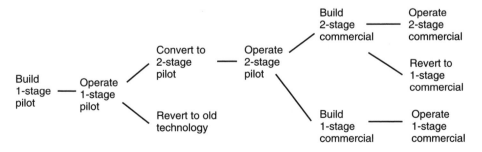

Figure 22.9—Phased options for selecting a process technology

A phased, toe-in-the-water approach like this provides flexibility to adjust the project according to the outcomes that are obtained at intermediate points, taking advantage of information gained in earlier stages and lowering the overall risk compared to building a full-scale commercial plant in one step. While a staged approach sounds generally attractive, simple economic analyses that ignore phases and uncertainties often indicate a single-step large-scale project development would be worthwhile.

When a compelling argument has been made to proceed with a major project as a simple single-stage development, it is usually hard to justify considering let alone adopting a phased approach. Quantitative risk models can be used to determine a value or price for the flexibility associated with project phasing, in a form that is similar to the outcomes obtained from a 'real options' approach. A traditional attachment to simple large developments may be denying sponsors significant value associated with the options offered by a staged approach.

Typically, a quantitative risk analysis of potential project outcomes would be undertaken for each of the main paths in Figure 22.9, and for the other main options (such as developing a 1-stage or 2-stage commercial process without testing in a pilot plant). These would be combined with the probabilities at branch points in the diagram to assist with decision choices.

Figure 22.10 shows a similar model for the phased development of an established oil field with new gas injection wells to enhance oil recovery. The lozenges represent decision points and the circles represent points at which a probabilistic branching takes place. For example, if a decision is made to proceed with a full development of gas injection across the field, the outcome might be a successful production enhancement ('Good field') with estimated probability 0.63, or the field may be below expectations ('Poor field') with estimated probability 0.37.

If a decision is made to drill test wells to trial the gas injection process, the outcomes might be favourable with estimated probability 0.49, in which case full development would proceed, and the estimated probability of this being successful across the field is now 0.97. The probabilities have been updated to take account of the additional information provided by the successful gas injection test, using a Bayesian revision process summarized in Figure 22.11.

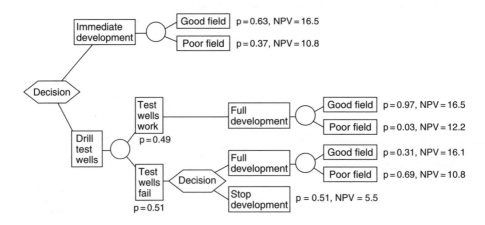

Figure 22.10—Options for an oil field development

Drilling outcome

	Prior probabilities	Test works Test wells flow at consistent high rates	Test fails Test wells do not enhance flow significantly	Key to conditional probabilities	
Good prospects for enhanced recovery across the whole field	63%	75%	25%	P(Test OK / Good field)	P(Test fails / Good field)
Poor prospects for enhanced recovery across the whole field	37%	4%	96%	P(Test OK / Poor field)	P(Test fails / Poor field)
Test outcome probabilities		49%	51%	P(Test OK)	P(Test fails)

Posterior probabilities

	Test works	Test fails		
Good prospects	97%	31%	P(Good field / Test OK)	P(Good field / Test fails)
Poor prospects	3%	69%	P(Poor field / Test OK)	P(Poor field / Test fails)

Figure 22.11—Probabilities for the oil field development

The NPVs associated with each branch in the tree in Figure 22.10 can be calculated from the capital and operating costs of each field development option and the revenues based on the expected production flows across the field. The NPVs and the probabilities all contain significant uncertainties, which can also be included in the decision model. This allows the options to be compared and decisions to be made about the best approach to select. In addition, it provides a process for justifying the field development strategy that is adopted.

Conclusions

DCF models that include risk are a basic tool for project capital evaluation in a wide range of sectors and circumstances. Sometimes simple analyses are sufficient to provide guidance on whether or not a large capital investment is worthwhile, but in most cases it is necessary to include the effects of risk and uncertainty explicitly, and to develop distributions of the principal values that support investment decisions, such as NPV and ROCE.

As project size and complexity increase, so the complexity of the models can be increased to support executive decisions. Financial, accounting and taxation matters are usually needed to support bankable feasibility studies, with associated balance sheet as well as cash flow models.

DCF risk models can be used to assist in other forms of management decisions. The incentive contract structure outlined under 'Incentive contracts' above illustrates just one of the ways models of this kind can be used to support contract negotiation and structuring. Other areas include the analysis of outsourcing contracts and public–private financing arrangements discussed in Chapters 15 and 16. As an extension of this, the technology-choice example noted in the early part of 'Technology choice' above mirrors some of the aspects of tender selection we have encountered, where a choice must be made between a high-cost tender offer for which the outcomes are relatively certain (for example, due to the quality management processes of an experienced service provider and associated contractual guarantees) and a tender with a superficially lower base price but high potential variability and a looser contractual arrangement.

The later examples in this chapter indicate some of the linkages between risk and uncertainty models based on discounted cash flows and the developing field of real options analysis. The approach is slightly different, though – whereas real options analysis usually links the value of choice to prices established in a real or notional market, DCF models often provide a more direct means of valuing the flexibility associated with different approaches to a project development path.

While this chapter has focused on resource projects, the principles and the approach can be applied to many kinds of projects that involve risk and uncertainty. Further illustrations are provided in the next chapter.

RISK ANALYSIS AND ECONOMIC APPRAISAL

23

Chapter overview

- ### Purpose

  This chapter outlines the role of risk analysis in the concept stage of a project, and the place of risk analysis in feasibility studies generally and economic appraisals more particularly.

- ### Rationale

  At an early stage in the development of potential projects, when there are significant risks and uncertainties remaining, decisions must be made in spite of the uncertainty. Risk analysis allows uncertainty to be quantified and included explicitly in the evaluation of a proposal. It permits decision-making to proceed in an orderly fashion even though major uncertainties remain unresolved.

- ### Method

  Standard approaches to economic evaluation and the assessment of costs and benefits are extended to consider potential sources of variation and uncertainty. Criteria such as net present values or benefit-cost ratios are calculated as distributions, and decisions are made that take risk into account.

Introduction

The concept phase of a project proposal is similar to a strategic planning activity. It involves setting objectives, comparing strategic requirements with existing capabilities, and identifying needs and gaps. From these steps emerge a list of the detailed objectives and general tasks necessary for achieving broad corporate and project goals.

A critical step in this concept phase is the conduct of a detailed feasibility study. The general process involves identifying the options that might meet the detailed objectives determined in the initial steps, assessing them and recommending the best option. The assessment should consider the project through its entire life, up to and including the termination, divestment or decommissioning of any associated facilities or assets and remediation of land. Key parts of the feasibility study are:

- Economic appraisal: This process identifies options and assesses their benefits and costs, both qualitatively and quantitatively, to determine the options with the highest net present values or the highest benefit-cost ratios. The appraisal process also involves sensitivity testing, which may use elements of risk analysis in its conduct and interpretation.
- Risk analysis: This process identifies major areas of uncertainty and risk, highlights key sensitivities and considers allocation of risk amongst the stakeholders. It also involves consideration of responses to risk, thus generating recommendations for risk management and control strategies. Quantitative risk analysis may be conducted as a key part of the economic appraisal, or as part of the financial feasibility analysis.
- Financial feasibility: This process examines the financing of the project and its cash flows, to determine whether it is financially feasible. (This contrasts with economic appraisal, where non-monetary factors are important; here the focus is on cash movements.) Outputs from a financial feasibility study may include recommended financing structures and debt to equity ratios.
- Environmental appraisal: This process examines the potential environmental impacts of the project and identifies measures for mitigating adverse effects.

These individual elements overlap to a great extent. It is the task of the feasibility study to integrate them and to develop a considered recommendation that takes all relevant factors into account. The recommendation should include not only a statement of the best option, but also an outline brief describing the purpose of the project, its integration with existing systems, an outline budget and key milestones including a target completion date.

Outline of the economic appraisal process

Cost-benefit analysis is the main tool for economic appraisal. Figure 23.1 summarizes the steps in determining the net benefit or cost associated with a specific option. The benefits and costs are identified, and then quantified, where possible, on a common scale of dollars. In some circumstances, it may be easier to do this in two steps, quantifying first in natural units (e.g. the amount of an output produced) and then transforming to a dollar scale using an explicit factor or rate (e.g. the economic or social cost per unit of that output), particularly when there is no well-defined or agreed factor. Time effects take into account the timing of cash flows, any escalation or inflation factors and the discount rate to be used to generate net present values or to set internal rate of return hurdle rates. Finally a net benefit or cost or a benefit-cost ratio is calculated, suitably discounted.

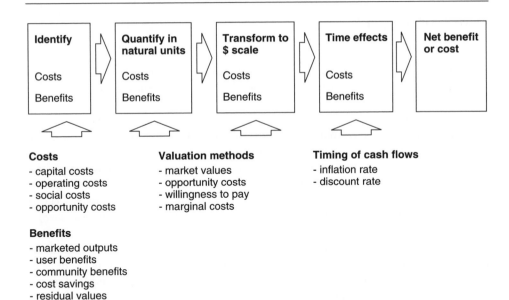

Figure 23.1—Summary of the steps in determining the net benefit for an option

When all options have been assessed in terms of their individual net benefits or costs, a decision must be made about the 'best' option. Decision rules may be based on net present values, benefit-cost ratios, internal rates of return or payback periods.

It is often assumed implicitly in this appraisal process that each measure of benefit or cost is a single numeric value, or that each measure can be assessed as a single point on a scale, albeit a subjective or descriptive one for some factors that may be difficult to value or quantify. Risk may not have been included in the analysis up to this point.

Risk and uncertainty in cost-benefit analysis

Many guides to cost-benefit analysis discuss risk only in outline and propose that aspects of risk can be addressed by sensitivity analysis. This approach is valid only in a limited range of circumstances, and even small projects benefit from a more detailed and explicit consideration of risk in the feasibility study.

Risk analysis has been used widely in the appraisal of capital works and in the comparative assessment of available options, as discussed in previous chapters. The remainder of this chapter is concerned with the contribution of risk analysis to the economic appraisal process.

Common approaches to taking risk and uncertainty into account in the cost-benefit process include:

- sensitivity analysis, including determining the effect of plausible changes in uncertain parameters on decision criteria such as NPV or ROR;
- loading the discount rate by adding a risk premium;

- scenario planning; and
- quantitative risk analysis.

Sensitivity analysis may be extended to the calculation of 'switching values', to determine the critical values for parameters at which it becomes worthwhile to switch to another option.

Sensitivity analysis may be a useful guide when there are only a few key uncertain factors with major influences on the outcome and the distribution or possible outcomes for these factors are easy to understand. However, when there are many uncertainties or where the uncertain factors are interrelated in complex ways, this approach becomes less suitable.

Loading the discount rate is simple, but it has many serious practical and theoretical difficulties, particularly when different kinds of variations are anticipated between benefits and costs. This approach also faces difficulties where the risk profile of a project changes through its life, as is often the case.

Scenario planning provides another way to select a preferred option. It involves describing possible future states and determining the potential consequences in terms of the decision criterion. This overcomes some of the problems of sensitivity analysis and loading the discount rate. It has the additional advantage that it facilitates the comparison of project options under similar conditions and assumptions. Nevertheless, this approach may be too simple for assessing risk in many large procurements or where the outcomes under separate scenarios are not clearly separated, such as where an optimistic outcome for one option is more attractive than a pessimistic outcome for another and it is not clear which is the most likely to arise.

Economic appraisal with risk

The process for economic appraisal can be modified to include appropriate risk analysis elements, within the same framework. The simplest extension to the standard cost-benefit process substitutes distributions for the single-value estimates of benefits and costs (Figure 23.2).

The distributions may be derived in several ways. Direct estimation of the distributions of benefits and costs may be possible where there are few sources of uncertainty or where the effects of uncertainty are well known or expected to be minor. In other cases a more formal risk analysis process is recommended. Previous chapters dealt with these topics in more detail. The distributions may also be generated from scenario analyses, discussed further below.

Where distributions are used instead of single values, the computational methods used in the appraisal process must be adjusted to handle distributions. Suitable software is normally required for this, but there are few conceptual difficulties. However, other adjustments may need to be made to the standard process.

- Transforming a single value to its dollar equivalent may involve several problems. The main issues centre around the value to be used as a multiplying factor to derive the dollar measure. This becomes a particular practical difficulty when the project's benefits and costs arise in different ways for multiple stakeholders or interest groups.

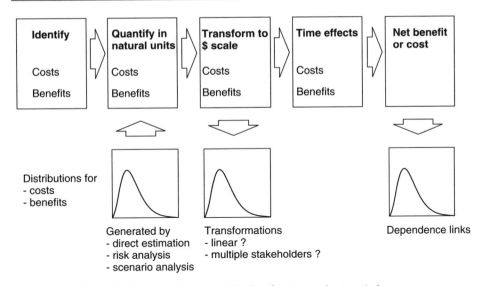

Figure 23.2—Extension to include distributions in the appraisal process

- In addition, when the 'natural' measure of benefit or cost is derived in the form of a distribution, it may be important to assess the linearity of the transformation, i.e. can the same factor be used to derive the dollar measure through the whole range of the original distribution, or do the marginal values of the benefits and costs change towards the ends of the range? In most cases linear transformations are appropriate, but the issue should be considered if distributions have wide ranges.
- Combining distributions must take into account the dependence links or correlations between them, otherwise risk estimates may be significantly in error. The ability to handle dependence properly and flexibly is a key requirement for risk analysis software. (Dependence has been discussed in previous chapters.)

Risk-based scenario analysis

Where there are major risks that might impact on a project, or where the range of potential impacts of a risk is very wide, a scenario-based approach may be appropriate. Natural disasters, large fires, industrial disputes, or major changes in the economic environment may have significant effects on a project as a whole. A scenario approach provides a flexible way of organizing the analysis in these circumstances.

The structure of scenario analysis is derived from probability trees. Figure 23.3 shows a simple probability tree structure for assessing the consequences of a risk in terms of the events that might occur, the potential outcomes associated with an individual risk event and the responses to it, and their cost implications. (In this example, the risk was that of a flood occurring, the event was the flood level, the outcome and

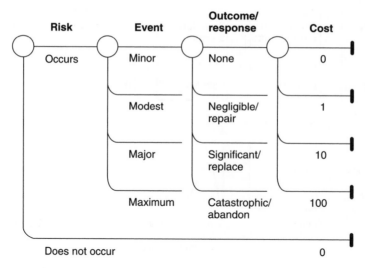

Figure 23.3—Risk event and outcome/response probability tree

response were the effect on a bridge and associated abutments, and the cost was the repair and recovery cost.)

Where the set of outcome and response scenarios is common across risk events, the probability tree structure may be simplified (Figure 23.4). For an individual risk, several steps are involved.

1. Identify a representative, mutually exclusive set of risk events.
2. Identify a set of non-overlapping outcome and response scenarios that might arise as a consequence of the risk occurring, and describe each in detail. The description should include a statement of the effect of the risk event, the main assumptions, possible responses to the risk event and the best response, any secondary risks that might arise as a result of the response mode chosen, and the consequences expressed in terms of the benefit and cost measures of interest.
3. Assess a matrix of conditional probabilities of each scenario arising, given that a specific risk event occurs.
4. Calculate the unconditional probability of each scenario arising.
5. Calculate the overall effect of the risk in terms of distributions of the benefit and cost measures.

The distributions derived from this process become the inputs to the appraisal structure of Figure 23.2.

The process illustrated in Figure 23.2 produces a distribution of the output measure of interest. For example, Figure 23.5 shows a cumulative distribution of net benefit for a project option, indicating the probability that the net benefit will be less than the value on the horizontal axis. Figure 23.5 shows the probability the net benefit will be negative, i.e. the likelihood that the option will generate a loss.

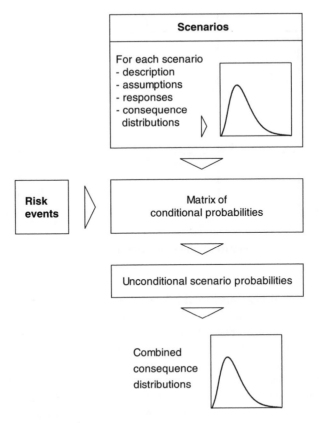

Figure 23.4—Simplified outcome/response scenario structure

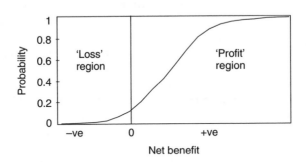

Figure 23.5—Distribution of net benefit for an option

River-crossing example

To illustrate some of the points discussed above, this section outlines the quantitative risk analysis that was used in the selection of a preferred option for a strategic river crossing.

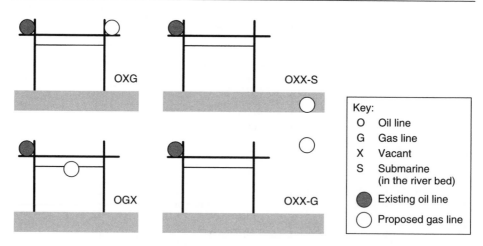

Figure 23.6—River-crossing options

The project involved a gas pipeline, the alignment of which was to follow an existing oil pipeline along most of its route. The oil pipeline crossed a large river on a pipeway cantilevered from a major bridge. Placing the new gas line on the bridge in the existing vacant pipeway on the other side of the bridge deck was an obvious solution, but it would increase the risk to the oil pipeline and to the bridge itself. Should the new pipe be placed on the bridge, under the bridge (to leave the existing pipeway clear for a potential third pipeline), on a new bridge some distance away, or submerged in a trench in the river bed (Figure 23.6)? A range of other minor options and variants were also considered, but they are omitted from this discussion.

This was a large and complex analysis, befitting the high-value and high-risk nature of the project. The results were subject to intense scrutiny by the stakeholders involved, as just one input to a wide-ranging decision-making process.

The analysis was complicated by a number of factors. Like many large projects, there was a range of stakeholders, and a diverse set of criteria important to each of them. The criteria themselves were not controversial, although estimating them was often difficult, but generating an agreed transformation from 'natural' units like barrels of lost oil production to a common numerical scale denominated in dollars raised many issues. For example, the 'value' of a barrel of lost oil production can be determined in several ways, depending on whose interests are concerned, as indicated in Table 23.1.

A risk-based scenario analysis was used, similar to that described in the previous section, supported by a large team undertaking numerous engineering and environmental studies, detailed risk and response analysis, and quantitative risk modelling involving software adapted specially for the project and the analysis structure. Extensive sensitivity analyses were performed.

Figure 23.7 shows typical results from the risk-based scenario analysis used for comparing options for the river crossing. The curves show, for each major option, the probability that the cost for the option will be less than the indicated value, so the preferred options are those towards the top (higher probability for the same cost) and the left (lower cost for the same

Table 23.1—Stakeholders and measures of the 'cost' of lost oil production

Stakeholder	Relevant measures
Producer	Current well-head price per barrel
	Discounted well-head price (as the production is not lost, only deferred to the end of the life of the oil field)
	Marginal profitability of a barrel of oil produced
Pipeline operator	Revenue per barrel transported
Local government	Royalty per barrel extracted
Central government	Strategic value of energy supplies
Refiner	Marginal additional cost of crude from the next-best source

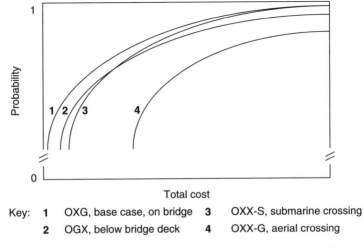

Key: 1   OXG, base case, on bridge   3   OXX-S, submarine crossing
      2   OGX, below bridge deck   4   OXX-G, aerial crossing

Figure 23.7—Comparison of strategic options for the river crossing

probability). The costs are the total annualized costs of construction, operation, maintenance and risk. These results indicate that the base-case Option 1 is preferred over the entire range of costs – it dominates the others. Option 4 is clearly not preferred to any other option and is dominated by them all. Had a choice between Option 2 and Option 3 been necessary, where the curves cross over one another, the risk preferences of the stakeholders would have been taken into account.

It is worth exploring Option 2 and Option 3 in a little more detail, as they illustrate the relationship between the risk analysis outcomes and the physical realities of the project. The curves in Figure 23.7 are shown in stylized form but in practice they were not as smooth as this.

- The curve for Option 2, with the gas pipeline below the bridge, had a marked kink to the right associated with the point at which flood risks start to have a major impact on the gas pipeline. As expected flood levels increase, the risk increases more-or-less smoothly until the level at which the pipe, suspended below the bridge, becomes exposed to floating debris and ice. At this point there is a step increase in the risk of physical damage and product release, with large associated costs. This risk was seasonal, associated particularly with the spring run-off.

- The curve for Option 3, the submarine crossing, also had kinks, but this time associated with the expected management response to risks. As problems with a pipe buried under the river increase, the risk increases more-or-less smoothly until it becomes cheaper to replace the entire pipe than to attempt to repair it.

Diagrams like Figure 23.7, and similar ones that showed the contribution of individual risks to the total cost, were also used to guide sensitivity analysis and re-examination of engineering and environmental matters. This example is described in more detail in Chapman *et al.*, 1985; and in Cooper and Chapman, 1987.

Summary

This chapter has discussed risk analysis and economic appraisal in the context of cost-benefit analysis (CBA), the preferred approach to economic evaluation of projects. Cost effectiveness analysis (CEA) is an alternative to CBA where the output of a project is not readily measurable in terms of dollars and it is necessary to compare the costs of project options having the same or similar outputs. Risk analysis can be applied to CEA in the same way as it is applied to CBA, generating outputs in a similar form for decision-making. In addition, distributions can be used to represent vague transformations of qualitative or social objectives to dollar scales, allowing the uncertainty in the scaling factors themselves to be included explicitly in the analysis.

In terms of risk analysis, the process described here is very similar to that discussed in previous chapters. Whereas in Chapters 20 and 21 there was a single criterion – cost – here there were several, and the structure was adjusted accordingly.

The scenario approach described here is an extension of the method described in Chapters 20 and 21 for cost estimation. Scenarios can also be used in the context of cost estimation, although they are not always necessary.

CONCLUSIONS

24

Chapter overview

> ● **Purpose**
>
> This chapter provides a short overview of some of the features of large projects and their implications for the selection of an approach to risk management.
>
> ● **Rationale**
>
> The risk management approach must usually be tailored for large projects. Large projects may require a combination of approaches, and careful thought about the emphasis that is placed on different aspects of the project and the risk management process. The initial context stage is critical.

Risk management for large projects

Large projects have characteristics that set them apart from 'routine' activities. Risk management for these projects usually requires careful selection of the approach to be used, and often the 'standard' approaches must be modified to suit the project and the context. Of course, many of the lessons apply to smaller projects too, but they are critically important as project scale increases.

The characteristics of large projects that set them apart from day-to-day activities include:

- many diverse and powerful stakeholders, inside and outside the sponsoring and project management organizations;
- complex technical requirements, often with flow-on complexity in contracts and insurances;
- large cash flows, that tend to be unbalanced, front-loaded and close to financial limits, with the potential for large financial gains or losses;
- scale effects in both the project management organization and the technology to be delivered; and
- intense regulatory scrutiny of safety, environment and probity aspects.

Stakeholders

Most projects have several stakeholders. With large projects:

- there are often many more of them;
- more of them must be actively engaged with the project to achieve success; and
- many of them have more power, including veto rights in some cases.

Stakeholders were discussed in Chapter 2. Stakeholders for a large project, some of whom may be antagonistic to project outcomes, may include:

- owners, sponsors and procurement teams;
- project delivery counterparties: contractors, equipment providers, materials suppliers, and their employees and unions;
- customers: purchasers of the products or services produced by the completed project asset;
- asset users: operators, maintainers, logistics support, employees and unions;
- suppliers of inputs to the completed project asset: materials, energy;
- advisers: technical, financial, legal, probity;
- financiers: financial and insurance markets, and providers of equity, debt and credit support;
- external: community, environment, media;
- regulators: planning, environment, safety;
- other companies, agencies, business units or projects that are competing for funds;
- competitors with a vested interest in project postponement or failure; and
- other entities with a vested interest in project success, or, in some cases, in frustrating the sponsoring agency.

With a large number of stakeholders, risk management processes must be structured carefully. There is a need to design governance structures and risk management processes that take account of the context, the stakeholders, the organization and the culture. For a detailed discussion of the design of risk management processes in different kinds of organizations and cultures, see Cooper (2003).

As discussed in Chapter 8, communication with stakeholders is critical at all stages of large projects (and see also Gough, 2003). Risk and project communication should be integrated, and integrated with other aspects of project management. The communication strategy for risk should:

- address both internal and external stakeholders;
- consider communication as a two-way process, involving consultation with stakeholders where appropriate;
- understand and take account of different perceptions of risk;
- foster ownership and engagement of stakeholders with the risk management process and its outcomes; and
- develop a consultative team approach.

Large projects require good communications strategies, and often a formal project communications plan. The communication strategy should incorporate media, community, government and regulatory liaison, as well as processes for involving internal stakeholders. Risk communication will be a core part of the overall strategy. (The environmental impact statement preparation and approval process is an important part of the public communication process for large projects in many jurisdictions.)

Stakeholder aspects should be included at all stages of the risk management process, and particularly as part of:

- context development (discussed in Chapter 2), where stakeholders' objectives and areas of concern should be incorporated in the development of criteria, scales and key elements;
- structured workshops for risk identification, assessment and evaluation (discussed in Chapters 3 and 4), to make the best use of diverse expertise; and
- risk treatment and change management (discussed in Chapter 6), to ensure that treatment options are understood and acceptable.

Processes for structuring problems to take account of diverse stakeholders, in a wider context than risk management, are reviewed by Mingers and Rosenhead (2004).

Complex requirements and contracts

Size and complexity often go hand in hand, and there are often more than just scale effects. Particular care is needed in tender evaluation, contract negotiation and risk allocation, topics discussed in Chapters 13 and 14. Large outsourcing and PPP arrangements introduce additional risks, as discussed in Chapters 15 and 16. The mine waste management case discussed in Chapter 18 involved many technical, environmental and social risks with complex interrelationships and feedback links.

In some circumstances, tender evaluation may be undertaken using very simple approaches. The objectives of the risk assessment in tender evaluation are:

- to provide an initial indication of where the major risks might arise in the project, prior to receipt or detailed examination of tender responses, based on a set of credible assumptions about how the project might be conducted;
- to develop a risk baseline against which individual tender responses can be compared;
- to assist the project team to focus on potential risk areas in their evaluations of offers and in their evaluation visits to tenderers' sites;
- to provide a risk profile for each tender offer submitted, developed on a consistent and justifiable basis; and
- to provide a documented audit trail of the project team's assumptions about potential risk areas and their reasons for adjusting their assessments in the light of individual tender responses or site evaluation visits.

In several projects, we have used semi-quantitative approaches for assessing risks at the tender stage, applied to Work Breakdown Structure (WBS) items (at an appropriate level) or work packages. In other cases, we have conducted more detailed analyses, based on specific

Table 24.1—Contract negotiation case example

Criteria	Extreme	High	Medium	Low	Total
Performance	1	22	78	56	157
Contract	2	8	77	70	157
Agreed priority	2	38	80	37	157

identified risks. This more detailed approach is necessary for contract negotiation, where risks must be considered explicitly.

An example of a qualitative rating process for guiding contract negotiation in a high-technology government acquisition is shown in Table 24.1. Two sets of criteria were used and applied to individual risks:

- performance criteria: functional capability, delivery schedule, life-cycle cost, supportability, safety;
- contract criteria: acquisition cost, industry involvement, good management, good contract. ('Good management' includes probity, processes, systems; 'good contract' includes being seen as beneficial and good value for money for the client and the nation, i.e. a political impact measure as much as anything.)

The five performance criteria were combined in the performance rating; the four contract criteria were combined into the contract rating; and these two ratings were combined into the overall agreed priority. Note the general increase in the agreed priority, compared with the individual components.

The outcomes from this risk assessment were used as one of the inputs for developing the contract negotiation strategy for the project.

More detailed quantitative risk modelling provides a basis for assessing the cost of risk, thus allowing preferred risk allocation structures to be developed prior to contract negotiation and facilitating the evaluation of their effects during the negotiation process. For example, Figure 24.1 illustrates schematically how the total cost of risk may change according to the degree of aggregation and allocation. As a general rule, the price attached to a set of risks

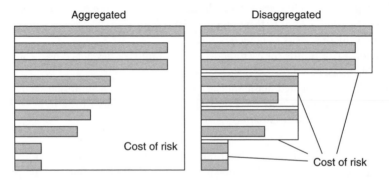

Figure 24.1—Notional effect of disaggregation on the financial cost of risk

by the financial markets is set conservatively according to the 'most risky' element, so the aggregated cost of the risks on the left-hand side of Figure 24.1 is relatively high; on the right-hand side, where the risks have been disaggregated, grouped and allocated to different parties with different appetites for risk, the total cost has been reduced because there is no longer a need to pay a premium for the low-risk elements that have been bought by other parties at a more appropriate and lower price.

This kind of analysis is relevant to some of the broad risk allocation and financial structuring matters discussed in Chapters 16 and 22. At a micro level, quantitative models provide the basis for evaluating potential contract incentive structures, also discussed in Chapter 22.

Large and unbalanced cash flows

Large projects often have large and unbalanced cash flows that are close to the funding limits of the proponents. Most projects involve initial spending, before any revenue benefits are realized, but for large projects this may be a critical factor:

- the initial spending requirements may be very high;
- there are usually large uncertainties in the size and timing of funding requirements;
- long construction and commissioning periods extend the payback period and reduce the NPV;
- construction incentives may be necessary;
- trading-off reduced construction costs and a faster schedule for increased through-life costs may be a false economy.

Large projects usually required detailed cash flow analysis that incorporates risk and uncertainty. Chapters 19 to 23 addressed aspects of quantitative risk analysis, and further examples of the use of quantitative risk models in the evaluation of public–private partnerships were provided in Chapter 16.

Simple quantitative project risk modelling is unlikely to be sufficient for large projects. It is often necessary to model financial structures and view the project on a business or enterprise basis. Further extensions to include tax and accounting matters are common, and financial risk allocation structures must be considered carefully.

Technology and scale

Large projects often involve complex technical and operating linkages, new technology and technology at new scales. Not all of the implications of scale and technology choice are obvious.

Risks and their implications must be specified in great detail. It is usually not sufficient to consider only primary risks and treatments: the causes and consequences of risks must be modelled more precisely, and secondary risks associated with treatment actions must be incorporated in the analysis.

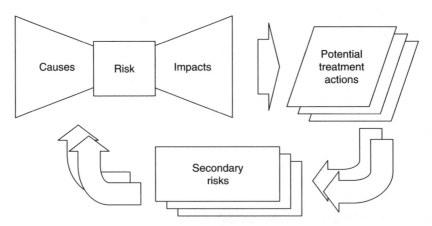

Figure 24.2—Primary and secondary risks and responses

The initial analysis structure is sometimes called a 'bow-tie' diagram (Figure 24.2, and refer also to Figure 17.8). The causes of risks may be modelled using fault tree analysis or some similar method that identifies and structures the precursors of the risk event. The impacts may be modelled using event tree analysis or some similar method that links the risk event to outcomes and consequence measures. Both the cause and impact models may use probabilistic approaches.

Because risks in large projects can have many links to other areas, there are often several potential treatment actions. These may be significant activities in their own right, and there may be a range of secondary risks that emerge as the outcome of choosing any particular course of action. These must be analysed and treated in turn.

Phased approaches to the introduction of new technology were discussed in Chapter 22. The quantitative risk analysis processes discussed in this book can be used to determine a value for the flexibility obtained by adopting a phased approach to a project implementation, compared to a one-phase project plan.

Intense scrutiny

Large and complex projects often involve major risks that are of interest to major stakeholders. This results in intense scrutiny from regulators and others with an interest in the project and its outcomes.

Regulatory scrutiny will almost always involve safety, environmental and planning bodies. Sometimes these bodies are in multiple jurisdictions, for example at national and regional or local levels. Other stakeholders may include local and regional communities, politicians, unions and the financial markets, or indeed almost any of the stakeholders noted in Chapter 2 and earlier in this chapter.

For example, the mine waste planning example that was discussed in Chapter 18 involved many stakeholders with keen and often divergent interests in the operation of the mine and the options for dealing with waste material. In addition to the stakeholders noted

Table 24.2—Stakeholders for the mine waste project

Stakeholder	Major issues
Board and shareholders	Option costs and benefits (value for money), economics, profit, reputation, accountability, image, environment, option costs
Mine managers	Reputation, accountability, image, environment, option costs
Employees	Job security, satisfaction, pride
Contractors	More contracts, spending shift to mitigation option, local partnerships and employment
Local community	Employment, business opportunities, cash compensation, development funds, future prosperity, option costs and benefits
Provincial community	Infrastructure including maintenance, sustainable industry, future prosperity, option costs and benefits
National public	Distribution of government funding (to other provinces)
International public	Environment, mine closure
Local government	Infrastructure including maintenance, sustainable industry, future prosperity
Provincial government	Infrastructure including maintenance, sustainable industry, future prosperity, option costs and benefits
National government (as shareholder and regulator)	Reduction in revenue, value for money, contribution to option costs, option benefits
World Bank	Environment, social effects of mine closure
Environmental groups and NGOs	Environment, mine closure
Shareholders of the corporate owners	Share price, corporate image

in Table 24.2, there were several groups of lawyers representing different interests in court actions involving the mine, and intense media scrutiny.

In circumstances like this, the development and implementation of a broadly based and effective communication strategy becomes critical. Because the company was subject to local and international scrutiny, the board wanted to demonstrate clearly that it was doing its best for all the stakeholders, particularly the local communities. To increase the transparency of the process, it took the step of making the results of the many scientific studies and the reports generated during the risk assessment available on its website, www.oktedi.com

Summary

There are many ways of looking at risks, from the riskiness of work items seen in the semi-quantitative and tender evaluation examples in Chapters 5 and 13 through to the detailed identification and inter-linkages seen in Chapter 18. In increasing complexity, they cover:

- riskiness of work items;
- lists of individual risks;

- risks considered in stages;
- primary and secondary risks; and
- very complex risk linkages and interactions.

Similarly, models may cover a wide range, from the very simple priority-setting approaches described in the early chapters of this book through to complex quantitative cash flow uncertainty models and financial models that include tax and accounting effects to form an enterprise view of the project. In increasing complexity, they cover:

- qualitative approaches for ranking risks and setting priorities;
- semi-quantitative models, also used for risk ranking and priority setting;
- quantitative models that deal with

  - costs only, starting with capital costs and then extending to through-life and whole-of-life costs,
  - cash flow models, where quantitative schedule models drive time-based consideration of costs and revenues,
  - more complex uncertainty models that incorporate tax and accounting effects to make projections of financial statements such as the profit and loss account, balance sheet, cash flow statements and financial ratios for the business; and
  - real options and related models to evaluate the value of the flexibility associated with staged approaches to project and business development.

There are many potential ways of looking at risk in projects. Many approaches to risk management are feasible, depending on the project, its scale, its level of development and the issues of concern, and there is no single 'best' method that suits all phases of all projects.

It is important to plan carefully the approach that is to be adopted, to make sure the one selected is the most appropriate for the circumstances. While this advice is certainly and obviously relevant for large projects that often involve complex risks through most of their stages, where sophisticated approaches to risk and uncertainty may be needed, it is also relevant for small projects, where the selection of simple approaches that suit the requirement and the circumstances may be the key to efficient implementation and organizational acceptability.

Plan the risk management process very carefully, start early in the project life, and select judiciously from the portfolio of available approaches.

Part IV
Additional information and supporting material

RISK MANAGEMENT PROCESS CHECKLIST **25**

Chapter overview

- **Purpose**

  This chapter summarizes the main steps in a simple risk management activity in the form of a process checklist.

- **Rationale**

  Checklists provide an easy way of ensuring all the steps in the risk management process have been completed.

- **Method**

  The process checklist here is a very simple one, and organizations that conduct projects regularly will need to tailor it to their own management processes and method of working. Refer to the preceding chapters for detailed descriptions of each step.

- **Documentation**

  Copies of the worksheets are contained in Chapter 26.

Initiation

[ ] Assemble the risk management team
[ ] Appoint the team leader
[ ] Ensure the team has a suitable breadth of skills and experience

Establish the context

Objectives

[ ] Familiarize the team with the project
[ ] Assemble documentation according to the requirement
[ ] Identify the main questions and issues of concern
[ ] Review the organizational and project environment
[ ] Specify the organization's objectives

Stakeholders

[ ] Identify the key stakeholders and their objectives
     Use the stakeholder and issues summary where appropriate
[ ] Develop a communication plan if appropriate

Criteria

[ ] Specify the criteria, linked to the project, organizational and stakeholder objectives
[ ] Develop scales for measuring the criteria, ensuring they are compatible, where relevant, with other scales used in the organization
[ ] Develop scales for measuring likelihoods that are appropriate to the project timeframe and the risk areas of interest
[ ] Develop a matrix for combining the criteria and likelihoods to derive levels of risks
     Use a simple matrix for combining them if appropriate, or develop a semi-quantitative worksheet
     Use the criteria summary where appropriate
[ ] Review the need for a more extensive quantitative risk analysis

Key elements

[ ] Develop an analysis structure (target 20–50 key elements, items or activities)
     Use the project element summary where appropriate
[ ] Number each element, describe it and list the main assumptions
     Use the project element description worksheets where appropriate, or refer to a WBS Dictionary if there is one

Risk identification

[ ] Select an appropriate process for risk identification
[ ] For each element, identify and number the risks
     Include opportunities as well as risks where appropriate

[ ] Describe each risk and list the main assumptions
[ ] Assess the implications for the project
Use the risk description and response description worksheets where appropriate

Risk analysis

[ ] Assemble data on the risks and their consequences
Most of this will be recorded on the risk and response description worksheets
[ ] Analyse the consequences of the risks in terms of the criteria
[ ] Analyse the likelihoods of the risks arising and leading to the assessed level of consequences
[ ] Summarize the analysis for each element on the assessment summary sheet
[ ] Combine the consequence and likelihood assessments to derive levels of risk
Use the assessment summary sheets

Risk evaluation

[ ] Rank risks in order of decreasing level of risk
[ ] Plot the consequence and likelihood measures on the risk contour diagram if required
[ ] Draw a risk profile if appropriate
[ ] Identify Extreme or High risks for detailed risk action planning
[ ] Identify Medium risks for management and monitoring
[ ] Identify Low risks for routine management
[ ] Specify the person responsible for ensuring each risk is treated appropriately (the 'risk owner')

Risk treatment

Identify feasible responses

[ ] For each Extreme or High risk, and for Medium risks if resources allow, identify and number the feasible responses
Response strategies include:

- risk reduction and risk avoidance
- impact mitigation
- risk sharing
- risk retention

[ ] Describe each response and list the main assumptions
[ ] Use response description worksheets for detailed analyses

Select the best responses

[ ]   Identify the benefits and costs for each response
      Take into account *all* the benefits and costs, including indirect ones
      Use response selection worksheets where appropriate
[ ]   Select the best responses for each risk

Develop Risk Action Plans

[ ]   Develop Risk Action Plans for all Extreme and High risks
[ ]   Actions (what is to be done?)
[ ]   Resource requirements (what and who?)
[ ]   Responsibilities (who?)
[ ]   Timing (when?)
[ ]   Reporting (when and to whom?)
[ ]   Use risk action summary worksheets for executive reporting
[ ]   Specify risk management responses for Medium risks
      Use risk action summary worksheets where appropriate

Reporting, implementation and monitoring

[ ]   For major projects, produce a formal Risk Management Plan
[ ]   For other projects, collate and summarize the Risk Action Plans
[ ]   Implement responses and action strategies
[ ]   Monitor the implementation of the Risk Action Plans
[ ]   Assign responsibilities for monitoring
[ ]   Specify reporting processes, frequencies and responsibilities
[ ]   Undertake periodic review and evaluation

WORKSHEETS AND EVALUATION TABLES 26

Chapter overview

> ### ● Purpose
>
> This chapter collects the worksheets provided through the text into one place.
>
> ### ● Method
>
> Table 26.1 summarizes the worksheets, and provides cross-references to the originals and examples of their use.
>
> ### ● Documentation
>
> Worksheets like these may form a major part of the documentation of the risk management activity for a project.

Table 26.1—Worksheets and cross-references

Topic	Description	Source	Examples	Chapter 26 reference
Stakeholders	Summarizes the key stakeholders, the issues of concern to them and their objectives	Figure 2.1	Tables 2.2, 2.3, 2.4, 24.2	Figure 26.1
Objectives and criteria	Summarizes the criteria, their definition and the method of measuring each one	Figures 2.2, 2.3	Tables 2.5–2.8, 4.3, 4.4, 8.2, 10.5, 17.6, 18.2, 23.1	Figures 26.2, 26.3

(Continued over leaf)

Table 26.1—(Continued)

Topic	Description	Source	Examples	Chapter 26 reference
Key elements	Provides the cross-reference between the element structure used for the risk analysis and the Work Breakdown Structure; summarizes the main features of each element of the project task and lists the main assumptions	Figures 2.4, 2.5	Tables 2.9–2.14, Figure 13.3, Tables 18.3–18.5, 20.2–20.4, 20.6, 21.2, 21.4	Figures 26.4, 26.5
Risk description	Describes risks, documents the initial thinking about mechanisms, and lists the main assumptions, for more detailed analyses of major projects	Figure 3.1	Tables 10.8, 10.9, Figure 21.3	Figure 26.6
Risk Register	Lists current information about the risks; summarizes the risks for a simplified assessment	Table 4.12, Figures 4.1, 10.2	Tables 10.10, 10.13, 11.3, 11.4, 11.7, 17.5	Table 26.2, Figures 26.7, 26.8
Semi-quantitative assessments	Sample assessment forms for risk assessments of systems and sub-systems; pictorial view of the distribution of risks for project elements in terms of likelihoods and consequences; summary sheets for recording workshop assessments	Figures 5.1–5.3, 13.3–13.5	Tables 5.1–5.7, Figures 5.4, 5.5, 5.7, 8.1, 13.9, 13.10	Figures 26.9–26.14
Risk treatment	Describes options for risk treatment and summarizes their benefits and costs; summarizes Risk Action Plans in the form of an overview or cover sheet for executive reporting of risk action plans for Extreme and High risks	Figures 6.6, 6.8	Tables 10.11, 10.12	Figures 26.15, 26.16
Project risk reporting	Provides a summary report for senior management commenting on the major risks and the risk management process	Figures 8.2, 8.3	Figure 8.1	Figures 26.17, 26.18
Hazop record		Table 17.5	Table 17.5	Table 26.3

Project:			Reference:
Stakeholder	**Key issues and objectives**		
Compiler:	Date:	Reviewer:	Date:

Figure 26.1—Stakeholder and issues summary (Figure 2.1)

Project name:	Reference:

Project description:

Objectives for the project:

Organizational objectives:

Business unit objectives:

Project objectives:

Objectives for the risk assessment:

Specific changes to criteria (if any):

Reference documents:

Compiled by:	Date:	Reviewed by:	Date:

Figure 26.2—Context review summary (Figure 2.2)

Project:		Reference:
Criterion	**Definition**	**Measurement method**
Compiler: Date:	Reviewer:	Date:

Figure 26.3—Criteria summary (Figure 2.3)

Project:			Reference no:
Element number	**Name and description**		**WBS references**
Compiler:	Date:	Reviewer:	Date:

Figure 26.4—Key element summary table (Figure 2.4)

Project: Element:			Reference no:
Description:			
Assumptions:			
Source material:			
Compiler:	Date:	Reviewer:	Date:

Figure 26.5—Key element description (Figure 2.5)

Project: Element: Risk: Manager (risk owner):	Reference:
Description and mechanisms:	
Key assumptions:	
Sources of information:	
List of attachments:	

Compiler:	Date:	Reviewer:	Date:

Figure 26.6—Risk description work sheet (Figure 3.1)

Table 26.2—Risk register columns and their contents (Table 4.12)

Column heading	Content and notes
E	The reference number of the key element (see Chapter 2)
Element	A brief description of the key element (see Chapter 2)
Group	This column is used for grouping similar risks as an aid to developing treatment options and action plans
R	A unique identifying number for the risk. This often has the form E.xx, where E is the element number from the first column and xx is a two-digit identifying number
Risk	A brief description of the risk, its causes and its impacts
Existing controls	A brief description of the controls that are currently in place for the risk. At an early stage in the life of a project, the controls may be those that are expected to be in place if normal project management processes are followed.
C	The consequence rating for the risk, with the controls in place, using scales like those in Table 4.3, Table 4.4 or Table 4.5.
L	The likelihood rating for the risk, using scales like those in Table 4.6, Table 4.7 or Table 4.8.
Agreed priority	The agreed priority for the risk, based on an initial priority determined from a matrix like Table 4.2, Table 4.9, Figure 11.1 or Figure 11.2, adjusted to reflect the views of the project team in the risk assessment workshop.
Inherent risk	The inherent risk rating for the risk, if there were a credible failure of controls or they failed to work as intended, using the scale in Table 4.11.
Action sheet	A cross-reference to the action summary for the risk, in one of the forms shown in Chapter 6.
Responsibility	The name of the individual responsible for managing the risk.

E	Element	Group	R	Risk	Existing controls	C	L	Agreed priority	Inherent risk	Action sheet	Responsibility

Figure 26.7—Format of a typical risk register (Figure 4.1)

Key elements and issues (Prompt list)	No.	Risks	Controls	C	L	Initial priority	Agreed priority	Actions and responsibility
Regulatory regime								
Business objectives								
Commercial								
Political and community								
Contractual and legal								
Safety								
Industrial relations and human resources								
Capital requirements								
Resources								
Timing and schedule								
Technical and performance								
Customers								
Suppliers								
Infrastructure								
Assets								
Monitoring and management systems								
Finance and administration								
Others								
...								

Figure 26.8—Example risk summary sheet for a simplified risk assessment process (Figure 10.2)

Project: Element:		Reference:	
Hardware maturity	**Software maturity**	**Dependency**	
Existing technology	Existing technology	Independent of existing system, facility, associate contractor	
Minor redesign	Minor redesign	Schedule dependent on existing system schedule, facility, contractor	
Major change feasible	Major change feasible	Performance dependent on existing system performance, facility	
Technology available,complex design	New software, similar to existing	Schedule dependent on new system schedule, facility, contractor, etc.	
State of the art, some research complete	State of the art, never done before	Performance dependent on new system performance, facility, contractor	
Other more substantial maturity risk	Other more substantial maturity risk	Other more substantial dependency risk	
Hardware complexity	**Software complexity**	**Commercial risk**	
Simple design	Simple design	No sub-contract element	
Minor increase in complexity	Minor increase in complexity	Minor sub-contracting of non-critical elements	
Moderate increase in complexity	Moderate increase in complexity	Minor sub-contracting of critical elements	
Significant increase in complexity	Significant major increase in number of modules	Significant sub-contracting to accredited supplier, not single source	
Extremely complex	Highly complex, very large data bases, complex operating executive	Single-source accredited supplier of critical elements	
Other more substantial complexity risk	Other more substantial complexity risk	Other more substantial commercial risk	
Technical factor	**Cost factor**	**Schedule factor**	
Minimal consequences	Budget estimates not exceeded	Negligible schedule impact	
Small performance reduction	Over budget by 1–5%	Minor slip (less than 1 month)	
Some performance reduction	Over budget by 5–20%	Small slip in schedule	
Significant degradation in technical performance	Over budget by 20–50%	Schedule slip more than 3 months	
Technical goals cannot be achieved	Over budget by more than 50%	Large slip, affects segment milestones	
Compiler:	Date:	Reviewer:	Date:

Figure 26.9—Assessment form for technical projects (Figure 5.1)

Project:								Reference:	
Element:									
Likelihood indicators	**Rating** **(High – Low)**						**Discussion, key assumptions and responses**		**Score**
	A	B	C	D	E	F			
	A	B	C	D	E	F			
	A	B	C	D	E	F			
	A	B	C	D	E	F			
	A	B	C	D	E	F			
	A	B	C	D	E	F			
							Average likelihood score:		
Consequence indicators	**Rating** **(High – Low)**						**Discussion, key assumptions and responses**		**Score**
	A	B	C	D	E	F			
	A	B	C	D	E	F			
	A	B	C	D	E	F			
	A	B	C	D	E	F			
	A	B	C	D	E	F			
	A	B	C	D	E	F			
							Average consequence score:		
Scoring:		A	B	C	D	E	F		
		0.9	0.8	0.7	0.5	0.3	0.1		
Risk Factor:									
Likelihood score + Consequence score – Product of scores									
Compiler:		Date:			Reviewer:			Date:	

Figure 26.10—An alternative assessment sheet (Figure 5.2)

WBS number:	Element:		Page 1 of

WBS dictionary:

Project team assumptions:

Assumptions continuation pages: Yes/No

Assessment summary

Likelihood measures		**Impact measures**	
Hardware maturity		Performance	
Hardware complexity		Cost	
Software maturity		Schedule	
Software complexity			
Dependence			
Integration and interfacing		**Risk factor**	
Management processes			
Compiler:	Date:	Reviewer:	Date:

Figure 26.11—Summary sheet for recording workshop assessments (Figure 13.3)

WBS number:	Element:		Page of
Project team assumptions			**Rating**
Likelihood, hardware maturity			
Likelihood, hardware complexity			
Likelihood, software maturity			
Likelihood, software complexity			
Likelihood, dependence			
Compiler:	Date:	Reviewer:	Date:

Figure 26.12—Detailed assumptions and ratings, sheet 1 (Figure 13.4)

WBS number:	Element:		Page of
Project team assumptions			**Rating**
Likelihood, integration and interfacing			
Likelihood, management processes			
Impact, performance			
Impact, cost			
Impact, schedule			
Compiler:	Date:	Reviewer:	Date:

Figure 26.13—Detailed assumptions and ratings, sheet 2 (Figure 13.5)

Project:

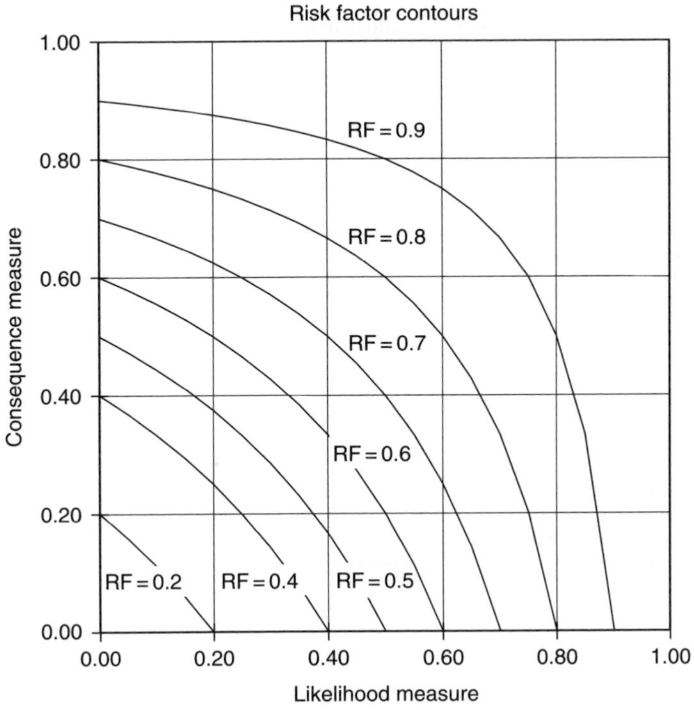

Risk factor contours

Special features and observations:

| Compiler: | Date: | Reviewer: | Date: |

Figure 26.14—Risk contour diagram (Figure 5.3)

Element:	Risk:		Action sheet:
			Risk register number:
Likelihood:	Impact:	Agreed risk level:	Inherent risk level:

Risk description (causes, consequences, implications):
Current controls and plans:
Possible additional actions:

Response	Effectiveness	Cost

Comments and recommendations:
Sources of information and list of attachments:

| Compiler: | Date: | Reviewer: | Date: |

Figure 26.15—Risk treatment options worksheet (Figure 6.6)

Element:	Risk:		Risk register number:
Likelihood:	Impact:	Agreed risk level:	Inherent risk level:

Risk description (causes, consequences, implications):

Current controls and plans:

Additional actions recommended:

Responsibility:

Resources required:

Timing (key milestones, closure):

Reporting (to whom, when, in what form):

References (to other documents or plans as appropriate):

Compiled by:	Date:	Reviewed by:	Date:

Figure 26.16—Risk Action Plan summary (Figure 6.8)

Project summary risk report		Period:	Submission date:
Summary of Extreme or High risks			

Risk number	Risk description	Risk treatment and control summary	Responsibility

Commentary on significant changes during the period:

Commentary on the status of the Risk Management system in the project:

Project Manager:	Reviewer:
Date:	Date:

Attachments: Risk Action Plan summaries for Extreme and High risks

Figure 26.17—Project summary risk report (Figure 8.2)

Major project periodic risk report	Period:	Submission date:
Commentary on Extreme or High risks to the project and their management:		

Summary risk profile:				

Agreed Priority	Impact			The number of risks in each inherent risk rating	
Likelihood ⇩	High (A or B)	Medium (C)	Low (D or E)	Extreme	
High (A or B)				High	
Medium (C)				Medium	
Low (D or E)				Low	

Summary of Extreme or High risks:

Risk number	Risk description	Risk treatment and control summary	Responsibility

Commentary on significant changes during the last period:

Commentary on the status of the risk management system in the project:

Project Manager:	Reviewer:
Date:	Date:

Figure 26.18—Major project periodic risk report (Figure 8.3)

Table 26.3—Hazop record sheet (Table 17.5)

Project:			Section:			Date:	
Drawing:						Revision:	
Node	Guideword	Causes	Consequences	Safeguards	Action	Manager	Comments and status
1							
2							
3							
4							
5							
6							
7							
8							
9							
10							
...							

Examples of Risks and Treatments

27

Chapter overview

- ### Purpose

  This chapter contains lists of risks derived from a wide range of projects, including risks associated with out-of-area projects, and examples of potential treatments for a small selection of them.

- ### Rationale

  Risk lists can simplify the risk identification process, and provide a useful check on its completeness. Treatment lists provide guidance on options that might be considered when developing action plans.

- ### Method

  The use of checklists is discussed in Chapter 3, as are some of their limitations.

- ### Documentation

  Organizations should develop their own lists of risks and treatments appropriate for the most common projects they undertake. Checklists may be part of the organization's quality assurance procedures and documentation.

Project risks

The lists of risks in this section have been derived from a wide range of projects. There are many other ways of classifying them.

These are not intended to be exhaustive lists. Organizations should develop their own lists of risks, appropriate to the kinds of projects in which they engage. Other examples of risks for specific kinds of procurement activities are provided in Chapters 15 and 16.

Commercial

- Competing projects
- Competitive pressures
- Demand management
- Innovation
- Market growth
- Market share

Contract general conditions

- Arbitration, courts
- Changes to standard general conditions
- Commercial issues
- Common use contract
- Conditions for acceptance
- Contractor to inform himself
- Delay due to principal or other factors
- *Force majeure* events
- General conditions (and are we aware of contents and implications)?
- Insurance, indemnities
- International contract terms
- Legal, regulatory
- Legally binding
- Liquidated damages
- Practical completion date
- Prompt payment
- Safety
- Scope
- Security, warranties
- Specification requirements, quality
- Variations

Counterparty

- Ability to meet contract commitments
- Attitude to litigation
- Client business failure
- Client change of ownership
- Client inability to take delivery of project
- Client misunderstanding of needs and scope of work
- Client speed of response

- Creditworthiness, ability and willingness to pay
- Experience with organization
- Failure to pay or delayed payment
- Future business
- Loading or preferential treatment of bids
- Payment delay history
- Payment philosophy
- Principal interaction
- Principal's attitude to changes in scope
- Project culture and attitude: environment, quality, safety, time

Economic

- Commodity prices
- Currency stability, exchange rate variation
- Demand growth
- Demographic trends
- Discount rate
- Energy price
- Inflation rate
- Interest rates

Environment

- Amenity values
- Conservation
- Contamination of land, water, air (deliberate or inadvertent leak, spill or release)
- Dust
- Endangered species
- Hazardous chemicals and materials
- Heritage values
- Latent conditions
- Legislative and regulatory constraints
- Noise
- Recycling

Financial

- Debt:equity ratios, gearing
- Equity funding and ownership
- Financing costs

- Funding sources
- Funding withdrawn or delayed
- Investment conditions
- Taxation effects
- Working capital requirements, liquidity

Industrial relations

- Award suitability
- Flow-on effects
- Job security
- Labour laws, regulations
- Loss of management control
- Strength of unions
- Strike leading to delays
- Strike settlement leading to higher costs

Interpretation of the brief, understanding the requirements

- Interpretation may cause overestimation and low value for money
- Misunderstanding of user expectations
- Poor technical knowledge in new area
- Quality and detail of specification
- Quality level not met
- Requirements not understood fully
- Timetable not met
- Users' expectations not met, different user groups have different expectations
- Variations in contract

Joint venture, partnership

- Complexity of the agreement and documentation
- Complexity of the business structure
- Level of control
- Level of responsibility
- Partner financially unstable
- Partner lacks technical resources
- Partner withdraws from joint venture
- Potential for litigation
- Probity

- Requirement for skills or equity contribution
- Staging aspects

Legal/regulatory

- Approval processes
- Conflicts of interest
- Inadequate terms and conditions
- Lack of knowledge of applicable laws and regulations
- Unclear contract

Natural events

- Drought
- Excessive heat, cold
- Fire
- Flood
- Landslip, subsidence
- Lightning
- Seismic event, earthquake
- Storm

Political and social

- Community consultation
- Community support
- Government endorsement
- Government or political intervention
- Policy change
- Political change (effect of change of Government)
- Pressure groups
- Public misinterpretation of decision without all facts available

Product life cycle stage

- Mature
- New
- R&D required

Resources

- Additional capital investment needed
- Availability of critical components or materials
- Availability of critical equipment
- Availability of funds (internal, external)
- New plant or equipment required

Safety

- Contract safety
- Drugs (use, testing)
- Equipment failure
- Human error
- HSE processes
- Legal requirements, local regulations
- Product contamination
- Project safety
- Safety guidelines issued in or referenced in contract

Security

- Community security
- National security
- Sabotage
- Site security
- Vandalism

Skills

- Adequate prior experience
- Availability of skilled staff
- In-house, external provision
- Inappropriate mix
- Learning curve effects
- Loss of critical skills (to illness, competitor)
- Poorly defined skill requirements
- Potential professional liability
- Recruitment
- Staff turnover
- Training (timeframes, availability, effectiveness)
- Training of contractors, suppliers

Software

- Database complexity
- Development required
- Management ability
- Software complexity
- Software maturity
- System size
- Telecommunications aspects

Suppliers and sub-contractors

- Ability to deliver, skills, quality of equipment
- Accreditation
- Alternate suppliers, sub-contractors
- Availability
- Claims, variations
- Commercial terms
- Control and supervision
- Cost of goods and services provided
- Delivery of goods and services provided
- Failure of critical supplier, sub-contractor
- Flow-on conditions from prime contract
- Lead times for orders
- Limited number of suppliers or producers
- New or existing sub-contract
- Overseas vs. local sub-contractors
- Quality of goods and services provided
- Reliability of supplier
- Safety attitude
- Special conditions
- Stability of joint ventures, partnerships
- Timeliness
- Transferability of warranties and guarantees
- Warranty of goods and services provided

Technology

- Availability of key components
- Failure rates
- Lack of technical knowledge
- Maintenance
- Need for further development

- New or non-standard performance or quality requirements
- Obsolescence
- Reliability, availability, maintainability
- Spare parts and support
- Specification does not reflect client needs
- Specification incomplete or misleading
- Technical standards or regulations change
- Technical standards or regulations unclear
- Technological change
- Technology not available

Transport

- Acceptable forms of transport
- Availability
- Duration
- Local conditions
- Loss in transport
- Police requirements
- Product dimensions
- Road, bridge, tunnel constraints
- Site access
- Special equipment
- Weather effects

Out-of-area project risks

This section contains lists of risks associated with projects out of the region or country of the implementing organization.

Communications

- Channel
- National/international
- Reliability
- Security

Culture and customs

- Agents' fees
- Clothing and dress codes
- Demoralization

- Family dislocation
- Food and alcohol
- Foreign business culture (including corruption)
- Hours of work
- Language
- Miscommunication
- Pay and conditions
- Quality culture
- Quality of business agent
- 'Rubber time'
- Staff rejection
- Standard of living
- Working conditions

Health

- Disease
- Hospitalization
- Injury
- Lack of sanitation
- Medical treatment facilities and equipment not available or of low quality
- Occupational health requirements
- Personal health decline
- Poor accommodation
- Poor working conditions
- Repatriation
- Safety problems
- Vaccinations

Language

- Accuracy of technical translation
- Body language
- Channels of communication
- Facial expressions
- Humour
- Translation
- Use of interpreters

Legal/regulatory

- Ineffective legal regimes
- Local bias in application of laws and regulations
- Unfamiliar legal environment

Offshore location

- Availability of suitable accommodation
- Communication (remoteness, poor infrastructure)
- Costs of accommodation, health, travel
- Dangerous sites
- Emergency response
- Equipment (will it operate?)
- Import/export restrictions
- Material availability
- Need for additional resources or time
- Proximity to our offices
- Support (hardware, software, spares, expertise)
- Support from embassy or trade commission
- Timeframe
- Voltage compatibility
- Weather, climate (monsoon, temperature)

Offshore skills

- Personnel leave after training
- Skills do not fit project work breakdown
- Skills not available at the site
- Suitable personnel to be sourced from elsewhere

Political

- National or racial preference
- Policy on repatriation of profits
- Project award on basis of political factors
- Relationship with home country
- Stability (unrest, riots, civil war)

Religion

- Holy days and festive seasons
- Prayer periods
- Fasting
- Births, deaths and marriages

Security

- National and community acceptance of foreigners
- National and community security
- Political situation
- Safety of staff and family members
- Security of staff and family members
- Site security

Staffing

- Domestic visits and communication
- Stability of employment
- Staff absences (e.g. illness, holidays, long service, leaving employment)
- Staff unwilling to take overseas assignments

Potential treatments

This section offers examples of potential treatments for a small selection of risks. Organizations should develop their own lists of treatments for the most common risks they expect to face.

Treatments for technical risks

- Assess technical skill requirements through the life of the project, develop a skill requirement profile for the project, identify critical skills and resources
- Buy or lease rights to technology
- Design redundancy into system
- Hire internal or external technology experts
- Monitor technical standards and regulations
- Plan integrated logistics support (ILS) at project start

Treatments for delivery risks

- Analyse brief and specification carefully
- Assess technical skill requirements through the life of the project, develop a skill requirement profile for the project, identify critical skills and resources
- Consult closely with users and suppliers to ensure mutual understanding
- Develop and maintain detailed resource plans

- Establish a register of pre-qualified or accredited contractors, suppliers
- Establish and maintain an internal skill and resource database
- Offer alternative solutions
- Plan internal skills development
- Provide suitable management tools
- Provide training to meet projected skill requirements
- Re-allocate internal staff, replace lower skills with contractors
- Rearrange other commitments
- Review procurement plan in context of user needs

Treatments for supplier risks

- Appoint supplier liaison managers
- Assess supplier's technical expertise
- Determine supplier attitude to safety, quality, environmental aspects
- Determine supplier credit rating and business strength
- Ensure supplier takes out appropriate insurance
- Establish appropriate business structure
- Negotiate terms and conditions, including warranty periods and coverage
- Provide for compensation or liquidated damages in contract (enforceable in practice?)
- Provide for payment and delivery terms in contract
- Take suitable legal advice
- Third-party or bank guarantees, insurances, confirmed letters of credit

Treatments for project structure risks

- Check the regulatory terms and requirements
- Determine contract terms and general conditions of contract
- Determine creditworthiness and reliability of contractors and suppliers, and their technical expertise
- Draft business agreement to allocate risks and rewards explicitly, prior to commitment
- Engage specialist expertise to develop the project structure, including legal, taxation, accounting and consulting skills
- Establish an agreed approval and governance structure, and an agreed internal management structure
- Establish back-to-back contracts with sub-contractors and suppliers
- Establish liaison and briefing processes to expedite approvals
- Identify responsibilities for liaison and negotiation with users, contractors, suppliers and partners
- Obtain guarantees from contractors and suppliers
- Review previous projects

Treatments for client quality risks

- Appoint client liaison managers
- Assess client's technical expertise
- Determine client attitude to safety, quality, environmental aspects
- Determine client credit rating and payment history
- Establish appropriate business structure
- Negotiate terms and conditions, including warranty periods and coverage
- Provide for compensation or liquidated damages in contract (enforceable in practice?)
- Provide for pre-payments in contract
- Take suitable legal advice

Treatments for out-of-area location risks

- Assess sovereign risk, political and currency stability
- Build additional contingencies into budget
- Contract with tropical diseases centres to establish health guidelines
- Determine applicable tax regime and government regulations
- Engage local agents
- Engage local legal and commercial advisers
- Establish procedures for staff to work under non-standard safety conditions
- Evaluate cost implications of location on operating budgets and overheads
- Evaluate security situation in target markets
- Hedge foreign exchange exposures
- Nominate own currency as currency of contract where possible
- Obtain third-party or bank guarantees, confirmed letters of credit
- Pre-fabricate where possible
- Provide staff with medical and health supplies and facilities
- Provide training for local employees and contractors
- Reduce amount of on-site work
- Take out appropriate insurance (e.g. with trade facilitation agency)
- Train expatriate staff and their families prior to departure
- Train staff in first aid
- Train staff in relevant health and safety matters
- Use local contractors

GLOSSARY

ALARP: As Low as Reasonably Practicable, a set of criteria for evaluating risk reduction strategies on the basis of their potential effectiveness, cost and practicality.

Bioaccumulation and **bioconcentration**: potential for material to accumulate and concentrate within components of the ecosystem.

Boolean algebra: a branch of mathematics describing the behaviour of binary variables (either on or off, open or closed, true or false). Boolean algebra is used in the quantitative analysis of fault trees; all fault trees can be converted into an equivalent set of Boolean equations. (See, for example, Tweeddale, 2003.)

Brainstorming: an interactive technique for developing new ideas with a group of people.

Configuration item: a collection of hardware or software items that satisfies an end use and is designated for configuration management, usually identified explicitly in the Work Breakdown Structure.

Consequence: outcome of an event. There may be one or more consequences from an event. Consequences are usually expressed in terms of organizational or project criteria, qualitatively or quantitatively. They may range from positive to negative.

Correlation: a measure of a statistical or dependence relationship between two items that must be estimated for accurate quantitative risk analysis.

Cost and schedule control system (CSCS): a formal system for recording, analysing and reporting the progress of a project and its component work elements, usually linked to the project Work Breakdown Structure.

Dependence: the correlation or linkages between uncertain variables that must be estimated for accurate quantitative risk analysis.

Environmental aspect: element of an organization's activities, products or services that can interact with the environment.

Environmental impact: any change to the environment, whether adverse or beneficial, wholly or partially resulting from an organization's activities, products or services.

Event tree analysis: a form of analysis that identifies and quantifies the potential likelihood, range and sequence of the outcomes that may arise from an initiating event, often with a graphical model in tree form.

Failure modes, effects and criticality analysis (FMECA): a systematic analysis of the ways a component or system might fail and the causes and effects of failure, with the aim of identifying and documenting potential weaknesses.

Failure rate: the number of failure events that occur divided by the total elapsed operating time during which these events occur or by the total number of demands, as applicable.

Fault tree analysis: a systems engineering method for identifying, representing and quantifying the probability of occurrence of the logical combinations of events, system states and possible causes that may lead to a particular failure outcome or specified event (called the top event).

Fractional dead time (FDT): the fraction of time in which a component or system is unable to operate successfully on demand.

Frequency: a measure of the rate of occurrence of an event expressed as the number of occurrences of the event in a given time. See also likelihood and probability.

Hazard: a physical, biological or chemical condition that has the potential for causing harm, danger or loss. In operating plants, the term hazard is often used to describe an event that might lead to an uncontrolled release of energy or production inventory, with on-site or off-site consequences for people, buildings, plant, equipment, materials or the environment.

Hazop: a Hazard and Operability (Hazop) study is a structured approach, using a series of guidewords, that systematically analyses every part of a process to identify how hazards, operability problems and deviations from design intent may arise.

Impact: another word for consequence.

Individual risk per annum: the risk of killing a person in a particular situation or area over the period of one year.

Key elements: project activities, phases, issues or other aspects used to disaggregate the project for structuring the risk management study.

Likelihood: used as a qualitative description of probability or frequency.

Mutagen: an agent that raises the probability of mutations, often with effects on offspring.

Opportunity: a risk with positive consequences.

Persistence: the length of time a hazardous item will remain hazardous before decaying, commonly used in relation to releases of toxic material to the environment.

Potential loss of life (PLL): the calculated number of fatalities for a defined group of people in a defined circumstance over a period of one year or over the entire life of the project.

Probability: the extent to which an event is likely to occur; mathematically, a probability is a number in the scale 0 to 1 that refers to the chance of a random event occurring. In risk analysis, probabilities may be derived from statistical analysis of historical data, or they may be estimated, usually by people with experience in the area concerned.

Programme: a collection of projects, usually related and often drawing on common resources.

Project: an organized endeavour to use resources to achieve a specific objective, usually limited in time and scope and often unique in nature.

Project Risk Management Plan (RMP): a plan at the project level to provide an overview, direction and specific processes for risk management, and in which priority risk areas are identified.

Quantitative risk analysis: detailed modelling and simulation to generate quantitative measures or distributions of key project outcomes like profitability or rate of return.

Residual risk: that risk remaining after all risk treatment measures have been implemented.

Risk: the chance of something happening that will have an impact upon objectives. It is measured in terms of consequences and likelihood. In some situations, risk arises from the possibility of deviation from an expected outcome or event, such as a deviation from the project plan. The consequences may be positive or negative.

Risk acceptance: an informed decision to accept the consequences and the likelihood of a particular risk. Risk acceptance occurs when risks cannot be avoided or transferred, or the costs of doing so would be high; the organization must then accept the risks.

Risk Action Plan: a plan for reducing or mitigating the risks associated with an individual item or functional area where major or critical risks are anticipated; sometimes called a Risk Treatment Plan.

Risk analysis: a systematic use of available information to determine how often specified events may occur and the magnitude of their consequences.

Risk avoidance: a particular case of risk reduction, where undesired events are avoided by undertaking a different course of action; an informed decision not to become involved in, or action to withdraw from, a situation with potential risks.

Risk communication: exchange or sharing of information about risk between the decision-maker, often the project manager, and other stakeholders. The information can relate to the existence, nature, form, probability, severity, acceptability, treatment or other aspects of risk.

Risk criteria: terms of reference by which the significance of risk is assessed. They may include corporate and project objectives, associated cost and benefits, legal and statutory requirements, social and environmental aspects, the concerns of stakeholders and other inputs to the assessment.

Risk evaluation: the process used to determine risk management priorities by comparing the level of risk against predetermined standards, target risk levels or other criteria.

Risk financing: the methods applied to fund risk treatment actions and the financial consequences of risk.

Risk identification: the process of determining what can happen, why and how.

Risk level: the level of risk calculated as a function of likelihood and consequence.

Risk management: the culture, processes and structures that are directed towards the effective management of potential opportunities and adverse effects.

Risk management process: the systematic application of management policies, procedures and practices to the tasks of identifying, analysing, evaluating, treating, monitoring and communicating risk.

Risk owner: the manager responsible for dealing with a specified risk and ensuring effective treatment plans are developed and implemented.

Risk perception: the way in which a stakeholder views a risk, based on a set of values or concerns. Risk perception depends on the stakeholder's needs, issues and knowledge; it can differ from objective data.

Risk reduction: a selective application of appropriate techniques and management principles to eliminate sources of risk, or to reduce substantially the likelihood of an occurrence or its negative consequences.

Risk retention: intentionally or unintentionally retaining the responsibility for loss or financial burden of loss within the organization.

Risk sharing: sharing with another party the burden of loss, or benefit of gain, for a risk, usually through contract, insurance or other means. Legal or statutory requirements can limit, prohibit or mandate the transfer of some risks. Risk sharing can create new risks or modify existing risks. (Relocation of the source of a risk is not risk sharing.)

Risk transfer: a term often applied inappropriately to risk sharing. In practice it is very difficult, if not impossible, to transfer a risk completely.

Risk treatment: the selection and implementation of appropriate management responses for dealing with risk.

Risk Treatment Plan: see Risk Action Plan.

Scenario: a description of how a risk might arise, the responses that might be taken and their consequences.

Scenario analysis: a process that uses descriptions of how a risk might arise, potential controls, responses and consequences for a broad examination of non-standard events or events that are hard to quantify.

Sensitivity analysis: a form of quantitative analysis in which the effects of changing the inputs to a model on the model's outputs are examined systematically.

Societal risk: a measure of risk to a population. It is often expressed in terms of a graph of cumulative frequency versus the number of fatalities on logarithmic scales, sometimes termed an f-N curve, and often with acceptable and unacceptable thresholds marked.

Stakeholders: those people and organizations who may affect, be affected by, or perceive themselves to be affected by, a decision, project, activity or risk. The project team are also stakeholders.

Technical hazard assessment: applies specific tools and quantitative techniques to the identification, analysis and assessment of risks, often associated with safety matters and hazardous processes.

Teratogen: an agent that raises the probability of congenital malformations in offspring.

Threat: a risk with negative consequences.

Watch list: a list of major risks examined at each monthly project review meeting.

WBS Dictionary: a definition and specification of the work involved in a project activity or process; the WBS Dictionary may contain, either directly or by reference, work requirements and expected outcomes, anticipated inputs, resources and equipment lists, process specifications and directions, and quality and other standards.

Work Breakdown Structure (WBS): a systematic definition of all the activities or work elements in a project or process, usually in the form of a 'family tree' of hardware, software and other individual work elements and the way they are combined to define intermediate sub-systems, systems and end products. The WBS is usually the basis for cost estimating. WBS items are often identified by a nested numbering scheme, which may be linked to the project cost and schedule control system.

REFERENCES

AS/NZS 4360 (2004). *Risk Management.* Standards Australia, Sydney, NSW.

Association for Project Management (1997). *Project Risk Analysis and Management (PRAM) Guide.* (See also http://www.eurolog.co.uk/apmrisksig/publications/minipram.pdf for a 'mini' guide.)

Bowden, A.R., Lane, M.R. and Martin, J.H. (2001). *Triple Bottom Line Risk Management.* Chichester, UK: John Wiley & Sons.

Chapman, C.B. (1979). Large engineering project risk analysis. *IEEE Transactions on Engineering Management,* **EM-26(3)**, 78–86.

Chapman, C.B. and Cooper, D.F. (1983). Risk engineering: Basic controlled interval and memory models. *Journal of the Operational Research Society,* **34(1)**, 51–60.

Chapman, C.B., Cooper, D.F., Debelius, C.A. and Pecora, A.G. (1985). Problem-solving methodology design on the run. *Journal of the Operational Research Society,* **36(9)**, 769–778.

Chapman, C.B. and Ward, S.J. (1997). *Project Risk Management: Processes, Techniques and Insights.* Chichester, UK: John Wiley & Sons.

Chapman, C.B. and Ward, S.J. (2002). *Managing Project Risk and Uncertainty: A Constructively Simple Approach to Decision Making.* Chichester, UK: John Wiley & Sons.

Cooper, D.F. (1997). *Applying Risk Management Techniques to Complex Procurement.* Canberra: Purchasing Australia, Australian Government Publishing Service.

Cooper, D.F. (2003). Organisational and cultural aspects of risk management implementation. Paper presented to the Centre for Advanced Engineering workshop on Integrating Risk Management Processes into Project Management, Christchurch, New Zealand, 5 November 2003. Available at http://www.broadleaf.com.au

Cooper, D.F. and Chapman, C.B. (1987). *Risk Analysis for Large Projects: Models, Methods and Cases.* Chichester, UK: John Wiley & Sons.

Cooper, D.F., Macdonald, D.H. and Chapman, C.B. (1985). Risk analysis of a construction cost estimate. *International Journal of Project Management* **3(3)**, 141–149.

Cullen, W.D. (1990). *Public Inquiry into the Piper Alpha Disaster.* (Department of Energy.) London: HMSO.

Department of Defence, Australia (2003). *Environmental Risk Management.* For an outline of environmental risk management in defence, see http://www.defence.gov.au/environment/ and http://www.defence.gov.au/environment/risk_management/risk_management_framework.pdf

Department of Defense, USA (1989). *Risk Management: Concepts and Guidance.* Defense Systems Management College, Fort Belvoir, VA, USA, MDA 903-87-C-0781.

Department of Defense, USA (1998). *Risk Management Guide for DoD Acquisition.* Defense Acquisition University, Defense Systems Management College, Fort Belvoir, VA, USA.

Environment Australia (2000). *A Framework for Public Environmental Reporting—An Australian Approach.* See http://www.deh.gov.au/industry/finance/publications/framework/

Environmental Protection Agency, USA (1998). *Guidelines for Ecological Risk Assessment.* Risk Assessment Forum, US EPA, Washington, DC, USA, EPA/630/R-95/002F. See http://www.epa.gov/ncea/ecorsk.htm

Goodwin, D., Cooper, D.F., Cross, J., Knight, K.W. and Walker, T. (2000). *Guidelines for Managing Risk in Outsourcing.* HB 240:2000, Standards Australia, Sydney, NSW.

Gough, J. (ed.) (2003). *Sharing the Future: Risk Communication in Practice.* Christchurch, NZ: Centre for Advanced Engineering.

Gough, J., Anderson, E., Beer, T., Bickford, G., Cross, J., Harding, R., Collins, D., Keey, R., Moy, D., Zaunbrecher, M., Ziolkowski, F. (2000). *Environmental Risk Management—Principles and Process.* HB 203, Standards Australia, Sydney, NSW.

Green, A.E. (ed.) (1982). *High Risk Safety Technology.* Chichester, UK: John Wiley & Sons.

Grey, S.J. (1995). *Practical Risk Assessment for Project Management.* Chichester, UK: John Wiley & Sons.

Hawksley, J.L. (1987). *Strategy for Safety Assurance for Existing Installations Handling Hazardous Chemicals.* WHO Conference on Chemical Accidents, Rome, July.

Hillson, D. (2004). *Effective Opportunity Management for Projects: Exploiting Positive Risk.* New York: Marcel Dekker Inc.

IEC 61025 (2004). *Fault Tree Analysis (FTA).*

IEC 61508. *Functional Safety of Electrical/Electronic/Programmable Electronic Safety-related systems.* IEC 61508 covers all safety-related systems that are electrotechnical in nature, including electromechanical systems, solid-state electronic systems and computer-based systems. The standard is in seven parts whose titles are:

Part 1: General requirements
Part 2: Requirements for E/E/PE safety-related systems
Part 3: Software requirements
Part 4: Definitions and abbreviations
Part 5: Examples of methods for the determination of safety integrity levels
Part 6: Guidelines on the application of IEC 61508–2 and IEC 61508–3
Part 7: Overview of techniques and measures

IEC 61882 (2001). *Hazard and Operability Studies (HAZOP Studies)—Application Guide.*

IEC 62198 (2001). *Project Risk Management—Application Guidelines.*

ISO 14001 (1996). *Environmental Management Systems—Specification with Guidance for Use.* The ISO 14000 series of standards cover many aspects of environmental management. For a summary, see http://www.iso.ch/iso/en/prods-services/otherpubs/iso14000/index.html

Merrett, A.J. and Sykes, A. (1973). *The Finance and Analysis of Capital Projects.* 2nd edn. London: Longman.

Mingers, J. and Rosenhead, J. (2004). Problem structuring methods in action. *European Journal of Operational Research*, 152, 530–554.

New South Wales Government, Australia (1993). *Risk Management Guidelines.* NSW Public Works Department, Sydney.

OGC (2002). *Management of Risk: Guidance for Practitioners* (Office of Government Commerce). London: The Stationery Office. See also http://www.ogc.gov.uk/sdtoolkit/workbooks/risk/index.html

OGC (2002). *Managing Successful Projects with PRINCE2: Reference Manual.* Revised edn. (Office of Government Commerce). London: The Stationery Office. See also http://www.ogc.gov.uk/prince/index.htm

Palisade Corporation (2002). *@Risk Advanced Risk Analysis for Spreadsheets.* Newfield, NY: Palisade Corporation.

PMI (2003). *Project Management Body of Knowledge (PMBOK)*, particularly Chapter 11, Risk Management. Upper Darby, PA: Project Management Institute. Available from http://www.pmi.org

Standards Australia (1999). *A Basic Introduction to Managing Risk*, HB 142-1999. Standards Australia, Sydney.

Treasury Board of Canada (2001). *Integrated Risk Management Framework.* Cat. No. BT22-78/2001. Available from http://www.tbs-sct.gc.ca/pubs_pol/dcgpubs/RiskManagement/rmf-cgr_e.html

Tweeddale, H.M. (2003). *Managing Risk and Reliability of Process Plants.* Amsterdam: Gulf Professional Publishing.

Tweeddale, H.M., Cameron, R.F. and Sylvester, S.S. (1992). Some experiences in hazard identification and risk shortlisting, *Journal of Loss Prevention in the Process Industries*, 5(5), 279–288.

Vose, D. (2000). *Risk Analysis: A Quantitative Guide.* 2nd edn. Chichester, UK: John Wiley & Sons.

Index